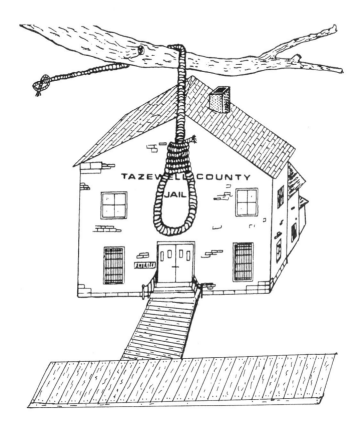

LYNCH LAW

Published by Lynch Law Productions
3 Reuling Court,
Pekin, Illinois 61554
December, 1998

1ST Edition

Library of Congress Catalog Number: 98-96953

ISBN: 0-9669-472-0-7

Illustrations by Jim Conover

Cover design by Jim Conover

First Printing - December, 1998
Second Printing - July , 1999

Printed in the United States

We dedicate this book to our families.

On the Conover side, wife Judie Conover, daughters, Kimberly Conover Moore, and Tammie Conover Fletcher and also for their loyal support and encouragement, sisters, Barbara Conover Watkins, Carmelita Conover Nash, Linda Conover Jones and Sherry Conover and brothers, Dennis Conover, and Rob Conover

On the Brecher side, wife Marilyn Brecher, daughter Katie Brecher and son Philip Brecher

ACKNOWLEDGEMENTS

We are deeply indebted to many people who gave us help and advice to make this book possible. Though we can't name them all, we do want them to know their help and advice was, and is deeply appreciated. There are a few to whom we would like to give special acknowledgement.

In particular, to two wonderful people who took so much of their own time to not only type this manuscript once, but to type it a second time on computer discs so that we could better handle the writing of it. Our deepest gratitude goes out to MICHAEL AND KRIS DUNLAP of Tremont, Illinois. Many thanks, you guys, for a job well done!

To BRIAN ADDY, our business partner, friend, and legal advisor, who helped edit the manuscript. His suggestions made the book much better reading. He not only helped edit the book, but handled our legal needs as well. Thanks again, BRIAN ADDY!

Thanks to RICHARD SHARP, Sr. and RICHARD SHARP, Jr., two computer geniuses at Sharp's Electronic Measurements, who came to our aid so many times when the computer failed to cooperate with the writing of this book.

Our thanks goes out to the great people of the TAZEWELL COUNTY GENEALOGICAL SOCIETY and the TAZEWELL COUNTY HISTORICAL SOCIETY, in Pekin, Illinois, who were so helpful every time we called upon them for information. We also thank them for the great opportunity afforded us in allowing us to attend meetings and speak about the writing of this book.

We wish to extend a very warm thank you to a gracious lady who was so helpful to us in our research. That lady, MILDRED

FORNOFF, owns most of the land Circleville Township once flourished on. MILDRED, we hope you enjoy this book as much as we have enjoyed your company. Thanks!

PAUL CROSS, who helped us get some sense of the feeling the lawmen had as they made that fateful trip to Circleville exactly 120 years earlier. He provided us with a team of fine horses and a wagon, then drove the team the eight miles, through heat, rain and wind. Thanks again, PAUL.

BILL FURROW, who was kind enough to allow us to use several photographs of old Circleville buildings as well as allowing us to photograph the Colt .44 caliber revolver once owned by Bill Berry.

GENE ABBOTT of Pekin and his sister, VIRGINIA, get our thanks for the information and pictures of William Fletcher Copes!

MRS. HENRY [MARGARET] BOORSE, of Leonia, New Jersey. She was gracious enough to provide us with photographs of George Washington Pepper.

MRS. MARIE PEMBERTON of Pawhuska, Oklahoma, who sent us genealogy on the William Berry family. Thank you, MRS. PEMBERTON, wherever you are!

Many thanks to M. CODY WRIGHT, of the Illinois State Archives; who was extremely helpful in locating information in that huge building. CODY was able to show us different fields to research and in fact located some top material for us. Thanks for all the help, CODY!

And last but not least, we want to acknowledge HEATHER BURDICK for her great work in proofreading and editing.

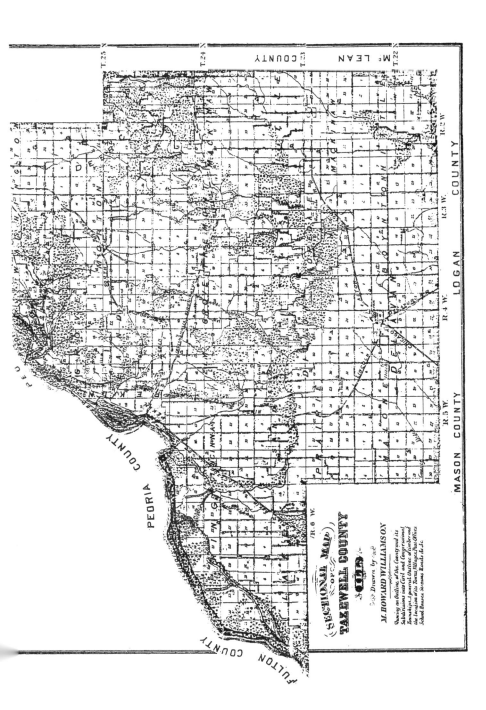

(SECTIONAL MAP)
OF
TAZEWELL COUNTY
ILL.

Drawn by
M. HOWARD WILLIAMSON

Showing an Outline of the County and its
Subdivisions into Civil and Congressional
Townships, a general Outline of Timber and
the Location of its Towns Villages Post-Offices
School Houses Streams Roads &c &c.

INTRODUCTION

Pekin, Illinois, in Tazewell County, was a rapidly growing city in 1868, on the very edge of the western frontier. Nestled along the east bank of the Illinois River, half way between Chicago and St. Louis, it had become home for approximately 5,650 citizens. This was a time when the people were trying to rebuild their lives after the Civil War that had so divided and devastated their world. Life was relatively good and would have been rather pleasant were it not for the constant torment of outlaws.

In the three years after the war's end, the crime rate had steadily increased, getting worse in 1868. Perhaps it was a result of the rapid growth in population over the same period of time. The population of Pekin had doubled in the ten years from 1858 - 1868. Many were people who came only to carve out a simple living in the new country, but there were others who came to prey upon those people. These were outlaws who knew that where there were people, there was money to be had.

As crimes increased, people became frustrated as one lawbreaker after another was arrested and jailed, only to escape punishment by engaging the services of a shrewd attorney. Through intimidation, payoffs, or political pressure on key people, the attorneys gained the outlaws' release. When this method did not work, either the lawyer, a member of the outlaw's family, or his friends, would start petitions for "Executive Clemency". By the same intimidations, payoffs, or political pressures, they also forced citizens to sign them, thereby gaining a pardon for the criminal from some unsuspecting governor.

Crimes became so frequent and so open that the residents could tolerate it no longer. They took the matter into their own hands by forming groups proclaimed in the local papers as "secret societies", found throughout the county. The idea was that anyone who wanted to help lawmen stop the outlaws, but didn't want to do it openly for fear of retaliation, would have their identity remain a

I

secret. In anonymity, they would use whatever trivial reason available to create problems for known outlaws. Reasons such as swearing to petty arrest warrants, filing lawsuits, foreclosures and the likes were often used against any suspected criminal, so the lawmen could arrest them.

Members of the secret societies especially wanted to get those in the small township of Circleville, some eight miles south of Pekin, which had become headquarters for a bunch of horse thieves and cutthroats. In haphazard control of this bunch of desperados were the Berry brothers, Isaac, Emanual and Simeon. The bunch had become known as the Berry Gang.

There was talk around the county that older brother William, known to all as "Bill", might even be the leader of the gang. He was well respected in Tazewell County as a farmer and businessman, and was always lending a hand to those who fell upon hard times. His only downfall was that three of his much younger brothers, Isaac, Emanuel and Simeon, were among the worst of road agents and horse thieves.

Standing between this bunch and the citizens was a handful of lawmen who tried to keep the peace. In Pekin, there was a tough City Marshal, Alfred Stone, and an Assistant City Marshal, Rudolph Kessler, as well as two policemen. In the Tazewell County Sheriff's Department, there was the newly elected sheriff, Edward Pratt; and two deputies, one of which was Henry Pratt, brother to Edward, and George Hinman, who also doubled as jailer. Each outlying township had a constable. Most were good men who tried hard to ride herd on the criminals.

Robberies, rapes, horse stealing, and even murder had been blamed on the Circleville bunch, but at the time Stone nor any other lawman had been able to get enough evidence to put a stop to them. A fatal battle in a Delavan saloon, and the injustice of the court system that followed, weighed heavily on the patience of the citizens.

On July 28th, 1869, in Circleville, Isaac Berry, an ominous looking "stranger" known only as "Frank", and William Shaw, made plans to steal two teams of horses, complete with harness, from Wilbur Clary, a young farmer who lived nearby. The theft of the horses was to take place the following evening.

Unfortunately for the outlaws, Marshal Stone got wind of their plans and on the night of July 29th, he took two of his men to the Clary farm where they waited for a crime that never took place.

This seemingly insignificant occurrence was to set into motion a bizarre chain of events that is unparalleled in the history of this county. For over the ensuing three days, the Berrys would be arrested, then released. A deputy sheriff would be murdered, and another one wounded. Over five hundred armed men would scour the countryside in a massive search for the suspected killers. Hundreds of those same men would assault the jail and an "innocent" man would be lynched. Three people would be stabbed and at least one would commit suicide.

In the story that follows, the exact dates, times and locations for the various events are uncertain, unknown or the sources disagree. We have, of course, scoured the available official records for any and all information concerning our subject matter, and have been greatly disappointed in finding the details we were seeking. Names, dates, and places are usually there, but testimony, significant details and even final dispositions of cases are usually lacking.

It is for this reason that much of the facts, as presented here were taken from newspaper accounts. The newspaper reporters possibly in search of the "big story" seemed to have taken far more care in documenting and describing the significant occurrences and testimony concerning these events than the officials who were actually charged to do so. We also believe that for the most part, they are no less accurate. This event is true. It actually happened. We present it using all the factual information available and as we believe it had to happen.

- Jim Conover
- Jim Brecher

1

The last rays of the setting sun danced off the bright steel blade of Bill Berry's knife as he glided it smoothly across the honing stone. "I will not return until my blade has drawn blood!" he was heard to say. It was September 1st, 1868, in Circleville, Illinois, and Berry was preparing for a trip to Delavan, a small prairie town some eight miles to the southeast, to attend one of the many political speeches that created much excitement among the citizens of Tazewell County during the 1860's.

* * *

The speech was a fine one, with all the hand shaking and backslapping that goes with such political gatherings. When it was over, many of the onlookers, including Bill Berry, retired to a local saloon for drink and relaxation.

Standing at the bar enjoying a cool drink, Bill glanced around the room. The saloon was full of men from all walks of life; prominent businessmen, politicians, farmers, and field hands. Continuing his gaze around the room, Bill suddenly spied the very man he had come looking for - George Washington Pepper. His blood began to boil as he stared at the man.

Pepper, a big, brawny, handsome young man, very popular around Delavan, was drinking with some friends across the room and must have felt the piercing eyes upon him, for he looked around and met the icy glare. He bristled.

There was a longstanding feud between the two, one that had begun several years earlier over a woman at a ballroom dance in Delavan, and had continued to build over the years.

Recently, while attending another political rally such as this one, Pepper had been involved in a heated altercation with two of Bill's brothers, Isaac and Emanuel. Words had been exchanged between the three men until, finally, Pepper in his foulest language, had openly made insulting remarks about Bill Berry's family being nothing but a bunch of horse thieves. Why Isaac or Emanuel, fighters that they were, had not settled the matter then and there is a mystery to this day. One can only guess that it was something only Bill could settle. Isaac had told Pepper that Bill would be coming for him to avenge the family name.

Now, Pepper glared at Bill, he thought of all the rumors going around that he was a coward - rumors that had been started by Bill Berry. Perhaps tonight he would prove differently.

The two men continued to stare at each other as they drank down more liquor, their anger growing with each swallow. By now everyone in the saloon was watching them. They were all aware of the animosity between them, and expected trouble any time. Tension was thick and trouble was indeed brewing.

Finally, unable to suppress his anger any longer, Pepper marched across the room toward Berry. The floor cleared instantly and a hush fell upon the room. Pepper was a life long resident of the area and knew well the reputation of the Berrys. But being the bigger man, well over six feet tall, he showed no sign of fear as he marched up to Berry and demanded to know if he had in fact been calling him a coward.

Berry stretched his five feet ten inches as much as possible to compensate for the difference in height. He looked Pepper right in the eye and shouted back at him that he had in fact said those very words to anyone who would listen. He then challenged Pepper about his insults toward him and his family, and returned the insult - whatever it was.

Pepper could restrain himself no longer. He struck Berry a mighty blow with his fist.

Berry reeled under the force of the blow, but recovered like a cat and before Pepper realized what was happening, Berry jerked his razor sharp knife from its sheath and slashed out at him. The knife's fine edge etched a long deep wound across Pepper's midsection. Pepper was stunned. He looked down at his stomach as his intestines began protruding from the great cut that gaped across his abdomen. Blood gushed forth spattering the men who stood nearby and spilling upon the dank floor of the saloon.

Nathan Caswell, a bystander to this violent battle, tried to step between the two men.

Berry, still waving the knife in a menacing manner, his black eyes darting about the room, saw Caswell coming and struck out again.

Seeing the steel blade streaking toward him, Caswell threw up his arm in self-defense and received a terrible and crippling cut across the arm. The cut spilled much blood as it had severed the arteries, letting the blood gush forth to mingle upon the floor with that of Pepper's.

Several people had rushed forth to separate the two combatants, but now backed away, the results of Berry's revenge obvious. Finally, some men were able to get to Pepper and assist the bleeding man. Some assisted Caswell, while others ran for the doctor and the law.

It had been a ruthless attack upon the two men by Berry, who took advantage of the mass confusion surrounding him to escape out the door. Once outside, he headed for his homestead in Circleville, well satisfied that he had made good his earlier boast - that his knife would draw blood before his return.

Inside the saloon, Jacob Pepper, who had witnessed the attack upon his nephew, told his story to Justices of the Peace, J. Appleton and Burt Newman when they arrived. He swore before them a complaint for a warrant for Berry's arrest, for assault with a deadly weapon. The warrant was given to Delavan Constable, A. Culver to execute, but they discovered that Berry had already left town.

Fearing that Berry might decide to leave the territory, Henry Wilson, another relative of Pepper's, told the crowd that he would finance the tracking down of the scoundrel no matter the cost.

Constable Culver knew that to attempt a search in the darkness was foolish, and decided it would be best to wait until dawn to go after Berry. This went against the grain of several men in the crowd who wanted to rush right out into the night and grab Berry, some because of their anger for the terrible deed done their friend, and others hungry for Henry Wilson's money. Culver however, managed to convince the crowd to wait until daylight.

* * *

Early on the morning of September 2, 1868, Constable Culver and a small posse of men rode into Circleville to arrest Berry. Much to their surprise, they found Berry at home as though nothing had happened.

Culver read Berry the warrant and placed him under arrest. They were again surprised when Berry submitted peacefully to the shackles.

Berry was taken back to Delavan, where he was placed in the local calaboose to await the arrival of Tazewell County Sheriff's deputies. They would take him to the county jail in Pekin, some twenty miles to the northwest, where he would be held until his trial.

2

William Berry, born in Three Churches, Hampshire County, Virginia, in 1828, son of James and Rachel (Larimore) Berry, was but three years old when, in 1831, Rachel's father, William Larimore, decided to travel to Illinois to start a new life. Daughter Rachel and her husband, James Berry, along with their three children, James, William, and Harriet, decided they to would join the family trek westward.

Besides William Larimore and wife, Nancy (McMann), and nine Larimore children still at home, another daughter, Elizabeth and her husband, Samuel Berry, brother of James, decided to travel with them.

Headed by the senior Larimore, the troupe formed a small wagon train and headed for Illinois, more than six hundred miles due west.

* * *

For several weeks, averaging only about ten miles a day, the tiny wagon train wound its way over the mighty Appalachian Mountains, forded the wide Ohio River, and rumbled onto the great prairies of Illinois, finally reaching Tazewell County.

* * *

It had been a long hard trip, but each family eagerly rushed to the government land office in the County Seat in Pekin and applied for land grants. This land was located just north of the Mackinaw River at the edge of virgin timber and was bordered on the north side by tall prairie grass, in Sand Prairie township, near the small settlement of Circleville.

Here the families desperately struggled for several years, surviving the Indian wars of 1832, the dreaded cholera outbreak of 1834, and one hardship after another, until finally the hard toil of the land claimed the life of James Berry. Rachel and the children who now numbered six were left to struggle with the farm.

Shortly after his father's death, Bill went to work on his Uncle Samuel's farm in Elmwood Township a few miles east of Circleville. A number of factors motivated him to leave. He wanted to supplement his mother's meager income from the farm and yet wanted to prove his manhood by staking out a claim in life independently. And last, but not least, he was greatly attracted to one of Uncle Samuel's housekeepers, Nancy Welsh.

Sometime later, when Bill had established himself as a man, he and Nancy got married and bought a forty-acre farm adjoining the western boundary of his mother's farm. Here, he and Nancy settled down and soon had two children - Albert and Ellen.

7

Bill prospered as a farmer and became well respected around the county as a good businessman. The only downfall he had was the way he rushed to the aid of his brothers, Isaac and Emanuel. Being the oldest, he tried to be a father to them, so every time they were jailed for some crime, it was Bill who had to travel to Pekin and post bail for them. Isaac and Emanuel, always in some trouble with the law, took advantage of this and Bill soon gained the reputation of being their guardian; and with that came the notion that perhaps he, too, was involved in their criminal activities.

It had cost Bill a lot of money to bail out his brothers over the years, especially for Isaac who was in trouble most often. It was so often in fact, that he had to commit more crimes just trying to repay Bill.

Isaac "Ike" Berry was a mean, tough outlaw, who at thirty, although claiming to be a farmer, dedicated his life to being a road agent, horse thief, and cattle rustler. He was so notorious, even the local newspaper reported him as being by far the worst of the lot. According to the paper, "he was a rough looking sort, but still a rather handsome man, standing five feet ten inches tall with a muscular built - strong and hearty with a mild expression. He was not a vicious looking man by any means."

Though Ike was not a vicious looking man, he was a scraper. He often boasted of how tough he was, how he feared no man, and more often than not, had to prove this when he went out drinking.

Ike was not totally ignorant, for he could read and write, as his trial records would later point out. Isaac married twice. The first marriage, to Elmyla Stockton on November 22, 1852, ended in 1861, when her clothing caught fire and she burned to death.

Perhaps her death had some bearing on the life he chose to lead for Isaac drank too much, fought too much, and stole too much. But somehow, for all the crimes he had committed, he had little to show for them. It seemed he was always broke, never having the money for the household needs or bail, and always needing money from Bill for these matters. This was, according to the local newspapers, due to his love for drinking and being generally a bad character.

Some time later, Ike met his second wife in Mason County, where he had been spending a considerable amount of time. Together, they were the parents of three children.

Uneducated as he was, Ike was far more literate than his younger brother Emanuel "Man" Berry, who could not write and could only read a little. As a Jacksonville newspaper reported later, "Emanuel was no doubt the dumbest of the gang." He was also the ugliest, standing five feet nine and three quarters of an inch in height, heavy set, with brown hair and hazel eyes set deep under an over hanging forehead, giving him a vicious primate look. He was a brawler and had sustained many scars over the years from knives, bullets, and other weapons used against him. To further his ugliness, he sported a goatee and mustache. He was a road agent, thief, and rustler.

Simeon "Sim" Berry, was the youngest and the most handsome of the Berry brothers. He was twenty-three years old, tall, thin, with a very youthful look. Although he ran with the wild bunch and drank far too much for his age and acted mean, most people knew he was not a bad sort. In fact, he was very likeable. Sim married Amanda E. McCain on October 15, 1868 in Pekin, and they lived on a farm near Circleville. He was educated to the point of being able to read and write.

Another brother, James (Ked), was never involved with the other boys in their criminal ways and little is known about him. He and Sister Harriet, who later married Reuben Hatfield, a well respected farmer around Circleville, were in good standing with the citizens of the county. Only Bill, Ike, Man, and Sim were the troublemakers of the family, and that was enough.

Bill Berry was not just a farmer, but a businessman as well. He owned several pieces of property and was half owner of a saloon. He and Matthew McFarland had purchased the old Murphy Saloon located on East Street in Circleville. Bill was also a fine dresser. He always wore a suit with hat and tie. And rather than ride a horse like his brothers, he drove around in a buggy, as did all the important men of the time.

Bill rubbed shoulders with all the politicians and businessmen in Tazewell County. It seemed that when he was not pursuing the needs of his brothers, he was very involved in politics. He attended many of the political rallies that were held throughout the county, listening to the speeches of the many speakers of the different political parties as they traveled through the state.

Almost every night, in some nearby town, someone was giving a speech. Newspapers would list the speakers and towns they would be in, and on what date, much like present day theater listings. The local people could then pick the one they wanted to hear, and go there for their evening entertainment. An example of the newspaper's entertainment listings appeared in the Peoria Transcript on August 31, 1868:

> General McCook, of Pekin, has entered upon his duties as collector of internal revenue for the 8th District. The Pekin Tanners have voted to attend the LOGAN meeting in this city, next Friday. The REPUBLICAN says 'Peoria may look out for a right smart chance of tanners from the celestial city' Very well let' em come. The more the merrier.
>
> Hon. S.C. PARKS, Republican candidate for Presidential elector in the 8th District, will

speak at Delavan this (Monday) evening
Hopedale, Tomorrow (Tuesday) evening;
Minier, Wednesday evening, Hittle's Grove,
Thursday evening; Green Valley school
house, Saturday evening and at Pekin next
Monday Evening.

This ad included some nasty remarks about one of the local political organizations known as the Tanners. Exactly what the Tanners represented is unknown, but it presented a problem for many people as is shown in an article from the same paper, the same date:

HOW TO MAKE REPUBLICANS VOTE

The Pekin Republican gives the following as the
mode that the Copperheads have adopted to
make Republican votes:' Thursday night the Tanners
had Their weekly meeting, after which the company
turned out on parade. At first all went smooth
enough barrin' the fact that a number of scalawags
of tender growth, employed by certain imitations of
manhood, and who followed alongside the
procession, kept up the cry of 'wooden shoed
Dutch nigger worshippers etc., which was, we
suppose, intended to provoke retaliation. Their
shouting and blackguardism failing to irritate the
tanner boys, some of the elder masculines, who
profess to belong to the Democratic Party,
determined to adopt different Tactics, stationed
themselves behind a number of ladies and children
in front of the residence of Judge Harriott, they,
on the approach of the procession, assaulted

the members with a shower of eggs. The
company, under the strict discipline of its
officers, marched on down toward the river.
Arriving opposite the Democratic headquarters from
hence the 'Greenback Club' was just issuing, they
were again attacked with eggs, clods of dirt, pieces
of brick, etc. Still the procession moved quitely on,
and cowardly miscreants, who from behind the
shelter of the women's forms, and in darkness, dared
to do the dirty work assigned them, but who would
tremble at the assault of a school boy, scattered to
their dens. Of the conduct of the cowardly sneaks
of the attacking party we have no remarks to make.
A simple statement of facts will show them up in all
their hideousness.

It was newspaper articles like this that fired the blood of
citizens and moved them to action. As one can see, there were
not only political differences, but racial differences as well. At
these speeches, tempers flared as the speeches became hotter
and hotter. Verbal arguments, as well as fights, broke out
among the attending audience, and all the while the speaker,
like a hellfire and damnation preacher on a roll, would continue
with his lecture.

It was at these speeches during the summer months, when
the crops had been planted, plowed, and laid by for the long
wait until harvest, that Bill had time to socialize with the
important people. After the speeches, the men would retire to a
local saloon for something to drink to cool Flemming tempers
as well as the body in the summer heat.

Partaking of alcoholic spirits is known to ease the minds
and muscles of the weary, but reek havoc with the mental state
of those who imbibe too much. On rare occasions, Bill Berry
was known to partake of the spirits; and when he did, people

who knew him tried to avoid crossing his path, for he would become a violent man. It was while partaking of the spirits in Delavan, Illinois that fateful night in September, that Bill reached a great turning point in his life.

3

Nestled along the east bank of the beautiful Illinois River, half way between Chicago on the Great Lakes, and St. Louis on the Mighty Mississippi, is the city of Pekin, Illinois. A city that had a population of 3,467 people in 1860 and was now, in 1868, home for approximately 5,650 citizens.

Pekin was a peaceful place, as was evident around the town square with its wooden sidewalks, dirt streets, and hitching posts along the store fronts, and typical of most towns situated on the very edge of the undeveloped frontier. Just a couple of hundred miles west, Indian wars were still raging and local papers carried daily reports on the battles and of the deaths incurred. Here in Pekin however, it was quite. Oh, there was noise, but it was a peaceful noise. A slow, laid-back lifestyle noise that would be the envy of many today.

One might hear the whinnying of a horse standing at a nearby hitching post, the squeaking wheel of a wagon lazily making its way along the street, or perhaps the distant slamming of a door, as someone made an effort to keep the hot, humid September air from his place of business. The loudest noise was music coming from the many saloons that were always busy. As the September wind blew down the street, whipping up tufts of dust from around the corners of buildings, one might smell the scent of fresh hay from all the livery stables around the square. There were one or two in every block, like the one owned by Benjamin Stickney, just to the north of the intersection of Fourth and Court. That stable was located beside one belonging to the American House Hotel, where most new arrivals to town were directed for lodging.

On the north east corner of the intersection of Fifth and Court streets just one block away, stood the huge Height's livery stable, a two story building, extending a full city block. Several saloon signs hung across the sidewalks. If there were any businesses in greater number than the livery stables, it was the saloon businesses. At one time during those years, there were twenty-eight saloons, or tippling houses, in and around Pekin.

Both the Courthouse and the county jail buildings were located in the very center of town, creating the town square. The jail was built in 1854 for $7000 to house twenty prisoners. It was a two story red brick and white stone building with the sheriff's office and a cell block located ground level and his living quarters upstairs. The design of the jail had been quite popular during that era of the mid-nineteenth century, and was used for many jails across the United States. The building was situated in the center of three lots on Court Street, its entrance to the north. An alleyway behind the building extended from Fourth street west to the court house property. The trees in the side yard of the jail gave the only shade other than from the buildings.

15

The jail was headquarters for not only the county sheriff, but for the past few years, Pekin City had been using it to house their prisoners as well. It seemed the local city calaboose, built in 1849 at a cost of $48.00 and described in W.H. BATES' HISTORY of PEKIN, as being, "long considered, especially by evil doers, a noisesome pestilential nuisance", had been burned to the ground by a drunk, sometime around 1858.

In 1868, three men frequently used the quarters at the county jail to discuss local problems that ranged from politics, horses, and women, to the one thing they were all familiar with; the local crime problem that had been getting out of hand. The three men were all peace officers. One was the Tazewell County sheriff, Edward Pratt. There was also his brother Henry, a deputy sheriff, and there was Pekin's ex-city marshal, Alfred U. Stone. He had recently resigned as city marshal because of political problems and was a full time deputy sheriff. These three men often worked together combating local criminals who had become more active during the summer months of 1868.

This was a most memorable period in the history of the growing city, a time when the people were all trying to rebuild their lives after the great Civil War that had so divided and devastated their world. Life was relatively good since the war ended, and would have been rather pleasant were it not for the constant torment of outlaws. In the preceding few years the crime rate had steadily increased, particularly in 1868. Perhaps it was the result of the rapid growth in population over the same period of time. In ten years, the population of Pekin almost doubled. Many were simple people who came only to carve out a simple living in the new country, however, there were others who came to prey upon those simple people. These were outlaws who knew that where there was a crowd, there was money to be had.

16

The outlaws committed crime after crime as the local people watched. The crimes became so frequent and so open, the residents decided they had tolerated it long enough. It was time something was done. It had become apparent that the lawmen could not handle the outlaws alone.

The people had become more and more frustrated as one criminal after another was arrested, only to escape punishment by engaging the services of a shrewd attorney, who through intimidation, payoffs, or political pressure on key people, gained their release. When this method did not work, either the lawyer, a member of the outlaw's family, or his friends would start petitions for "Executive Clemency".

By the same intimidations, payoffs, or political pressures, they also forced citizens to sign them, thereby gaining a pardon for the criminal from some unsuspecting governor, such as their current governor, Richard J. Oglesby.

The people formed organizations throughout the county which were proclaimed in the local papers as "secret societies". These secret societies were formed to protect decent local people who wanted to help stop the outlaws but did not want their names known for fear of retaliation. They would use whatever means available to create problems for the outlaws. Problems included such trivial things as swearing to arrest warrants for petty offenses; filing lawsuits for any money owed; filing foreclosures; and the like; against any suspected criminal, especially those in Circleville.

Down in Delavan, yet another crime had been committed, and this time by the very man suspected of being leader of that gang of horse thieves in Circleville. Sheriff Pratt, although in sympathy for Pepper, was elated when he heard the news. The perpetrator, Mr. William Berry himself, had just been arrested and was awaiting transportation to his jail. Sheriff Pratt had been looking for a break in the fight against crime, and perhaps that break had finally come.

He immediately dispatched Deputy Alfred Stone to retrieve Berry from the calaboose in Delavan. Pratt felt the Berrys were less likely to cause trouble on the return trip, knowing Stone's reputation as a tough, no nonsense lawman. Stone hailed from Kentucky, where he had settled after travelling west from his home state of Rhode Island. Not happy with Kentucky, Stone gathered his wife Eliza and son William into their wagon and headed across the Ohio River to Illinois, where he settled on a piece of ground near Delavan.

In Delavan, Stone tried his hand at farming once more, but, like before, he found that it was not what he wanted out of life. He wanted to be a lawman, so he moved to Pekin where he managed to land a position as police officer. Although he was only twenty-three years old when he came to this county, Stone had quickly become known as a man not to tangle with. He was a quiet man. He was not the biggest man in the county, standing five feet eleven inches in height with a stocky build, but perhaps he was the toughest when it came to fighting. This reputation had followed him to Pekin and was an asset in his work as a law enforcement officer.

It was January 11, 1864, when he got his first chance at being a lawman. That was when Benjamin S. Prettyman, a wealthy and influential politician, was elected mayor. He promptly appointed Stone to the night force of the police department at a salary of forty dollars a month.

Before long, Stone became well known throughout Tazewell County as an outstanding lawman. He was sought after by several politicians who wanted him as city marshal, or at least, on the city police force, should they be elected as mayor. That top position in town was up for election each year. The sheriff swore him in as a deputy that same year, even though he knew he could only work part time.

Stone served on the night force until April of 1865 when William Sellers, a local newspaper owner, was elected mayor and promptly appointed Stone as city marshal, with a salary of seven hundred dollars a year. That was a far cry from the salary he earned as a farmer. The increase in pay would later allow him to purchase a house in the three hundred block of Caroline Street only three blocks from the jail.

During his tenure as city marshal, he also kept the position of part-time deputy sheriff. This would insure that he would have a job should a new mayor get elected who might not want him as marshal. Politics made that job very unstable and an election was held in April of every year. Stone maintained his position as marshal off and on over the following years. In 1968, however, when he was dispatched to Delavan to bring in Bill Berry, he was a deputy sheriff.

* * *

It was Saturday, September 2, 1868, when Stone rode to Delavan. He received custody of Bill Berry at two o'clock in the afternoon and immediately started on the long trek to Pekin. He expected trouble from Berry's brothers along the way and wanted to make the trip before dark, or it would afford the outlaws a much better advantage. His dark eyes scanned the prairies as he rode quitely beside Berry. He encountered no one at all during the twenty-mile ride, however and Berry was tucked safely away in a cell to be taken before the judge at the earliest opportunity.

Assault with a deadly weapon was nothing to be concerned about, not in these dangerous times, and especially not for Bill Berry who had a lot of pull about town and would probably be out in a day or two. On September 3rd, however, a dark shadow fell upon the unconcerned Berry. It was in bold print in a local newspaper: "Young George Washington Pepper has succumbed to his injuries."

The charge would now be manslaughter. Berry was destined for the penitentiary. Now he was worried.

4

George Pepper had been a popular young man around Delavan, and much excitement prevailed there during the next few days following his death. On more than one occasion, there was talk of violence in the form of a lynch party for Bill Berry. The Pepper family, especially George's uncle, Jacob Pepper, who had witnessed the attack, was extremely upset.

Word spread of Pepper's death and, for a time, it did in fact, look as though there might be a lynching. There had never been a lynching in Tazewell County, and only one legal execution by hanging was on record. That one was also for a murder, or, rather, multiple murders. That crime, committed eight years earlier in 1860, was heinous. A young mother and her two daughters had been hacked to death with an old rusty axe. The victims were Mary Orendorff and daughters Emma, age nine, and Ada, age seven. They were the family of one of the earliest settlers of the Delavan prairie, Richard Orendorff; a highly respected farmer and civic-minded man who had been away on business when the tragedy struck.

Citizens of Delavan, having found the three victims, formed a search party and soon discovered a local man, John Ott, hiding in the cornfield near the house. There was blood on his clothing and upon further searching, the bloody axe had been located not far from where he had been hiding. Ott was arrested and transported to Pekin to stand trial.

The trial was rather short and Ott was found guilty by the jury and sentenced by the judge to death by hanging. The judge ordered the sheriff to build a scaffold in the yard of the county jail for Ott's execution. He also ordered, as per the recently enacted "execution law" for the State of Illinois, that a structure be built around the scaffolding as to "render it impossible for the execution to be viewed by the public." The last order was something the public did not want, and they quickly started a petition drive to amend the new law so that the public could view the Ott hanging.

The petitions were sent to Springfield, but nothing was heard in reply, and the day of the hanging was near. The sheriff ordered the scaffolding built and the structure, a tall wooden stockade, was built around it. The stockade was the last thing built and it was finished just two days before the execution was scheduled.

This so infuriated the people who had been trying to abide by the law and get the amendment through, that they gathered in the streets the night before the hanging. Angrily, they stormed the jail yard and tore down the wooden wall surrounding the scaffolding.

The sheriff, fearing there would be more violence and that the crowd might even storm the jail and lynch the prisoner, sent to Peoria for local troops, equivalent to the present day National Guard. The troops arrived, consisting of the Washington Rifles, The German Rifles, and the National Blues.

They came under the able command of the Quarter Master General, as well as the Adjutant General. Immediately the troops were disbursed around both the jail and the scaffolding to prevent any further damage by the mob.

News of the pending execution and the assault on the stockade around the scaffolding spread like wildfire. On the scheduled day of the execution, an estimated five thousand people poured into Pekin to watch. People came from as far away as St. Louis and Chicago. There was a gala carnival atmosphere throughout the town. The buildings surrounding the jail were crowded with people perched on rooftops and hanging out of windows. Everyone was ready and anxiously waiting to watch a man die.

The sheriff had long since decided to let well enough alone and go against the State laws, rather than have the people rioting again. He did not order the wall rebuilt, figuring that if they wanted to watch the man hang that much, then so be it.

At eleven o'clock in the morning on March 1, 1861, John Ott was marched from the jail to the scaffolding by the sheriff and his deputies. Ott was placed on the trap door under the hanging coil of rope. From the bottom of the platform, a Reverend climbed slowly upward, saying a prayer for this condemned man. After the prayer sessions, Ott was asked if he had any final words he wished to say. John Ott told the huge crowd that he was sorry for what he had done and hoped he would be forgiven in Heaven. He said he alone had committed the crimes. There had been much talk that he was with another person, perhaps his cousin, when the murders were committed. Now he denied this for the last time, clearing anyone who might have been with him.

A black hood was slipped over his head. Next came the rope that was tightened firmly around his neck. At a nod from the sheriff, the trap door was sprung, hurling Ott's body down with such force that the scaffold shook. There were a few twitches from his bound legs and he hung still.

Thus ended the murdering life of John Ott, going down in history as the first and only man in Tazewell County to be executed by hanging. The only legal one, that is.

In September 1868, for a short time, it looked very much like there would be another hanging. This time an illegal one - a lynching.

After much debate on the issue, however, and being decent law-abiding citizens, they felt justice would prevail in Bill Berry's case. They decided to allow the court system to handle this murderer just as it had done with John Ott.

5

Less than a week after George Pepper's death, as Bill Berry remained confined in the Tazewell County Jail, members of the Berry gang were at it again. Three men beat, and robbed Ed Howard, a black laborer from Pekin.

Three days later, a grand jury indictment was handed down naming Mathew McFarland, William Taylor Shay, and James Jones as being responsible for that attack.

Mathew McFarland, dubbed "the saloon keeper," was a partner of Bill Berry in ownership of old Murphy's Saloon and Hotel, a sleazy place, long known to be a hangout for drunks, bums, and outlaws. He was thirty-three years old, stood five feet eleven inches tall, had dark hair and gray eyes. He had a dark complexion and a slim build, was married, and had four children. He had been involved with the gang for several years and according to the local newspaper was regarded as a "generally bad character," and always in some scrape with the law.

William Shay and James Jones were only shirttail members of the gang. The only description of them is that they were members of the so-called Berry Gang and were bad characters.

The attack, a racial incident involving men of the Berry gang, makes one wonder if the Berrys were not members of the southern sympathizing organization known as the "Serpents" or "Copperheads," which seemed to be popular in the area.

The "Copperheads" were a secret organization consisting of northern sympathizers of the south. Also know as the "Knights of The Golden Circle", these people had plans to accumulate enough money by hook or by crook, to finance the "uprising of the confederacy".

One objective of the Copperheads was to harass families of northern soldiers who fought in the war and by use of political pressure get members of their society appointed or elected to key official positions. The position of postmaster was just one of them, but a very important one as you can imagine.

These people pressured everybody. In fact, tucked away in a court document in the case of John Orrel that State's Attorney C.A Roberts was prosecuting, was a hand written letter from local a businessman named John Eades.

Eades reminded Roberts in the letter that he had to try to get the position of postmaster filled by one of their own men. Eades signed the note *"Copperhead."* After more than 120 years the original letter is still in the records at the Tazewell County courthouse. The letter read (exactly as written) as follows:

San Jose June 14/68

Friend Roberts--
I forgot to call and see you that morning in regard to our post office, but it was not

necessary to get another petition for the reason there is one there that has been there for some time in favor of Charles D. Knopp the man we want for post master and all that is necessary I suppose is to get them to act on it.

I hope you will at once write to MAS Reps Congress for the Mason County District is also write to Randolph or another man that will attend to at once and for God's Sake let us have a man that can read the address on a letter and not turn the letter over to every man that comes in and let him take any and all that he chooses to take.

Doc, if you will fix this matter up at once you may consider me indebted to you the biggest drink you ever took when Pendleton is nominated in New York---

The reason I am in hurry about this is there is a move on foot here to have another man than Knopp and I want you acting on the petition before this new move gets there.

Don't fail to have this attended to and oblige the Democracy.

Thos. Eases
Copperhead

Though indictments had been handed down for Mathew McFarland, William Shay, and James Jones, these defendants would have to wait for their day in court because the Berry-Pepper manslaughter case held center stage.

Court proceedings on the Pepper case got under way on September 12, 1868, when William Berry was indicted for manslaughter. On the same day, several subpoenas were issued for witnesses for the State.

A day or two later, William Berry posted the $500 bail bond and was released from jail. Just fourteen days after the death of George Pepper, Berry was a free man. The justice system was at work protecting the rights of the accused while the victim lay in a fresh grave atop a small hill in Weyrich Cemetery, hardly a mile from Berry's farm.

As States Attorney Cassius G. Whitney prepared for court in the days that followed, he issued subpoenas for George Yeoger, Hugh Wilson (a relative of Pepper's), William Caswell (the brother of one of the victims), Nathan Caswell (one of the victims), F. Connett, Bishop Addington, John Meyers, and James Farr, each to testify for the State.

Later more subpoenas went out for James Farrow, Mathew McFarland, Taylor Shay, Doctor Grote (the physician who treated both George Pepper and Nathan Caswell), Thomas Eades (the local politician and high ranking member of the Copperheads), William Addington, William Woolford, Samuel Laman, Creed Browner, and James A. Jones. Several other subpoenas came back unserved because the witnesses could not be located in Tazewell County.

Berry enlisted the aid of Attorney John B. Cohrs and his assistant, W.N. Green, to defend him in the action. Right away Cohrs filed motions for a continuance, claiming Berry had been incarcerated for two weeks and was therefore unable to locate the addresses of witnesses he would need for this case. Cohrs had already subpoenaed for the defense William Daughtery, Martha Daughtery, George Daughtery, and Jacob Pepper. As one can see by the number of subpoenas issued overall, there had been a large crowd attending the speech that bloody September night.

On November 30, 1868, a special term of the Circuit Court in Tazewell County began. Judge Charles Turner presided, with Cassius G. Whitney prosecuting and Benjamin S. Prettyman assisting the prosecution. Two bailiffs were appointed to serve the court during this session, B.F. Stickney and J.B. Reeves, both respected businessmen and former lawmen.

Before the trial could begin, however, more subpoenas had to be issued. This time those subpoenaed for the defense were William T. Edds, the mayor of Pekin, C. Bode, and Walter McLaughlin. John Orr had not been located, and Wiley Storm had to be arrested to get him into court to testify. John Baily, Robert McClintock, William Larimore, Charley Murphy, Bert Newman, Evert Montgomery, and Abram Wiseman were additional defense witnesses, as were Benjamin Priddy, Wily Horn, Hollis Rockhold, James Briggs, Jack Michael, Henry Sutton, Joseph Stephens, Oliver Jones, Mary Hamson, and a man named Dawson and his wife. With that many witnesses to testify, the trial would be a long one.

On December 11, 1868, Attorneys Cohrs and Green filed motions to quash the indictment for manslaughter against Berry on the grounds that; "(1) The indictment does not appear entitled of any terms as by statute required and (2) It does not appear with sufficient certainty by said indictment that said George Pepper died through or in consequence of the injuries the said indictment alleges to have been inflicted upon said George Pepper by said William Berry." The motion was summarily denied and the trial began.

Witnesses tramped through the courtroom one after another for the next four days testifying as to what they had seen or heard. Many would testify as to Berry's "good character," and on December 14, 1868, the trial finally came to a conclusion.

After hearing closing arguments from both sides, Judge Turner issued several pages of instructions to the jury. These were statements made to the jury by the Judge explaining the State statutes and how they were to be interpreted. In short, if the jury believed from the evidence and testimony that Bill

Berry killed Pepper without provocation, or reasonable cause, they were duty bound to find him guilty. If, however, they believed from the evidence and the testimony that Berry acted only in self-defense and could not have otherwise escaped Pepper's attack, even by fleeing the scene, they were duty bound to find him not guilty.

With instructions given, the jury at last retired to deliberate Berry's fate.

Within three hours they returned to the court room with a verdict of guilty, and to the astonishment of some, especially the Pepper family, recommended a sentence of one year in the penitentiary with the first day served in solitary confinement and the remainder to be served at hard labor.

After the announcement of the sentence, turmoil erupted in the courtroom, as it upset both sides. The Berry family was shocked that he had been found guilty of manslaughter instead of being released for an act of self-defense, and Pepper's family was shocked that he received such a light sentence. How could the court justify giving Berry just one year, 365 days, for the taking of a man's life?

Dismissing the jury, the judge allowed post trial arguments and motions by the defense that he promptly denied, then sentenced Berry to the one year in the penitentiary at Joliet, Illinois, as the jury had recommended. He further ordered Sheriff Edward Pratt to deliver Berry to the proper officer in charge at the penitentiary within ten days.

Bill Berry's bond was revoked, and he was once again incarcerated until arrangements could be made to transport him to Joliet.

Immediately, petitions sprang up all over the county, sworn to by Berry's family as well as members of his gang, seeking executive pardon.

On December 19, four days after the conclusion of the Berry manslaughter trial, the court entertained a motion filed by

Cohrs and Attorney Saltonstall to quash the indictment against Mathew McFarland. Judging from the incomplete records, it appears the case was quashed and the charges against Jones were dismissed. The charges against Taylor Shay were changed from "riot," a statute covering a situation where more than one person is involved in an altercation, to "larceny."

This modification against Shay implies that the black man, Ed Howard, was not only beaten, but robbed as well, and that Shay had been left to take full responsibility for the acts. The offense occurred within a few days of Bill Berry's arrest and he was bailed out just a day or so after the incident. Perhaps it wasn't an intended racial incident after all. Perhaps the men were merely harvesting bail money for their leader.

Still, just four days later, Mathew McFarland and A.B.C. Knott, a close friend of McFarland's and another member of the gang, secured Shay's release from jail by posting the $100 cash bond. At least they were all free now except for Bill Berry, who was prison bound.

Continuing with the great petition drive, on December 28, 1868, Reuben Hatfield, Bill's brother-in-law, swore before the Notary Public, Henry Spoonhoff, to the validity of over 80 signatures, with names such as W.H.H. Larimore, Justice of the Peace of Circleville, William Shaw, Charley Murphy, and others.

Next came Isaac and Simeon Berry to swear before Notary Spoonhoff to the validity of a dirty, wrinkled petition with over a hundred and twenty names. Listed were names like Henry Pratt, deputy sheriff of Tazewell County, Nathan Caswell, one of the victims of the fight, and the man rendered a cripple for life by the huge wound on his arm; Theis Smith, a wealthy businessman of great influence, Benjamin Priddy; and others, including Edward Pratt, the Sheriff, who had been elated when Berry was arrested.

The testimony during the trial must have painted Bill's a very bright portrait and Pepper's one of darkness. On the petition was also the name of William T. Edds, the Mayor of Pekin.

With the many petitions came as many personal letters to the governor. One letter was from Charles Turner, the Judge who presided over the trial. His letter to Governor Richard J. Olgesby read:

>Sir-
>At the request of friends interested on behalf of one William Berry a citizen of Tazewell County who was tried and convicted at the November Special term of the Circuit Court of Tazewell County of manslaughter, for the killing of one GEORGE PEPPERS, and sentenced for one year in the penitentiary. I desire to say that I fully concur in the recommendation of the jurors who tried him as well as others who join in recommending him to Executive Clemency. There were some strong mitigating circumstances connected with the case not sufficient in my opinion however to render the killing justifiable) which taken in connection with his general good character I think are sufficient grounds for recommending his pardon.
>
>I am Respectfully Your Obt. Servt.
>
>CHAS. TURNER
>Judge 21st Circuit

Next came the letter from the ex-mayor and local newspaper owner, W.H. Seller, who wrote:

In the application that will be made for the pardon of
BILL BERRY, convicted of manslaughter in the
Circuit Court of this county, and sentenced to one
year of imprisonment in the penitentiary, I am of the
opinion that there are just grounds for the exercise
of Executive Clemency. There seems to be
circumstances connected with the unfortunate affair,
which, if not sufficient to render the killing entirely
justifiable ought to at least to greatly mitigate the
offense. The entire jury, together with many of our
best citizens have signed the petition for pardon, and
it is the general impression of all whom I have heard
express themselves concerning this case, that to
pardon BERRY would be an act of mercy well
exercised and wholly justifiable on the part of the
Executive.

> Respectfully
> Your Obt. Servt.
> W.H. Sellers

Not to be out done by the judge, another letter to the
Governor was from none other that the prosecutor, State's
Attorney, C.G. WHITNEY, and he wrote:

Dear Sir,
My attention has been called to the case of William
Berry who was tried at the Special November Term
of our Circuit Court and convicted of manslaughter,
and who has been recommended for Executive
Clemency. I do heartily concur in the opinion
of Judge Turner that the circumstances disclosed
in the trial were of a character well calculated to
mitigate the offense. While I did not nor cannot

believe that the killing was justifiable, yet under the circumstances I cheerfully recommend that BERRY have the interposition of Executive favor on his behalf.

His character heretofore has been irreproachable and I believe the ends of justice would be fully served if He were pardoned from the penalty of his offense.

Respectfully your
C.G. WHITNEY
State's Attorney
21st Judicial Circuit

There was even one from all the court officials, which read:

To His Excellency, the Governor of the State Of Illinois

The undersigned being somewhat acquainted with the facts as given in evidence to the jury in the case of the people VS William Berry, convicted of manslaughter at the Special November Term, A.D. 1868 of the Tazewell Circuit Court for the killing of George Peppers, and knowing the general good character of the said William Berry; concur in the opinion that his case is a proper one for the excuse of Executive clemency and pardon, and to that end do join with the jurors who tried the case and the Judge before whom it was, in the petition that your Excellency will grant a full pardon to the said William Berry.

S.E. Barber - CO. Treas.

M.A. Henry - Magistrate Chancery, Tazewell
Co. Illinois
W.W. Charmus - County Clerk
Edward Pratt - Sheriff T.C.
H.P. Finigan - Clerk Circuit Court

    The preceding letters were from men of high position and power. Those letters, along with the petitions, would no doubt have been enough to effect the pardon; but, just to put the icing on the cake, the "entire jury," as W.H. Sellers had written in his letter to the Governor, wrote their own letter of petition. That letter to the Governor read:

> To his Excellency the Governor of the State of
> Illinois
> The undersigned respectfully petition that your
> Excellency will pardon William Berry a citizen of
> Tazewell County, Illinois, and who at the Special
> November Term A.D. 1868 of the Circuit Court in
> and said County of Tazewell was found by the jury
> guilty of Manslaughter of George Peppers upon an
> indictment by the Grand Jury of said County found
> against him the said William Berry, and his term of
> confinement in the penitentiary fixed at one year-and
> your petitioners, the undersigned represent to your
> Excellency that we were of the jury which tried said
> case and found said verdict that we have no doubt
> upon the evidence that William Berry the defendant
> is a man of unquestioned and unimpeachable good
> character as a citizen and the offense for which he
> was convicted was done in the heat of passion and
> under provocation of an assault and attack upon
> him, and that we only found him guilty under the
> imperative sense of duty under the law and we

believe no good will be accomplished by his confinement in the penitentiary.

H.B. Barnard	Albert Frazer
Reuben Hyers	J.D. Warburton
Fred Schaefer	Henry Crall
Franklin Michael	Steven Stevens
Wm. H. Still	Lorenzo Nass
David Shuttleworth	L.B. Chamberlain

All the letters and petitions noted the "general good character" of William Berry and begged the Governor to pardon this poor family man. Richard Olgesby, governor at the time, no doubt knew nothing about the character of this man, but with all the very top-notch people in Tazewell County signing petitions and writing letters, he would feel obliged to look into the case.

Their reasons for signing the petitions or writing the letters is unknown, but one might want to look once more upon the political pressures, intimidation, and payoffs that prevailed so during those young years of the State of Illinois and the County of Tazewell for the answers.

Human beings have long been noted for being followers and it usually takes only a slight effort to cause frenzy among them. Believing they were doing the right neighborly thing, the entire county was caught up in the whirlwind of signing the petitions and writing letters. That is, all except one man.

That man, Tazewell County Deputy Sheriff Alfred Stone, knew well the man everyone was dumping praise upon; the man everyone was talking about; the man who had managed to make a mockery out of the judicial system, with his "general good character;" and the man who had conned an entire society. Stone knew this man for what he was - a dangerous criminal who had a persuasive nature about him that most people could not resist.

36

Deputy Stone, you see, was a rather unique figure in his day. As a top law enforcement officer of Tazewell County, despite the various chaos and political shenanigans that were ripe at this time, Deputy Stone could not be bought by anyone. He was a man who had worked his way upward through the various law enforcement agencies in order to achieve his position as a highly respected lawman, depending on no one but himself to achieve his goals. The populous of the county knew him to be a tough, unyielding enforcer of the laws. His concept of the law of the land was such that, if there were a law proscribing an illegal activity, he would enforce that law in a tough and aggressive manner. Simply put, he refused to sway to the winds of political pressures.

It was with this background that Stone watched as the people signed the petitions with such vigor. He simply could not understand how anyone could look upon Berry as a hero instead of the cold-blooded killer he actually was.

On January 1, 1869, acting on the orders of Judge Charles Turner, Sheriff Edward Pratt delivered William Berry to Joliet where he handed him over to the Officer in Charge. He was given a receipt for the delivery of his body as ordered. The Officer then turned to Berry and handed him a pardon from Governor Olgesby.

Berry had not even been locked up. He had slipped through the fingers of justice again, this time on the most serious of crimes, the killing of another human being.

With the pardon in hand, Berry walked out of the prison a free man and accompanied Sheriff Pratt back to Pekin on the same train. And why not? Sheriff Pratt had signed the petitions for that very pardon.

6

Had justice been done in this matter? Did the people think they had done a good Samaritan deed? Perhaps so, but that deed would come back to haunt them in less than seven months. Perhaps the good people who petitioned the Governor felt the pardon would change Bill Berry's ways; and if that was the case, they were right.

The change, however, was not one to their favor, for Bill Berry began to brag openly about the "great crime" he had committed and gotten away with. Over and over he told the story of killing Pepper and soon began to think of himself as a great criminal mind. His farm was soon overrun with cutthroats and thieves from all over the county, and then some.

There was John Orrel, a young man who had been hanging around for years. Most often Orrel was involved with his brother Henry, or with a fellow named Conner, with whom he committed several crimes. John Orrel, his brother Henry, and Conner were arrested and convicted of burglaries in Pekin as well as in Mason County.

Some of the goods stolen in the burglaries had managed to find their way to the Berry gang, as was apparent by the rather unique clothing worn by Emanuel and Isaac Berry. Both wore clothing made of bed ticking.

Several bolts of bed ticking cloth had been stolen from a downtown Pekin store by Orrel and his friends. Bed ticking cloth was rarely used to make clothing. Its usual use was coverings for mattresses and pillows.

John and Henry Orrel, arrested in the Pekin burglary of the bed ticking cloth, filed a motion for a change of venue to Mason County and it was granted. John Orrel had already escaped from the Mason County jail several times, and had acquired the title of "escape artist." He was transported to Mason County and shortly afterward managed to escape again.

Josiah Coombs was another horse-thief who spent a lot of time at the Berry farmhouse and was considered to be a strong member of the gang.

In addition, "ole man Lane", was another strong member. There were others involved, but these were the most active, and one can see why the local decent people were frightened of them.

Although Bill Berry never actively participated in criminal acts, his home became the rendezvous for such men. When they were in trouble with the law, Bill would hide them out, or his attorney, John B. Cohrs, would bail them out. The number of burglaries, horse and cattle thefts, incidents of passing counterfeit money, and other crimes, began to climb in the area. As usual, though everyone knew it was the Berrys, the law was unable to get the proof necessary to make an arrest.

It was at this time that the citizens began to realize just how wrong they had been in begging the Governor for a pardon. They began to see that Bill Berry had conned the entire society of Tazewell County.

News of Bill Berry's pardon was met with mixed reactions in Tazewell County. Many citizens of Pekin, residing in the county seat and familiar with the testimony in the case, hailed the fairness of the decision. Likewise, many from Circleville were elated to see their friend, relative, or neighbor benefit from the Governor's justifiable act of mercy. Most of those who signed the petition for Bill Berry's pardon lived in these areas. The citizens of Delavan, however, felt differently. For many of them, Bill Berry's pardon represented the latest in a string of failures by the judicial system. For the second time in a decade, retribution for the most horrible of crimes had not been fully exacted. The executive privilege had been abused, and a murderer of one of Delavan's citizens, though found guilty in court, never spent a day in prison. The men of Delavan, were also haunted by the ghost of Abner Underhill, another unfortunate soul who had met a violent and untimely death, and whose murderer was never found, though many felt it was also at the hands of the Berry brothers. Now George Pepper's death was crying for justice.

Yet there was no indication that justice would be forthcoming. As the citizenry of Tazewell County welcomed the arrival of a new-year, the Circleville gang had much to celebrate. Bill Berry had killed a man, but had been quickly pardoned. John Orrel, the well-known thief, burglar, and escape artist was still free. And, although three persons had been charged with the beating and robbery of Ed Howard, charges against two had been dropped, and the third was out on bond.

If the Circleville gang felt any elation over these developments it would be short-lived; for even as Bill Berry stepped out of the gate of the state prison at Joliet, walls were beginning to tighten around his group.

As so often occurs in our history, the walls which ultimately lead to a criminal's downfall and confinement are not made of brick or stone and mortar, but of paper; and true to history, a wall of paper would soon close in on the Circleville gang.

Following his release from prison and the end of his ordeal relating to the Pepper killing, Bill Berry may have mistakenly believed his troubles were over and that better times lay ahead. It was at this time that Bill contracted with his brothers, Simeon and Emanuel, to pay $600.00 for their interest in four tracts of land totaling 68 acres, which had been a part of their father's estate.

It is not known whether payment for those transactions was made in cash, or if special terms were arranged. Either way, $600.00 represented a significant amount of money that would have to be accounted for at some time. The figure of $600.00 is even more significant considering the events that were to follow.

During the 1869 February term of court, William Taylor Shay failed to appear, leaving Mathew McFarland and A.B.C. Knox holding the bag for the bail money they had put up.

Mathew McFarland was served papers requiring him to appear in court and explain why the bond money posted on behalf of William Taylor Shay should not be forfeited.

Nathan Caswell, during the February term of court, also entered a suit against Bill Berry, seeking damages for treatment of the wounds inflicted when he attempted to intervene in the Berry-Pepper struggle of the preceding September.

Bill Berry, though out of prison, may not have been out of the paper walls, better known as debts.

As winter wore down and spring arrived, elections were held, and Alfred Stone was again appointed as City Marshal. Rudolph Kessler was appointed as Assistant City Marshal.

About the same time, property taxes became due. Some of the Berrys could not, or would not, pay. On May 14th, 1869 the Tazewell County Republican published a list of property owners delinquent in paying taxes. William Berry was listed as owing taxes totaling more than $30.00 on four tracts of land. Rachel Berry, Bill's mother was also listed as being delinquent on two tracts of land in the amount of $11.66.

As the spring term of the Circuit Court convened in Pekin in June of 1869, the financial woes of the Circleville gang became more apparent. Mathew McFarland and John Boyle were sued by R.S. Updike.

After a short jury trial, McFarland and Boyle were found liable in the amount of $112.15. As defendant in a lawsuit initiated by Aaron Shay, McFarland was able to obtain a continuance, but he was still on the hook for the bond posted on behalf of William Taylor Shay, who had still not appeared before the court.

Emanuel Berry had problems to contend with, as well. He was indicted for, of all things, "adultery" by the Grand Jury of the June term of the Circuit Court. That charge came from Pekin, where he had taken up with a woman even though he was known to be married. The affair had become so open and notorious that the people decided they could not allow it to continue, as it was causing a scandal. Emanuel was arrested and brought before the Tazewell County court for adultery in July of 1869. He appeared in court where the judge promptly read the charges against him, and recognized his appearance. Emanuel, not wanting a conviction that might land him in the calaboose for a year, plead not guilty; and his case was continued, giving the gang just one more problem to worry about financially.

Several suits were pending against William Berry. The Nathan Caswell suit for damages had not gone away. In addition, Bill was also being sued separately by his uncle,

Thomas Larimore, and his brother's mother-in-law, Harriet McKean. Could the "secret society" be working?

With aid from his attorneys, Cohrs and Saltonstall, Bill managed to have these causes continued, but the legal fees owed by Bill and others in the Berry orbit continued to mount.

In late June, Bill Berry was arrested on a charge of "harboring a common thief". Josiah Combs, Samuel Miller, and Jacob Terry, accused of assisting Berry, were arrested on the same charge. For what reason Bill had decided to hide or "harbor" a thief is unknown, but perhaps he had done what his brothers had always expected of him - to protect a member of the gang.

One Parker Vanorstrand, who on The 30th of June appeared before Justice of the Peace William H.H. Larimore and swore out the affidavit, initiated the charge against Bill Berry and the others.

Arrest warrants were immediately issued and promptly executed by Constable William Fletcher Copes, who brought the four accused before Justice Larimore in Circleville. Upon hearing further testimony from Samuel Miller and James Gordon, Larimore entered guilty verdicts against the four defendants. Josiah Combs was required to post $200.00 cash bond.

Bill Berry was required to post bond as well. Although the exact figure for Berry's bond is unknown, it is safe to assume that it was at least $200.00. He, after all, was the principal defendant. The others were merely accessories. Jacob Terry and Samuel Miller, who were somehow involved, were both charged and later released on $200.00 bonds - quite a considerable amount of money for a farmer to have to come up with in those days. All four were required to appear at the next term of the Circuit Court, where the final determination of guilt and judgment, if necessary, would be made.

As one can see, it appeared the secret societies and the lawmen had joined together to create problems for the gang. Most of the charges and suits were so petty, they were rarely used. Adultery? In those days when major crimes abounded, it was doubtful that anyone other than a gang member would have been given a passing glance.

Monies were paid out, or more commonly, owed by the gang on all fronts. Judgments, taxes, bail, and personal contracts totaled several hundred dollars. That represented an enormous amount of money at the time, when thirty dollars a month was considered very good wages.

Undoubtedly, the man deepest in debt was none other than Bill Berry himself. Bill's obligation to Simeon and Emanuel, whether it constituted an actual outlay of cash, or merely an informal agreement among brothers, was surely significant. Even more so was Bill's debt to the three persons suing him. His tax problems were a concern as well, as were those experienced by his mother, Rachel. Two hundred dollars of his own money was tied up in bond, payment to his attorneys was overdue, and judging from claims against his estate, Bill Berry owed numerous professional and businessmen hundreds of dollars.

Others in the gang had troubles as well. John Orrel was sought by the law, as was William Taylor Shay. Shay had also forfeited his bond of $100 for failure to appear at the last term of court. McFarland owed money, as did Boyle. Josiah Coombs had posted $200.00 bond money that he surely did not want to lose, and Samuel and Terry Miller each had $200.00 posted as bond they did not want to forfeit.

Emanuel Berry still had to be concerned about the upcoming adultery case. With debts and obligations combined, the Circleville gang was in desperate need of financial aid. They needed money and needed it fast. It seemed what they had been "harvesting" was being used up for bail as fast as they could obtain it.

At some point during the first six months of 1869, Bill Berry began to change. Perhaps driven to the point of desperation by all the lawsuits and arrests, Bill had long since stopped being the respected and successful farmer.

As evidenced by charges filed against him, newspaper accounts which recited popular opinions of the Berry family, and later court testimony, we know that by June of 1869 Berry's home had become a haven for criminals. Although there is no evidence that he was directly involved in stealing, he was in fact protecting the others in their criminal activities.

Having been sentenced to prison for simply defending himself from a larger, stronger assailant and a long time foe at that may have left a bad taste in his mouth for the judicial system. Perhaps the stigma he and his family experienced as a result of his being a convicted felon - a murderer - created in Bill Berry a sense of resentment for those "respectable" citizens who now regarded him and his family with contempt.

Besieged with insurmountable debts, William Berry saw no way out except to relinquish his role as his brothers' advocate, and to become, at the very least, a recipient of the rewards of their illegal deeds.

With his knowledge, Isaac Berry made plans that would bring in some money - some big money. That plan was to steal horses and cattle, and sell them, no questions asked, to someone with whom he had already made arrangements.

Ike begin a search for more men who were "business," as he called it, meaning men who could be trusted to do the job right. He was able to locate one man in short order. That man was Cornelius Daly, who was also known as the Peddler, gaining the nickname, no doubt, by peddling someone else's livestock. Daly soon became a fixture around the old saloon and at Bill's home.

Cornelius Daly, alias the Peddler, was very short, standing only five feet three and three quarters of an inch in height. He had a slim build and shifty eyes that made him look like he was ready to take flight. The eyes were light brown and his hair was brown. He was married and had two children. He could read and write and was the only member of the gang not born in the United States. Cornelius Daly had been born in Ireland.

On July 24th, 1869, to make matters worse for the gang, Justice William Larimore filed complaints against Bill Berry, and et al, for harboring a thief - John Orrel - wanted for escaping from the Mason County Jail.

Bill was immediately rounded up, arrested and taken before the court. He was released on bail, however, immediately afterward.

During the July term of the Tazewell County Circuit Court, Emanuel Berry went to trial for the Adultery offense. After evidence was heard, he was found guilty and received a substantial fine.

His wild romantic affair ended and Emanuel went back to Circleville to his wife, Mary (Farrow) Berry, whom he had married March 26, 1866, and to their three children. He was now in more financial trouble due to the fine levied on him by the court.

About this same time, on his mother-in-law's farm, near Forest City, in Mason County, Isaac Berry struck up a conversation with an odd, evil-looking twenty-one year old Irish immigrant whom he had became acquainted with during his lengthy stays in that county.

Robert Britton, the man with whom Ike Berry spoke that day, stood just over five feet eight inches tall. This "bullet-headed bully," as a Jacksonville paper later called him, possessed a roundish face punctuated by small deep-set eyes and a black mustache. His dark brown hair, combed back on the sides "ala pugilist," framed and provided contrast to his light complexion, giving his face a ruddy appearance. Robert Britton's "overall demeanor was by no means indicative of intelligence or any moral attributes".

He was, however, precisely the type of man Ike Berry was looking for. The same qualities that would later repulse reporters covering this event apparently attracted Ike, who approached this queer-looking man. Ike explained that he wanted him to go to Circleville and assist in stealing some horses and cattle.

Britton at first refused. In an attempt to reassure his reluctant would-be accomplice, Ike told Britton that if any problems developed, his brother, Bill, would swear them clear, or in other words, give them an alibi. A quantity of liquor was procured and the two acquaintances began to imbibe. After a time, Britton got tight and consented to follow Ike to Circleville. After all, any old horse would bring a quick $100.00 in those days, and two nice matched teams complete with harness would fetch a small fortune.

Late in July 1869, Ike and Britton arrived in Circleville. One of Ike's first stops was Bill's home, where he introduced Britton only as "Frank", a name no doubt decided upon to conceal his real identity since he was not known in the area. He explained that Britton was there to help steal the horses.

Accepting this, Bill offered Britton a place to stay, which Britton in turn accepted. All components for the tragedies to follow were now in place...

7

In 1848, a man named Harrison Clary had contracted for 212 acres of land southeast of Circleville, less than a mile from the town limits. He seemed to have been a reasonably industrious man, married, and the father of five children.

In 1853, Clary added to his property by contracting for several pieces of land that brought his property holdings within the town limits of Circleville itself. He had built a home for his family near the southern county highway that connected Circleville with Dillon, and seemed to be well on the way toward accumulating holdings sufficient to see to the future needs of his children.

All seemed to be going well for the Clary family until Harrison's untimely death. Harrison Clary died leaving the large tract of land to be managed by his widow and two sons, who were barely in their teens. That was not for long, as most of the land had to be sold in order to pay debts. The Clary family was able to salvage an 80-acre tract of land containing the family homestead, but a third of this land, being covered in timber, was untillable. They did not have much, but they did own the land and two spans of horses, complete with the best of harness. With seventeen year-old Wilbur being prematurely thrust into the role of head of the family, they were also easy pickings for thieves.

From the south side of McFarland's saloon, headquarters for the Berrys, the Clary homestead was clearly visible across the open fields that lay due north of it. It was easy to observe the comings and goings at the Clary place, and more importantly, it was easy to discern the exact location of their valuable livestock.

From the elevated vantage point afforded by McFarland's saloon, Ike Berry and Robert Britton gazed down upon the Clary farm and finalized their plans to relieve Wilbur Clary of his beautiful horses, both spans, as well as the harness and, perhaps as an after thought, a wagon as well. The proceeds from the sale of Clary's property would provide welcome financial relief for the monetary problems of the Berrys. Two matched teams complete with harness and a fine wagon would bring near a thousand dollars if sold to the right people, and apparently they knew just the right people in Mason County. A buyer had already been lined up, but two men could not accomplish the task. They would need help - someone they trusted who was familiar with the area.

That Ike and Frank sought assistance is understandable, their choice of an accomplice, however, was perhaps the most ironic development in this bizarre chain of events.

Circleville was a rogue's gallery of potential accomplices. Simeon and Emanuel Berry, "always regarded suspiciously" by the general population, were available. Cornelius Daly, the recently arrived peddler, was in Circleville making his temporary home at Bill Berry's place. Josiah Combs, Sam Miller and Matt McFarland, none of whom would be adverse to making a quick, dishonest buck, were available. Also available for service were William Taylor Shay and John Orrell, both fugitives from the justice system, but still in touch with their Circleville confederates and having little to lose and much to gain from the type of endeavor Ike and Britton proposed. A veritable who's who of criminals was available from which to choose. Yet Ike and Britton ignored the obvious talents of these needy individuals and chose instead the bartender at McFarland's saloon, William Shaw, the least likely candidate of all.

William Shaw was born in Illinois in 1832. He married Irene Welch, a sister of Nancy (Welch) Berry, thereby making him a brother-in-law to none other than Bill Berry.

In July of 1857, William Shaw was accused of stealing wheat from one Charles W. Morris, the affidavit having been sworn before none other than Charles Turner, a Justice of the Peace at the time, but destined to become a Civil War General and later a Circuit Judge. In the latter role, Turner would, of course, become well acquainted with the Berry's, the Orrell's, and the rest of the Circleville gang.

In October of 1857, the mittimus for Shaw's arrest was executed. He was arrested, brought before the proper authorities, and released on a $200.00 recognizance bond. The larceny charge was later dismissed, reportedly as a result of Shaw agreeing to compensate Morris for the missing wheat.

Sometime after 1860, Shaw moved his family to Peoria, but remained there for only a short time before returning to Circleville, where he bought a farm. How he had acquired enough money to purchase a farm while living for such a short time in Peoria had always raised eyebrows around Circleville. The farm was located about one-fourth mile north of Circleville, in the south east corner of Cincinnati Township.

In his spare time, Shaw worked as a barkeep in McFarland's saloon. As a relative of Bill Berry by marriage, he was considered family by Ike and was just the person he was looking for.

At McFarland's saloon, Shaw engaged in conversation with Ike and the stranger he introduced only as Frank. The meeting took place on July 28th, and after some preliminary conversation, Ike, Robert Britton and Shaw retired to a private place where Ike detailed their plan.

Shaw was surprised when he heard it was to be Wilbur Clary's horses. It happened that he had always liked the family and respected young Wilbur for taking over as head of the family when his father died. He knew what the family had been through already, and knew that if they lost those horses it would be devastating. Shaw made his mind up. This theft was something he would not let happen. Though disgusted with the two of them, Shaw feigned interest in the scheme.

Perhaps seeing the look of disgust in Shaw's eyes and mistaking it for doubt about his own ability to handle the job, Ike thought it necessary to tell a bit about his past escapades. During the course of this conversation, he told Shaw that he had been engaged in stealing horses and cattle for some time and that during all these times he had never been caught. If just by chance, however, problems did develop, he could get Bill to swear them clear. He'd give them an alibi.

Satisfied Shaw was in, Ike set plans for the theft to take place the following night. Shaw, still pretending to be interested but claiming a prior commitment for the present, left the meeting.

Shaw went home and gave the matter much thought. He was determined to stop them from stealing Clary's horses. After much inner deliberations, considering Ike was nearly his brother-in-law, he went to W.H.H. Larimore, the local Justice of the Peace and told him the contents of his conversation with Ike and Britton.

Larimore was certainly not a fan of the Berrys and was a full-blown member of the secret society. He was excited about the chance to grab a Berry, and urged Shaw to inform the authorities of Ike's plan.

Heeding this advice and doing what he would later call his "duty," Shaw mounted his horse and rode to Pekin to talk to the authorities. He went to Pekin's newly re-appointed city marshal, Alfred Stone, and provided him with a detailed account of his conversation with Ike and "Frank," including what Ike had told him about his career of stealing horse and cattle.

Stone was well acquainted with the Berry family and the Circleville gang, but did not know who "Frank" was. Excitement ran through him as he listened to Shaw's story. It certainly rang of truth, and he was determined to do something about it.

Stone went to Sheriff Pratt, explained the situation, and together they made plans for the coming night. Because Stone had developed the information, Sheriff Pratt let him handle the case.

On July 29, 1869, enlisting the aid of his two trusted night officers, James Milner and Lewis Cass, Stone decided to go to the Clary place where he would wait for the rare opportunity of catching a Berry in the act of committing a crime.

It was well after sunset when Stone, Milner, and Cass slipped quitely into Circleville and positioned themselves in and around Clary's barn to watch the horses. They had a clear view of McFarland's saloon and could easily detect any movement around the place.

The saloon had several patrons that night. Knowing something might happen, Justice Larimore was the first to arrive that evening. "Frank" and Ike were there, as was Josiah

Coombs, Mathew McFarland, and one of the Miller brothers. Shaw did not show up.

Unfortunately, the lawmen positioned about Clary's barn were too far away to recognize specific individuals as they waited anxiously, battling not only the July heat, but also mosquitoes and other flying insects as well.

Shortly after midnight, Stone saw the lights from McFarland's saloon began to flicker and die. He watched several men leave the saloon and finally he could see the outline of Ike Berry and another man (matching Shaw's description of the stranger named "Frank") step off the porch and head northward on East Street - the opposite direction of Clary's place. They were not going to steal the horses.

Stone reasoned that perhaps they were spooked when Shaw didn't show up. It was possible they saw the lawmen, or perhaps Shaw had a change of heart and told Ike about his trip to Pekin. Then again, maybe they were heading over to Shaw's house and would then go steal the horses. It was several hours before sunrise. He decided to follow them.

Maintaining a safe distance, Stone and his men followed Ike and Frank as they staggered north on East Street, then turned westbound on William Street where they continued on toward Bill Berry's house.

As the small posse silently stalked Ike and Frank, the lawmen suddenly realized they were not alone. Justice Larimore and a couple of other local citizens, who recognized Stone and, knowing the rarity of such a late night appearance by him in Circleville, cautiously trailed behind.

Knowing Larimore to be the local Justice of the Peace as well as the Post-Master, Marshal Stone cautioned him and the others to be quiet, and allowed them to tag along.

When Ike and Frank entered Bill's house, Stone motioned his men into position to watch it. He needed to be patient, for it was possible that Ike and the stranger might be going to pick up an accomplice to replace Shaw - one of the many common thieves said to be staying at this house, or maybe even Bill himself.

Stone watched with disappointment as the lights from Bill house faded and died, and the area became shrouded in darkness. No one had left the house. It seemed the effort to catch a Berry in the act of committing a crime had been thwarted. There would be no attempt on Clary's property that night.

Considerable amounts of time, energy, and manpower stood to be wasted if an arrest was not to be forthcoming. It would do no good to wait for another night. The posse had already been spotted by citizens and the word would certainly get back to Ike. Word would also spread that the gang had once again escaped arrest and might well be, as popularly assumed, invulnerable to prosecution.

Stone had a decision to make. He could take his posse and leave, but such an act would certainly be interpreted as a sign of defeat on the part of the lawmen; or he could initiate an arrest. The charge would not be larceny, but rather the very rarely used law of "inciting to commit a felony," a common law offense. This, for trying to get Shaw to help steal horses.

Stone pondered these thoughts as he, his posse, and a few curious onlookers stared at Bill Berry's darkened farmhouse. Finally, unwilling to accept defeat, Stone chose his course of action. He had no warrants and he had viewed no crime being committed, but he had probable cause to believe that a crime had been committed. Not the crime of larceny, but that of inciting another to commit a larceny. This he had in statements from Shaw himself, and he would use this as his cause for arrest. He had set out to arrest Ike and "Frank" tonight and he fully intended to do just that.

Stone gave his men the high sign and they approached Bill Berry's house. As they neared the building, Milner and Cass took up positions around it, and Stone went upon the porch and boldly pounded on the front door.

Bill Berry answered the door and acted shocked by the sight of Marshal Stone, standing there, with gun drawn, demanding to see Ike and the stranger. Impatiently, Stone pushed Bill aside and entered the house. Milner and Cass hurried behind him, as the onlookers still hiding in the darkness pressed forward to view the proceedings.

Ike Berry and Britton rousted from their beds by the noise, staggered forward to meet Stone who informed them that they were under arrest. Caught unaware, drunk, and facing three armed men apparently intent on fulfilling their mission, Ike and Frank had no opportunity to resist.

Resistance was ill-advised on other counts as well, for a crowd of witnesses were present and any violence conducted in view of such a group might later come back to haunt the pair in a court of law. Still, there was another reason they decided not to resist. That was Stone. He was well known to the Berrys, and in fact the only man in the whole county that Ike actually feared.

Bill, being the businessman he was, questioned the validity of the arrests. Stone, fully aware of the fact that the arrests would be meaningless unless William Shaw swore out affidavits and the appropriate warrants were issued, ignored Bill's protests. Ike and Britton were placed in irons and prepared for transport to the county jail.

On the way to Pekin, Stone sent Cass to Shaw's place with a message. He was on notice to appear in Pekin in a few hours to swear to warrants against Ike and "Frank," or Stone would personally come for him.

Ike Berry and Britton were marched on foot the eight miles to Pekin where, by four o'clock in the morning, they were lodged in jail. Robert Britton refused to give any name other than "Frank". He was booked simply as "Frank".

As the steel jail doors slammed shut in front of them, Ike Berry reminded Britton of his earlier promise - that their incarceration was only a temporary inconvenience and, come morning, Brother Bill would swear them clear.

8

Well aware of the circumstances behind the arrests, Bill Berry, immediately sprang into action making plans for getting the boys out of jail. Only one man could have supplied the information to the law that led to the arrest of the pair. That was William Shaw. Now he knew why Shaw had failed to show at the saloon.

The remedy seemed simple to Bill on that already hot Friday morning. He had to get Shaw to change his story. If he did, there would be no basis for the arrests, and the arrests would be illegal. Besides, the horses were still secure within Clary's pasture and no harnesses had been stolen, therefore, no crime had been committed. Indeed, the suspects had overdone it at McFarland's saloon the night before. They were far from able to commit a felony and were merely searching for a place where they could sleep off the ill effects of their indulgences. At least that would be Bill's story.

Bill knew Shaw could be stubborn when he made up his mind about something and persuading him to change his story might not be easy, but, still, it was worth a try. And what better way to do this than to offer Shaw a ride to town as a token of their continued friendship. While alone during the eight dusty miles to Pekin, he would convince Shaw that it would be in his best interest to proceed no further with the affair.

Berry drove his horse and buggy to Shaw's farm and offered him the ride. Shaw accepted and, once aboard, they headed for Pekin. Berry talked to Shaw about the matter, but talk as he would, Shaw could not be convinced to change his mind. He told Berry that, for the sake of justice, he could not change his story. Besides, if he did, Stone might jail him for lying or, even worse, obstruction of justice, since he had already told him about the incident.

Stone had made it very clear that he would testify, or he would have to deal with him later; and Shaw had already decided that he would rather deal with the Berrys than with Stone.

When they arrived in Pekin, Bill pulled up in front of Attorney John Cohr's office, just a few doors away from the jail.

Shaw hurriedly departed in the direction of Marshal Stone's office in the Town Hall.

A short while later, both Isaac Berry and Robert Britton were grinning from ear to ear as they were led from their cell to Sheriff Pratt's office to be released. Brother Bill and Attorney Cohrs had "sworn them clear" again.

Ed Pratt could do nothing but grit his teeth as he slowly started gathering the personal property taken the night before, trying to buy time for State's Attorney C.G. Whitney and Shaw to locate Esquire Glasgow to swear to complaints for warrants. Pratt had hoped they could get it done before he had to release them.

Bill Berry and Cohrs were enjoying this little victory very much, and Pratt wondered again, as he had many times in the past, how the Berrys could afford the services of Cohrs, who did not come cheap. It seemed as though Cohrs, or his associate, N.W. Green, always represented not only the Berry brothers, but their friends as well. Pratt knew the gang had to be stealing to pay his fees.

Sheriff Pratt stole glances out the window of the jail, looking for some sign that Whitney and Shaw were on their way, and wondering what was taking so long. He could wait no longer. He had been a sheriff for only a few months and he was still not sure about the legality of arrests without warrants. Cohrs had already warned him that it was "false imprisonment," and Cohrs would know because he had only recently represented the victim of an arrest without warrant incident, in which two Pekin Police officers had been indicted and ordered locked up for unlawful arrest. This was still fresh in his mind and he did not need that problem right now. That would mean the end of his political career. He could only hope that Shaw did not change his mind about testifying. His testimony would be their only chance to get the warrants and lock these two up again. He hated to see the Berrys get off, but he had no choice.

Gritting his teeth, he handed the two outlaws their personal belongings and watched as the four men walked out of the jail into the street, where they stopped and began talking and laughing.

Out on the street, Bill argued with Ike, trying to convince him that Shaw was getting two warrants right this minute and that if they did not leave town soon, the Sheriff would be out to lock them up again.

Ike wanted Bill to drive them home in his buggy because he and Britton had been forced to walk the eight miles earlier, but Bill insisted he had to stay in town to talk Shaw out of testifying before the Justice of Peace.

Ike and Britton reluctantly stomped off, both dreading the long hot walk back to Circleville.

Bill and Cohrs strutted off down the street, knowing the Berrys had scored yet another victory over the law.

When Shaw first arrived in Pekin that morning, he had gone to Marshal Stone's office. Stone had taken him directly to the courthouse to meet with Cassius Whitney, the State's Attorney.

In Whitney's office, Shaw again related what he had told Marshal Stone. Hearing this, Whitney took Shaw to Justice of Peace J.W. Glasgow's office, where, once again, Shaw told his story, this time under oath.

Justice Glasgow, acting upon this information, issued warrants for both Issac Berry and, having no other name, "Frank," for soliciting another to commit a larceny.

With warrants in hand, Cassius Whitney and Shaw left the office and headed for the jail. Suddenly, Bill Berry and Cohrs blocked their way.

Berry asked Whitney if he was going to get warrants for the arrest of Ike and his friend, Britton.

Whitney answered in a calm voice, saying that he had, in fact, already gotten the warrants issued.

Angrily, Berry inquired as to what the warrants were for.

Whitney told him it was inciting a man to commit a crime of larceny.

In a menacing tone of voice, Berry told Whitney that he should not give it to the Sheriff because the boys had not done anything. He threatened Whitney, saying there would be trouble. If the officers went out there trying to arrest the boys, someone would get hurt.

Seeing he was getting nowhere with the conversation, Whitney stepped around Berry and he and Shaw continued on to the jail.

They soon learned that Isaac and "Frank" had been released and had already left town. There was nothing Sheriff Pratt could do but go after them, and as it was only ten o'clock in the morning, he decided to wait until later in the day to serve the warrants.

When Shaw left the jail, Bill was waiting. He approached Shaw and asked if he was going home.

Shaw replied that he did not have a horse.

Bill went to his buggy, tied to a nearby hitching post, got in, and drove to where Shaw was walking along the street. He told him to get in the buggy.

Reluctantly, Shaw climbed into the buggy, and they headed out of town.

Shaw knew that Bill was mad and that there would be some trouble when they got to Circleville. He was not particularly afraid of Bill or any of the others individually, but together they could pose a problem.

During the trip back, Bill asked him why he had sworn to the warrants.

Shaw told him it was his duty.

Arriving at Circleville, Berry did what Shaw suspected he would do. He drove right up to the saloon where Isaac, Britton, and the others were sitting on the porch.

Shaw knew this would be the wrong time for a confrontation because Isaac and Britton would be tired and angry from their long walk and he could be in real danger.

As soon as the buggy stopped, Bill stepped out onto the porch, pointed his finger at Shaw, who was already walking away as fast as he could, and announced, "There goes the damned son of a bitch who got the warrants."

Shaw headed for old Andrew Ditmon's store. Ditmon was a friend and he knew he would be safe there until he could make his way home.

Once inside the store, Shaw watched the crowd gather at the saloon only a stone's throw away. Knowing it would be best if he was not seen for a while, Shaw slipped out the back door of the store and out through the woods to his house.

Shaw had been up most of the night before and was extremely tired. He lay down on a bed, but was unable to go to sleep. He could hear the ruckus being raised at the saloon and his name used many times in the foulest language, with threats on his life.

Finally, he fell into a half sleep only to be jarred awake minutes later by someone pounding on the door of his home. By their voices, Shaw knew it was Isaac and "Frank." They were trying to kick the door down as they yelled threats at Shaw.

Shaw knew better than to open the door, but just as he thought the door was going to burst open, they stopped pounding on it and he heard them leave. He lay back relieved and fell into a restless sleep.

Ike and Frank went to Ditmon's store where they threatened Ditmon with harm if he did not give them some liquor. Ditmon complied and the two men left the store, but continued to parade around the streets shouting obscenities and threatening resistance to any lawmen who come for them.

In the meantime, Justice William Larimore, hearing the threats of the Berrys to resist any officers coming to arrest them, mounted his horse and raced toward Pekin to warn Sheriff Pratt of the impending trouble.

9

The long hairy tail of the horse is provided to him to aid in his battle against insects. This held true on July 30th, 1869, for the team of horses pulling a wagon along South 14th Street, for their tails were in constant motion, swatting at the dust and insects that pestered their hind quarters and legs. Foam gathering around the harness where it rubbed against the hide of the horse soon turned brown as it became covered with dust. The day had been another long hot one, but hopefully it would cool down soon for the sun was sinking low in the western sky.

Recently, there had been something of a drought, as it had not rained for days, leaving the area dry and dusty. Nothing escaped the dust. It was so powdery on the roadway that it splashed like water around the hooves of the horses. The half-grown corn in the fields along the way was white from dust that had settled upon it from previous travelers.

Now, the dust rose almost straight up in the calm air, making the approach of the team and wagon visible for miles. That same dust, rose up from the hooves of the two large horses only to settle back upon the three men in the wagon, and yet they took no notice, for they were in deep thought of the task that lay before them.

Deputy George Hinman, drove the team as Deputy Henry Pratt, reached into his coat pocket and removed a memorandum book. A single sheet of paper was taken from this book, unfolded, and handed to Assistant City Marshall Rudolph Kessler who was seated behind Pratt.

Kessler recognized the paper as an arrest warrant of the type he had served so many times before. It was not necessary for him to read the entire document. Kessler's attention was drawn to one line about a third of the way down the page where he knew he would find the hand-written names of those to be arrested. The words Isaac Berry and "Frank," a stranger, promptly caught his attention.

Turning toward Pratt, Kessler nodded his approval, perhaps hiding his eagerness to fulfill the demands of the warrant. Refolding the document, he returned it to Henry.

Henry again placed the warrant inside the notebook, which in turn was returned to its place in the right breast pocket of his new black linen coat. Henry settled back as best he could on the hard wooden seat, took out a long thin cigar, and placed it in his mouth. He knew he had just about enough time to enjoy the fine cigar before they reached Circleville. The wagon lumbered its way southward, trailing a stream of gray smoke from Henry's cigar.

Although word had been received that the Berrys were going to resist, Henry wasn't worried about anything. He was experienced in fighting, having spent three years in the Civil War fighting with Company H of the Eleventh Cavalry. That unit had fought some of the most ferocious battles of the war.

His unit was first under fire at Shiloh. Later, they fought at Corenth, Mississippi, Bolevar, Iuka, Lexington, Jackson, Tennessee, and back in the second battle of Corenth They fought in General McPherson's expedition to Canton, Sherman's Meridan raid, and in the relief of Yazoo City. There were many other battles and skirmishes before Pratt was finally discharged on December 22, 1864.

Returning home, he had tried to settle into the normal routine of life. He purchased half ownership of a warehouse in Hopedale, Illinois, just few miles east of Pekin. He had yearned for something with a little more excitement, however, so when his brother Edward was elected sheriff, he took on the job of Deputy Sheriff.

Henry was well regarded by most of the townsfolk and had somehow remained single. He was tall, slim, good-looking, and much of the time had a cigar dangling from his mouth. He had undoubtedly become more striking to the ladies during late July, for he had donned a new black linen coat as well as a new hat - it too, was black. Sheriff Edward Pratt in an attempt to get some type of uniformity among his men, had purchased identical hats and coats for Henry and George Hinman.

On July 30th, 1869, they did in fact have uniformity, as they rode along the dusty road with Circleville on their mind. If this was the kind of excitement Henry had been searching for, perhaps he had just found it, for it certainly looked as though a fight was in the making. They knew all too well from Justice Larimore's information that the Berrys were armed and had boasted all over Circleville that no law was going to take them. The officers also knew they would be greatly outnumbered, but figured they might surprise the boys and, having had no prior resistance from them, felt it might be just drunken boasts and no real resistance would come from the gang. It was on their minds as they slowly made their way south.

The little posse still looked ahead with anticipation to their arrest of Isaac Berry and Frank on the charges of inciting Shaw to commit a larceny, only this time with a warrant. To some, this may have seemed a frivolous charge, but it was all they had at the time, and the officers wanted to show the Berry gang and the citizens of Tazewell County they meant business. From now on, every time they broke the law, the law would be right there to snatch them up and lock them away.

Make no mistake. The officers held no notions that these criminals would remain in jail for any length of time. In fact, they knew that big brother Bill and his trusty lawyer would no doubt have the boys out again by morning; however, the officers would be satisfied just to get them locked up for a day or two to show the Berrys that law does exist in Tazewell County.

The three lawmen rode along silently in the sheriff's wagon, amid the dust, the heat, and the insects. They were approaching the farm of William Fletcher Copes, the local constable of Circleville. He would be needed to help locate the suspects and to make identifications, as well as assist in making the arrests. Besides, Sheriff Pratt had ordered the three young lawmen to pick him up on the way. Though unafraid, they welcomed the presence of an older and more experienced lawman when they faced the Berry gang.

Minutes later, the wagon left the main road and turned west onto the lane leading to the Copes farm. From the yard where he was enjoying the cool shade of the late afternoon, Copes watched the wagon bounce and buck its way up the rough dirt path leading to his house, perhaps wondering who might be paying him a visit on such a hot afternoon. As the wagon drew nearer, he recognized the occupants and immediately suspected the purpose of their visit.

Earlier in the day, Copes had heard talk of Ike Berry's arrest and subsequent release. As Constable of Circleville, he had also heard rumblings concerning the threatening actions of the Berrys in Circleville that afternoon from Justice Larimore. He had ridden past Cope's place on the way to Pekin. Copes had wondered just how long it would be before the sheriff came calling.

Now, near sunset, three armed lawmen sat perched in a wagon in Copes' yard and he knew it was no social call. This was a posse.

Copes' suspicions were soon confirmed by Pratt's first words, "I want you to go with me to Circleville to arrest Isaac Berry and a stranger named Frank. I have a warrant."

A long time resident of Circleville, Copes had grown up with the Berry family and could easily identify any of the clan, including their friends, on sight. He might even be able to identify the stranger, who had been frequenting McFarland's saloon of late. Besides, he might enjoy a little action. It had been a while since he had been involved in a good fight.

Copes was unarmed at the time and had to go back inside his house to get his gun. While he did this, the men in the wagon climbed down for a short but much needed stretch before continuing on. As they moved about, they kept a wary eye toward the south, where they could just make out Bill Berry's house. It was perched on a small rise in the landscape less than a mile away. They could detect no activity around the house.

When Copes came out, he was armed and ready to go, a gunbelt containing his old military 44 caliber colt revolver strapped to his waist under the dark gray suit coat he always wore.

The others liked and trusted Bill Copes. He was a huge, red-haired, honest and friendly man, standing six feet-five inches tall, with a long thin nose, bent slightly to one side, that gave him the look of a prize fighter. He was no nonsense and could be trusted to do the right thing in a fight.

The men climbed into the wagon for the final mile or so of their journey. The ride from Pekin to Copes' place had been bumpy and uncomfortable. They had brought the wagon along to haul the prisoners in. They would have preferred to ride their horses, as they would have been much more comfortable, but the wagon offered more security for the prisoners they intended to take back. Their stop at Copes' place had taken only five minutes.

It took but a few minutes for the wagon to reach Townline Road, which oriented east to west and represented the boundary between Cincinnati and Sand Prairie Townships. The wagon turned east along Townline Road. Moments later, Bill Berry's house came into view.

Hinman slowed the team as the four lawmen gazed across the intervening field of corn plants and cautiously searched for some sign of movement at Bill's residence. Observing no sign of activity there, and having the earlier information from Larimore that the gang was at the saloon, the wagon continued eastward on Townline Road for a quarter of a mile.

McFarland's saloon was where the officers were expecting to find their prey. The saloon had long been headquarters for the gang. It was where they did their drinking, fighting, and general hell-raising. Oftentimes, shots were heard coming from the saloon.

A small cluster of unremarkable buildings soon became visible on a piece of raised ground immediately to the south, but quickly disappeared behind a curtain of trees as the wagon continued its trek eastward to Circleville.

Those precious minutes it had taken the posse to travel from Cope's farm to the outskirts of Circleville had not been wasted. A strategy had been devised. With the village in sight, each member of the posse felt a little surge of energy and excitement as the time neared when their plan would be put into action.

Outnumbered, and with their arrival expected, the entire Berry gang would be waiting for this test of wills on a site of their own choosing. The worst possible course of action under these circumstances would be to openly stroll into town and force a confrontation in the Berry's front yard.

The little posse needed something to shift the odds in their favor. They needed the element of surprise and had decided they would not brazenly and blindly enter the beast's lair. Instead, the approach would be secretive. The wagon would be hidden some place within walking distance of McFarland's saloon. From there, the posse would secretly advance upon the tavern, surprise its patrons and make the arrests before there was an opportunity to resist. Such a plan should work. All that was needed was a suitable place to hide the wagon and the team...a spot which could be reached undetected, yet offered concealment for both the team and the posse as it made its approach on the tavern.

Finding such a site might have presented a problem, but Copes had the answer - the widow Sarah McKasson's place. She and her husband Jacob had farmed the area for years, but after his death, she turned her home into a boarding house. She lived there with her daughter, Anna. Her home was the gathering place for the rest of the town. She lived on East Street just a few hundred feet from the town limits. Her place always had a lot of people coming and going. There would be less suspicion of a team and wagon with four people in it going to McKasson's than anywhere else in town.

From Townline road, Circleville could be entered by one of two narrow lanes, a quarter of a mile apart. The first lane marking the western boundary of Circleville's city limits led to a couple of small shops and to the eight or ten plain-featured houses which constituted the Village's residential district. The chances of finding the gang in this section of town was slim, but entering Circleville in this way had to be avoided for another reason as well.

To enter town by this route, it would be necessary to pass Rachel Berry's farm. If one of the boys happened to be visiting his mother and spotted the wagon, all element of surprise would be lost. The second lane, actually a county road which became East Street when it entered Circleville town limits, was the most logical for the posse to take. It was the most traveled and was in fact the main street of town.

Although the Town Square had been laid out two blocks to the west, it was never built upon and rarely used. The buildings scattered about East Street comprised the town's business district: the post office, two groceries, and the saloon-hotel all compactly housed in four buildings in that end of town. One of these buildings, standing alone on the west side of the street, contained Mathew McFarland's saloon.

On the opposite side of the street to the east was Andrew Ditmon's Grocery and Tobacco store. You could always find Ditmon, a short, chubby, balding man of forty, sitting on his front porch watching the activity at McFarland's. The saloon had been the center of excitement for a long time, even when Ole' Charley Murphy owned the place. Ditmon would be in his favorite chair, leaning back against the wall, watching, until he was forced to vacant his ringside seat by some farmer wanting liquor or tobacco.

As the wagon made its turn onto the north end of East Street, the posse found itself traveling southward down a narrow, dusty country road that darkened and grew more sinister as sunlight faded. It was excellent place for an ambush.

With daylight giving way to dusk, the road was all but covered in shadow cast by huge cottonwood trees and jagged corners of a zigzag-style split-rail fence that bordered the road on both sides near the crest of a gently sloping hillside. Adding to the sinister setting was a wooden bridge spanning a small creek. Beyond the bridge, on the west side of the road, was an apple orchard, which would also be an excellent spot for an ambush.

McKasson's house, east of the road, was still some three hundred yards away. The lawmen knew they had to be alert. George Hinman tugged at the reins. The team, obedient to their driver's will, slowed.

In the distance loomed the faint, darkened silhouette of McFarland's saloon perched on the crest of a much steeper hill directly ahead. The dark saloon was a bad sign. Larimore had said that the Berrys would probably be there, and the plan for making the arrests had been based on that assumption. The saloon appeared deserted, however, and, if truly empty, the lawmen's carefully planned tactics for making the arrests would be useless.

An alarming and worrisome question arose in the minds of the posse. If the Berrys were not at the saloon - where were they?

10

Darkened as it was, McFarland's Saloon was far from empty. Bill, Issac, Emanuel, and Simeon Berry, Matthew McFarland, Cornelius Daly, and Robert Britton lounged about the saloon's darkness. They had endured a long, tiring day. Since early afternoon, their drinking had been interrupted only by periodic displays of force as gang members paraded the streets in a show of unity and demonstrated their intent to oppose the posse.

Bill Berry, who had instigated this resistance, had also laid out plans to ambush the posse coming after them. No doubt their fear of Stone in a face to face confrontation played a major role in deciding on an ambush. The ambush would be along the road, at the rail fence that offered plenty of cover from both sides of the road. Here they could hold off a small army and they had no idea of the size of the posse that would be coming to arrest them.

Throughout the afternoon, however, the level of excitement ebbed and flowed as gang members marched, drank, and abused the citizenry as they awaited the posse's arrival. They made several trips up the road to the rail fence. There they waited and stared off into the distance toward Pekin, apparently watching for the posse. After a while, they would grow tired of waiting and return to the tavern where they indulged in more alcoholic beverages.

With their drinking and hell-raising, they paid little notice as the orange evening sun fell slowly and silently behind the tree line to the west. As sunlight waned and began to disappear, so did the gang's expectation of a showdown with the posse. They knew the warrant had been obtained early that morning and the sheriff had hours of daylight in which to attempt to serve it. It seemed doubtful that the officers would be foolish enough to attempt in darkness a task that would be difficult enough in daylight. Perhaps word of the gang's display of unity and defiance had reached the sheriff. Maybe he was reluctant...or even afraid to send men to confront the gang head on.

Sam Miller arrived at the tavern shortly before dusk. As Miller approached the saloon, he saw the familiar faces of the Berry boys - Bill, Man, and Sim. The Peddler and McFarland were also there, as was Robert Britton, who, curiously enough, had a revolver strapped to his waist. Miller remained at the saloon for a quarter of an hour, conversing with the other patrons, after which he watched as Ike Berry made his way toward the tavern. Ike was carrying a double-barreled shotgun.

From his tobacco store window, Andrew Ditmon also watched as Ike, making no effort to conceal the weapon, lugged it down the street past his store. Ditmon had seen enough. The day's events, even by Circleville standards, had been bizarre. The gang had been drinking, parading the streets, making threats and demanding more liquor. They had even attempted to kick in his door. Finally, the sight of Ike wielding a shotgun foreshadowed disaster and Ditmon promptly closed his shop and made his way toward a safer ground - McKasson's house, where he knew he would be out of both sight and shotgun range. A place where many other people would be gathered, offered safety in numbers.

Amanda Reed, who had witnessed the happenings from the window of her home across the street, bravely, or for lack of an alternative, remained at home to see what would happen next.

Upon reaching the saloon, Ike placed the shotgun up against the wall near the front door and immediately called for Britton. Britton left the tavern with Ike, and, after moving a distance away from the others, the pair engaged in private, hushed conversation.

Sam Miller had talked with the boys at the saloon long enough to discern their mood. Robert Britton, armed with a pistol, was a mere curiosity, but the sight of Ike Berry with a shotgun, especially in light of his frame of mind while at the saloon, was frightening. Miller decided he would be leaving as soon as an opportunity arose.

It was at this time that John Bailey arrived. As he reached the saloon, Bailey noticed the shotgun leaning against the wall near the front door. He watched as Britton pulled Ike to one side as the two of them talked in hushed tones.

On the porch, the Peddler and old man Lane were arguing over who had bought the last round of drinks, and Bill Berry, who was apparently bored with the argument, invited Bailey to treat.

Bailey's arrival was enough diversion to allow Sam Miller to slip away and return home.

Bailey soon became aware of the trouble in the wind. He remained with the gang briefly, but left for McKasson's as Ike and Britton threatened to "whip Shaw on sight" and talked of returning to Shaw's home to force a fight.

From across the street, Amanda Reed watched as one by one the men at the saloon - some grumbling, others whistling, hooting, or shouting - made their way down from the porch as if to leave. She watched as they gathered briefly at the corner of William and East Streets where Ike Berry launched yet another drunken tirade against Shaw.

Ike, with Britton backing him, had proposed another attempt to locate Shaw, the man responsible for their troubles, and give him a whipping.

Others in the group - tired, disappointed, and intoxicated - prevailed on them to call it a day and find a place to spend the night. It was suggested to Ike that he pay a visit to his mother. Perhaps, because it was so loudly discussed, it was a ploy intended to convince those listening that the gang was breaking up for the night, while in all actuality, they were setting up the ambush.

Emanuel and Simeon agreed to go along, as did Britton, who was dependent on Ike for a place to stay. McFarland would accompany them as far as Townline Road, as this route was his way home, as well.

Emanuel, Ike and Mathew McFarland headed north on East Street toward Townline road.

Simeon Berry and Robert Britton had remained behind and exchanged a few words with Bill Berry and Cornelius Daly - perhaps getting last minute instructions. Within a minute or two, they also headed north and followed the other men.

Samuel Miller and John Bailey, having left the saloon earlier, arrived at McKasson's where they intended to take their evening meals. Joseph Miller, (unknown if he was related to

Samuel Miller) whose farm lay a mile west of Circleville, was
already there.

The post office and Ditmon's grocery were closed, the
proprietors of each having long since abandoned their shops in
town to enjoy the relative security afforded by McKasson's.

From her window, Amanda Reed watched with relief as
the gang began to disperse. This disturbing, incredible day
finally seemed to be nearing an end.

11

A crowd had been gathering at McKasson's all afternoon and it was apparent they expected something to happen. Perhaps, they gathered there for protection as well.

Justice Larimore was fit to be tied. He had been involved for two days at that point, and knew something terrible was going to happen. He had been at Bill Berry's house the night before when Pekin City Marshal Al Stone and Officers Cass and Milner had gone there to arrest Isaac and the man he knew only as "Frank." He had been in Pekin earlier this day to watch as Bill Berry and his attorney John Cohrs had threatened Sheriff Ed Pratt with false arrest if he did not release Isaac and "Frank."

Next, Larimore had ridden back toward Circleville and encountered Isaac and "Frank" along the way. They were sitting on a fence resting when he stopped. Isaac, looking over the Justice's horse, had said to him, "If you had another horse, I would ride." Larimore, knowing the reputation of the two and that it was not beyond them to try and take his mount, even if he was the Justice of Peace in Circleville, hurriedly replied, "Bill will be along shortly with his buggy." With that, he had ridden on to Circleville where he watched as the gang paraded the streets, drinking, singing, and shouting, "No Lawmen are going to take us."

He had closed his office and gone to McKasson's house where he watched as the gang paraded past several times, then stopped just beyond McKasson's to stare off across the fields. He saw that they had guns and realized Bill Berry was serious when he told the gang, "Stand your ground. You have done nothing wrong. I have guns and revolvers."

Larimore, fearing an ambush, had jumped on his horse and rode once again to Pekin, where he met and told Sheriff Pratt what he knew.

It was then that Pratt decided to send George Hinman with Henry Pratt, and summoned Assistant Marshal Rudolph Kessler as well. They could stop along the way and pick up Copes. That would make four, enough to arrest Isaac and "Frank," and to discourage any other brave souls who might favor assisting the Berrys.

Why Sheriff Pratt did not go himself or ask Stone to go is unknown. One would think that knowing a resistance was planned, the sheriff would have sent more men. Perhaps, being familiar with the Berrys and knowing they had never really resisted to any degree, he felt four was enough. Besides, Pratt and Stone were tied up investigating an incest case, involving a father and his daughter; as well as a recently uncovered counterfeiting ring. Whatever the reason, neither Pratt nor Stone went, so four it would be.

After warning Sheriff Pratt, Larimore had ridden back to Circleville to continue his vigil on the Berrys from McKasson's front porch. He must have been tired, for he had ridden over thirty miles that day and it was not over yet. The gang had continued their partying, and Larimore had heard shooting over at Bill Berry's house where they had gone earlier for a short time. It was apparent that they were testing the guns and sharpening their skills in preparation for the upcoming resistance.

Warily, Larimore continued his vigil giving a sigh of relief when he saw the deputies' wagon approaching.

As the lawmen neared McKasson's gate, Copes recognized Andrew Ditmon, Joseph Miller, John Bailey, and William Larimore. They followed as the lawmen pulled their wagon into the yard and behind the house. Hinman halted the team behind the barn and was ordered by Pratt to take charge of the horses.

J.W. Burnham, who had followed the wagon around the house, stepped forward to assist Hinman in putting up the team. Hinman asked if he had seen the Berry boys and the others, and Burnham told him that they were all at the saloon.

As Pratt, Copes, and Kessler jumped from the wagon, Pratt inquired of the crowd that had gathered around, "are they near?" The crowd almost in unison told him they were.

Hinman and Burnham were left to hitch the team behind McKasson's barn as the rest of the posse and on-lookers intermingled and discussed the Berrys. They walked toward the front of the house.

Inside the house, Sarah and Anna McKasson had halted their chores briefly and looked outside as the wagon entered their barnyard. They watched as three men jumped down from the wagon and talked with the group in her yard. Unable to recognize the new arrivals in the fading light, Sarah inquired as to their identify. Once informed that the new arrivals were the posse sent to arrest some of the Berry boys, Sarah returned to her work, but stole an occasional nervous glance out the window.

The gang and the posse each had ample time to develop a plan. Indeed, the gang had thought of nothing else the entire afternoon, as was apparent by their actions. Ironically, neither side was able to employ its strategy, for when the confrontation finally occurred, it was brought about more by accident than conscious design with both sides taken totally by surprise.

Larimore paced nervously around the front porch as the situation developed. Straining his eyes in the dim light, Larimore made out several shadowy figures approaching from the south. Suddenly, Larimore recognized the figures and yelled out, "There go the men you want!"

Pratt, Copes, and Kessler headed out the gate to intercept the approaching men.

Larimore ran out the front gate behind the officers, who had confronted the men in the street. He heard Henry Pratt yell, "Hold on boys, I have some business with you".

The men refused to stop and continued to walk away, northbound up the country road, quickening their pace somewhat.

Pratt yelled out a second time for the men to stop, but instead they broke into a run. Finally in desperation, he shouted, "Halt or I will fire!" With the light of the day failing fast, it was difficult to recognize anyone from a distance, however, Larimore and Copes both were able to identify Isaac, Emanuel, Mathew McFarland, and Britton as the four men they saw running along the road. The Berrys were still wearing the same clothing they had on earlier that day - "bed ticking clothes."

A short way up the road, just across the small wooden bridge spanning the creek, Emanuel Berry and Mathew McFarland, upon hearing the last warning, stopped running and stood still in the roadway. The other two men continued on.

Pratt, Copes, and Kessler, all with guns drawn, ran up to the two men; and Pratt, looking them over, shouted, "Copes, these are not the men we want!" With that, he ran on after the other two. He yelled several more warnings, then fired into the air.

Immediately, one man jumped over the rail fence and disappeared. The other man continued running up the road.

Pratt fired directly at him.

Copes also quickly fired a round at the fleeing man, and then both he and Pratt let loose a volley of shots that should have been impossible to escape.

A shot rang out from across the fence on the opposite side of the road, causing the lawmen more alarm as they continued the chase.

As many as fifteen shots had been fired when the fleeing man suddenly jumped over the fence rail, spun around, laid his shotgun upon a rail, and faced the fast approaching Pratt.

Henry Pratt, weary from the fast pace, had been running with his revolver swinging at his side. Now, taken totally by surprise, he tried desperately to raise the pistol toward Isaac.

Before he could do so, a loud blast shattered the night, and Pratt stopped his running and staggered backward in the road, clutching his chest.

Another loud blast echoed, and Hinman, who had been last to run out of the gate but had pushed hard and caught up to the others, grabbed his face and fell backward. He remained conscious and soon regained his footing, though still trying to stop the flow of blood from his head and shoulder, where he had been struck by a blast of lead shot.

The other lawmen had ducked for cover and were watching as Pratt, still staggering in the roadway, clasped his hand over his heart, exclaiming, "Oh boys, I am shot."

Copes, who had fired until his piece was empty, was kneeling behind the fence, trying to reload and watch everything at the same time, especially Ike Berry. Even though Copes thought that the gun Isaac had was a double barrel shotgun, and knew Issac had fired two shots, he did not feel like charging him with his own piece empty. Copes' attention was diverted momentarily to his friend Henry Pratt, who was still staggering backward, staring down at his chest as if to examine it.

When Copes looked back, Isaac Berry had vanished into the darkness.

Kessler ran up to Pratt and caught him, crying, "Where are you shot?"

Weakly, Pratt answered, "Oh boys, I am shot through the heart." Those were the last words Pratt was to utter as he sank to the roadway.

Kessler, struggling hard to hold him up and in an attempt to keep Pratt alert, went on to ask, "Does it pain you?"

Pratt never answered. He was unconscious.

By now all the lawmen had gathered around Pratt, trying to help. Copes, by now reloaded, stood with pistol in hand between the men and the fence where Ike had been, and stared guardedly into the darkness in the direction that Ike had vanished watching for any sign of movement. Ike could easily reload that shotgun and return.

Kessler knew they had to get Pratt to the house where there was light enough to see how severe his wounds were. While cautiously watching for any sign of the gang, Kessler, Copes, Larimore and Hinman(who was also wounded), carried Pratt to the front porch of the McKasson place.

Several men at the house watched the roadway and woods for the approach of any members of the Berry gang, as Sarah hurriedly got some blankets and placed them under Pratt to make him as comfortable as possible.

A lamp was quickly fetched to the front porch for light. Frantically, they ripped Pratt's coat, vest, and shirt away to get to the wound, which they soon found to be a gapping hole in the upper right breast area. Seeing the severity of the wound, they knew there was not much they could do except to apply a bandage to it in an attempt to stop the flow of blood. They had to get Pratt to a doctor immediately.

Kessler and Copes, with the assistance of Mrs. McKasson, rendered what little medical attention they could to both Pratt and Hinman.

Hinman had been shot in the right shoulder and over the right eye, but painfully insisted he would be okay. Unfortunately, they found that Henry Pratt had been injured so severely that they could not move him for fear of causing his death. He would have to remain with Mrs. McKasson and the others until someone could ride to Pekin for the doctor. There were no doctors in Circleville.

While examining Pratt's wounds, they had discovered the book in the breast pocket of his coat had a large hole in it. Ironically, inside the book, was the warrant with Ike's name on it. It had been shot completely through with the same shot that entered Pratt's chest and pierced his heart.

With help from the local people, Kessler and Copes loaded the wounded Hinman into the wagon, jumped in, and raced for Pekin. It was 10:00 P.M.

Pushing the team at a full run, the three lawmen managed to make the eight-mile trip to Pekin in record time. The team was breathing hard and was well lathered with sweat as they slowed in front of Doctor Richard Charlton's office and residence on the corner of Sixth and Court Street.

Copes' tall frame was in full motion as he jumped from the still moving wagon and ran to the doctor's door. He pounded on the door as Kessler whipped the team down the street to the jail where Edward Pratt had been anxiously waiting for their return with their prisoners.

Seeing the way Kessler was running the team told Sheriff Ed Pratt that something was wrong. He could see that neither Henry nor Copes were in the wagon, and his jailer was hunched over with bandages on his head. He felt a sudden sense of dread come over him. His brother and Copes were missing and deep in his mind he knew what it meant. The thing he had feared most when he had hired Henry as a deputy - that Henry might get killed - was now a possibility. He could only hope it was not as serious as it looked. He soon learned, however, that it was, as the wagon jerked to a halt in front of him.

He heard Kessler's excited voice telling him that there had been a shooting, and that Henry had been gravely wounded. Pratt was jarred from the trance he was in as Kessler hurriedly told him of the ambush, of how Isaac Berry had fired the shotgun, of the shots that had been fired from across the road, and how the attackers ran into the woods afterwards.

Doctor Charlton arrived at the jail within minutes in his buggy, ready to ride. Copes had already told him of the severity of Henry's wound to the chest, and he knew they had to hurry if there was a chance to save him.

Edward Pratt wanted desperately to go to Circleville to be with Henry, but knew there was much to be done in town and that he would have to stay. He ordered Kessler and Copes to accompany Doctor Charlton back to Circleville, to insure his safe arrival, for it was felt there was still danger of more attacks, even if the suspects had fled into the country side.

There was not time enough to get more manpower. Henry needed a doctor fast, and George was still bleeding from his wounds. Another doctor would have to be fetched to attend him.

As the lawmen and Doctor headed for Circleville, Hinman was assisted into his quarters at the jail, and another doctor summoned to care for his wounds. The small entourage left Pekin at a run, with Kessler and Copes now on fresh mounts, leading the way.

Although it took only a short time for Doctor Charlton to reach Circleville, pushing the horses at a dead run, almost three hours had elapsed since the shooting.

Arriving at the McKasson place, Doctor Charlton found the crowd subdued and silent, some with tears in their eyes. He was told that Henry Pratt had died of his wounds some fifteen minutes earlier.

Doctor Charlton dropped to his knees beside Henry and quickly examined him. Henry was indeed dead. The wound was two and one half inches in diameter. The doctor, rising from the floor, told the others he could not have saved Henry had he been with him when he was shot.

They decided to send someone back to town to tell Sheriff Pratt and the others that they would wait until daylight to start back with Henry's body.

12

As soon and he learned of the ambush on his posse, Sheriff Pratt had sent word to Marshal Stone, who rushed to his office. Stone and the Pratt family had been close friends for years.

One can only guess what was on Stone's mind. Had he not made the arrest of Ike and Frank the night before, Henry would still be alive. At the very least, had he not spent the entire night completing those arrests, he would have had plenty of rest and would have gone with Henry. Perhaps he could have prevented this attack. Instead, however, in the predawn hours he sat waiting with his friend Edward to hear word on Henry's condition.

Then came word that Henry was dead. The mourning session was cut short, for there was work to be done. Marshal Stone quickly sat about rounding up a posse.

Word of the shooting was carried throughout the town, and, before long, forty or fifty men had gathered at the jail. Some were still tucking in their shirt tails and rubbing sleep from their eyes, for most had been sleeping soundly when the call went out.

They were scattered about the front lawn of the jail, some sitting quietly and checking their guns, some talking threats of revenge, while others on horseback were busy trying to keep their mounts under control as they anxiously awaited the ride to Circleville.

They were waiting for the dawn light to be able to see their way and identify anyone they might come across. They knew to ride off in darkness was not only dangerous, but a waste of time, for in the darkness they could ride past a man ten feet away and not see him.

They waited also for the warrants to be prepared by State's Attorney Whitney and Justice of the Peace Glasgow. The original charges being prepared had been for aggravated battery with the intent to kill, but when word came that Henry had died, the charges were changed to murder. Each charge would have to be sworn to by a witness to Henry's death, so the process halted until Henry's body was returned to Pekin and Doctor Charlton and the deputies could give testimony needed to complete the warrants. Each member of the gang would then have a murder warrant issued for him.

Never in the history of Tazewell County had so many men been charged with murder at the same time. This was no doubt an exciting time in the lives of most of the men. Perhaps to some, it was simply a rerun of the time a few years past; when they had been drawn together to fight in the great rebellion. To others it must have been simply mind-boggling.

Looking over the posse, Stone could see several men he knew. Some looked vaguely familiar and others were strangers to him. He had been around Tazewell County for many years and thought he knew most every man; however, there seemed to be a lot of strangers in the crowd tonight. Perhaps they were appearing publicly only in a sense of civic duty, in light of the murder of one of their lawmen.

Among the men Stone did know was John Berry. John was not a member of the Berry family they would be hunting. He was a tough saloon owner who had a reputation for being one not to cross. He had been in many scrapes with the local toughs and usually won those rounds, although it can't be said that he won them fairly, for John had been arrested on several occasions for the use of "iron knuckles." He was also Pekin's Chief Fire Engineer. Stone welcomed this man to his posse, for he knew he could depend on him when things got rough.

Others Stone would see in the crowd were his own policemen, James Milner and Lewis Cass. Both were good men, whom he trusted completely. He would also have Rudolph Kessler who without a doubt would want to ride with him even though he had already been up all night.

There were others in the crowd who could be trusted to do the right thing in a pinch, and Stone surely welcomed them all.

Most of the men present were from Pekin, but later there would be men riding in from all over the county as word spread of the shootout. They would flock into Pekin to join one of the posses being organized.

Stone decided that there would be three posses of not less than fifty men each, formed to search the vast prairies and thickets for the murdering outlaws. He would lead one, another would be lead by ex- lawman Benjamin Stickney, and the third by yet another tough ex-lawman Ben Towner.

Stone's posse, already fifty strong, was the first one ready to ride because he took all the local men. Stickney and Towner would have to wait for the men riding in from farms and other nearby towns. By the time they could gather enough men and were ready to ride, Stone would be far to the south searching the prairie for the killers.

At dawn, just as it got light enough to ride out, a small party of riders came into town from the south. A wagon drawn by two large horses lead the small procession. Doctor Charlton followed in his buggy. The riders were silent as they stopped in front of the jail.

Doctor Charlton stepped down from his buggy and approached Ed Pratt and Al Stone, who had been awaiting their arrival. Finally and officially, they heard from Doctor Charlton, himself, that Henry Pratt was really dead. His wounds had been too severe and he had died just fifteen minutes before Charlton's arrival. Doctor Charlton told Pratt and Stone that even if he had arrived while Henry was alive, he would not have been able to save him.

Pratt asked that Henry's body be carried to Hinman's room in the jail until he could make the necessary funeral arrangements.

Several posse members assisted in carrying the body inside.

Sheriff Pratt called for Whitney, Glasgow, and Stone to meet him in his office. The warrants would have to be sworn to by witnesses and signed by Justice Glasgow.

Assistant Marshal Kessler was chosen to give testimony to Esquire Glasgow and swear to the warrants. Glasgow issued warrants for murder for William Berry, who instigated the attack; for Isaac Berry, who pulled the trigger; and for Emanuel and Simeon Berry, Mathew McFarland, Cornelius Daly and Robert "Frank" Britton(Stone had learned "Frank's" real name was Robert Britton) for being accessories.. Glasgow also issued a warrant for Josiah Combs for horse theft, stemming from a previous incident.

With warrants in hand, Stone left Pratt's office. He knew Sheriff Pratt wanted to go, but also knew that he would better serve in the capture of the gang by staying back to coordinate the different posses that would be forming at later times. Besides, he had to make funeral arrangements for Henry.

Stone mounted his horse with a sense of determination, gave final instructions to his posse and headed toward Circleville, the most likely starting point for his search.

Fifty men strong, the posse rode southward. Their horses kicking up dust that rose high in the still early morning air. The sun was just beginning to show on the eastern horizon, casting long fingers of light though the sky.

Amid the squeaking of leather saddles and jingling of bridle bits and spurs, there was nervous chatter among the men as they rode. They mostly made small talk as they tried to cover their excitement and, yes, even fear, for they knew it was now war with the Berry gang. Though many of the men had fought in the battles of the civil war, there were some who had never fired a shot at a human being before.

These men, however, one and all, welcomed the chance to arrest a Berry. If it meant a shootout, they were prepared to accommodate them, especially under the expert guidance of Marshal Stone.

There were men in this posse who had heard of the Berrys, but had never seen them. They had no personal quarrel with them, but who had rode along out of friendship to Henry and George. Some rode just for the privilege of riding with a posse of the law. Others rode for the excitement it offered in an otherwise dull existence.

Marshal Stone rode in silence. He had dreaded the day when something like this would happen. He knew the Berrys and had warned many of the townspeople about them. He had been one of the few men who had not signed the petition for the pardon of William Berry in the Pepper killing a year earlier.

Stone knew Isaac Berry had always been capable of doing something like that. He had long expected it to happen, but never thought it would happen to a close friend. What made matters worse, was that Stone knew the ambush had been meant for him, not Henry. It was widely known that Ike hated Stone.

Stone felt a heavy weight on his shoulders - a weight that would be lifted only when Ike was in his custody and had paid for killing Henry. He was looking forward to confronting Ike again.

Though it seemed much longer, it had only been yesterday that he had arrested Ike and Britton at Bill's house, and he knew there was a good chance they would be there again. Even if they weren't there, Bill would be, and possibly other members of the gang. Besides, where better to start making arrests than with the leader of the gang?

* * *

In Circleville, Stone warily led his posse to the home of Bill Berry, where they surrounded the house with guns drawn and shouted for him to come out.

Bill Berry strolled to the door as through nothing had happened. Before he could react, several men rushed onto the porch. Some grabbed him, while others dashed into the house. Bill struggled and protested as they drug him to the horses, but it did no good. They slapped the shackles on him and threw him upon a horse, where his hands were secured to the saddle horn.

Nancy stood on the porch crying as she watched. There was nothing she could do.

Inside the house, members of the posse searched every room and crawl space, but found no other members of the gang.

The posse, with Bill in tow, rode to Rachel's house, located a short distance to the east. There, the men again surrounded the house, but with all due respect to her, as she was considered a good citizen, they searched her house. She told Stone she had not seen her sons since the day before. Finding no one, they rode on.

Cautiously, Stone and his men approached McFarland's saloon. Surrounding the saloon with guns drawn, the posse closed in.

With more guns outside trained on every window, Stone and his men rushed through the front doors expecting shots to be fired at anytime. The saloon was empty. Twenty strong, they started searching the rest of the hotel and found McFarland and Cornelius Daly cowering in a back room. Both men were immediately taken into custody. They were too frightened to offer any resistance.

Quickly, the posse searched the remainder of the saloon and the rooms of the hotel upstairs, but found no one else.

With three now in tow, they rode on to Emanuel's house, where the same tactics were used.

Emanuel's wife came out and told them he was not there.

Stone advised her that he had a warrant, and that Emanuel had been involved in the killing of Henry Pratt.

Mrs. Emanuel Berry, with tears in her eyes, stepped aside and pointed at the door. She told Stone that Emanuel had told her to tell them he was not there.

Several men rushed inside, and Emanuel was found hiding in the house. He offered no resistance as he was taken into custody.

The posse rode away, leaving Emanuel's wife crying and wringing her hands while his children stared after them, wondering what would become of their father.

A short time later, the posse surrounded Simeon Berry's place, and he surrendered himself into their custody without incident.

His wife and only child watched from the yard, as the posse rode away with him and his brothers in chains.

Next, members of the posse surrounded the home of the killer, Issac Berry. Using extreme caution, and at a distance from the house, Stone shouted at Ike and demanded his presence in the yard.

Ike's wife came out and told Stone that he was not there. She had not seen him since the night before. She said they were welcome to search the house.

Several of the posse members made a complete search of the house and out buildings, but were unable to find Isaac.

The posse rode back to Circleville with the Berrys in tow. There were more than fifty men in the posse now, for as time went on, more men rode up and were allowed by Stone to join their search.

Arriving back at Circleville, the posse made a complete search of the entire town, building by building.

Encouraged by seeing five of the gang in custody, grateful citizens joined the search. These local people had witnessed the slaying of the deputy sheriff the night before, but were unable to do anything for fear of retaliation. With all the manpower of the posse beside them, however, they showed their willingness to help, as well as their contempt for the Berry gang. They had been witnesses to all the other things the gang had done, including riding rough shod over anyone who disagreed with them, or, for that matter, happened to walk in their path when they were drinking. This was a chance to get even, a chance to repay them for all their cruel acts against the gentle town's people.

A thorough search, however, failed to turn up either Isaac or Frank Britton.

The posse, with five outlaws in tow, returned to Pekin and searched every cornfield and place along the way that a man might have concealed himself in.

By noon, Bill, Emanuel and Simeon Berry, Mathew McFarland, and Cornelius Daly had been locked away in the county jail. That left three warrants unserved, Isaac Berry, Robert Britton, and Josiah Combs.

By now, however, the other two posses, with one hundred and fifty men in each, were roaming the great Delavan Prairie searching for these men whose chances of getting away were slim.

That same day, one local newspaper reported that there were "hundreds of armed citizens starting to scour the countryside for the murderers." According to the newspaper, everyone the armed posse saw was chased, cornered, and interrogated.

With four to five hundred men roaming the prairie with guns in their hands and hate in their hearts, it was a dangerous time for anyone to be out of their homes. In fact, most people who were not riding with the posses, stayed indoors.

Shots were heard quite often, fired at someone too far away to catch, and more than likely totally innocent of the recent tragic events. It was only by the grace of God that no one was killed.

Much to the disappointment of the owners, young waist-high corn growing in fields was trampled flat under the hooves of their horses as members of the huge posses searched out the outlaws.

Late in the day, Josiah Combs was captured by one of the other posses.

By this time word had reached them of Stone's successful captures, and many men left the posses and rode to Pekin to get a glimpse of the outlaws already in custody.

Later in the day, several men from Delavan drifted into Pekin, where they gathered in local saloons, drinking and expressing their displeasure with the court system. They discussed what should be done with Bill Berry, who was at the time incarcerated in the jail, just a few yards from where they stood.

They fired up the George Washington Pepper case again, wanting satisfaction, even though Berry had been pardoned. The talk reached a boiling point as the liquor flowed. It was evident that yet another volatile situation was beginning to materialize. It was a situation that would have to be watched closely so that it did not get out of hand.

13

It was late afternoon when Al Stone left the jail after locking away all the Berry gang except for Isaac Berry and Robert Britton, but they were expected to be in custody very soon.

Tired and hungry, Stone was eating in the restaurant of the American House Hotel, where he lived, when word came that Robert Britton had been seen in Delavan only a short time ago. Stone knew he had to do something right away, as time was of the utmost importance. It was late afternoon and it was almost twenty miles to Delavan. Darkness would be upon them in a few hours.

Marshal Stone gathered what remained of his weary posse and headed across the hot dusty prairie for Delavan, Illinois, some twenty miles to the southeast. Most of his posse were men who had ridden with him all day and even though they were tired, hungry, and dusty, they were on the road again for another long, hot ride. There is no doubt that they would rather suffer the elements, than miss out on a chance to be in on the final capture. Stone himself had been up for almost two days, getting little food or rest, and saw little chance of getting any soon.

Mustering what strength he had left, he pushed on. The rest of the posse once again urged their mounts to their limits. Snorting, tossing their mighty heads, and sweating heavily in the sweltering heat, the horses doggedly moved along, and just over two hours later they were in Delavan.

Upon reaching the town-square, where a crowd had gathered after seeing the approach of the posse, weary men and horses took a short breather while Stone spoke with the man who had sent word that Britton was in town.

Stone learned, much to his dismay that Britton had but a short time earlier left for Mason City on horseback. Mason City was another twenty miles to the southwest.

According to witnesses in Delavan, Britton had purchased a change of clothing and put them on over the ones he already wore. Perhaps he had planned to change on the run, to throw off anyone who might be looking for a certain type or color of clothing. Whatever the reason, he had wasted little time before striking out for Mason City.

Stone knew he could not catch the man on the horses they had been riding. They had just been pushed hard for over twenty miles, not to mention the distance they had ridden earlier in the day. He knew he had pushed the horses and the men too hard already, and would have to allow them to rest for a few hours before continuing. Yet he feared that Britton would be moving further and further away and thought that perhaps they might not be able to catch him at all if he were to keep on the move.

Stone was deeply troubled by this inconvenience and impatiently pondered the situation as he walked about town. They were too close to Britton to lose him now. Stone knew he had to somehow make up some of the lost time if he was to catch up to Britton. Even with fresh mounts, however, it would be most difficult, for Britton had quite a head start on them

He continued his pondering of the situation. He walked to the train depot and looked around. If only the train was here and going that way, he could use it to get to Mason City and get there much faster than on a horse. Unfortunately, the train was not due for several hours.

Suddenly, perhaps by chance, or perhaps with a little help from above, he was struck with an idea that would allow him to catch up with Britton. The answer he needed had been right there in front of him - a railroad workman's handcar! Small, without question, but sufficient for what he needed. He was quite delighted with this wild idea. The Chicago and Alton Railroad had a line that ran straight across the prairie from Delavan to Mason City. Although powered by hand pumping, the small handcars could travel more than twice the speed of a running horse, and the tracks would be a more direct route than the roads they would have to travel on horseback. Besides, the men could rest while the railroad workers provided the power required to propel the car.

Now eager to get on the road, Stone rounded up two railroad workmen to man the car. There was only room for a total of five men on the car, so he picked two men from the posse to go with him - Lewis Cass and Deputy John Berry. He felt that the three of them could handle Britton, while the two railroad men only had to worry about powering the car to Mason City.

The three lawmen, each armed with revolvers and carrying long guns, as well as shackles, climbed aboard the handcar and were soon on their way across the vast open prairie lands headed for Mason City.

Although somewhat crowded, they had a spectacular view from atop the elevated railroad bed. They could see miles of tall buffalo grass bending ever so slightly in what little breeze there was. The view looked like a huge lake, with waves rolling endlessly across it. The wind created by the moving car blew through their hair and cooled the men after their long ride on horseback. Even with the hot sun beating down on them, the ride was not too uncomfortable for the men as they scanned the open prairie for any sign of Britton.

The unique little posse made good time, but it was not long before the railroaders needed water and a little rest. They had to hand pump almost constantly to power the car. Knowing the little settlement of San Jose was just ahead, they pushed on until they reached it. Climbing down from the handcar, they headed for a saloon and some much needed refreshment.

Inside the saloon, with cool drinks before them, Stone engaged in passing conversation with the bartender and told him of their mission, describing Britton. Much to his surprise and delight, the bartender told Stone that he had seen a man very much like he described arrive in town earlier and go into the Hicks House Hotel across the street. He told Stone he had not seen the man leave, and believed he was still there.

This caused excitement to rush through the men, and as soon as the drinks were downed, they made plans for their attack. Although they were in another county, Stone decided the three of them, without the aid of the local constable or sheriff, would confront the man at the hotel to see if it was in fact Britton. He instructed Berry to man a shotgun, while Cass would use his revolver. They would go to the room and try to get Britton to answer their knock on the door. They would have the element of surprise and get the drop on him. The railroad workmen would remain at the saloon out of harm's way.

Upon entering the Hicks House Hotel, Stone inquired of the clerk as to the room the stranger had taken. The clerk took them up the stairs and pointed out the room he had rented to Britton. He fled down-stair to safety as Stone knocked softly on the door.

A voice from inside inquired, "Who's there?" Stone answered in a voice not his usual, "The inn keeper."

Shortly, the men could hear footsteps as the man inside approached the door. When it opened, he was met with the barrels of three guns.

Cass immediately ordered, "If you move, I will hurt you!"

Britton, taken completely by surprise, surrendered without incident. After the shackles were in place, a search was made of the room, and a navy revolver was found under the pillow of the bed in which Britton had been lying. Had they not approached the room as planned, disaster could have struck again.

Marshal Stone, Officer Cass, and John Berry with Britton in shackles and marching at the end of the shotgun, left the hotel and walked to the livery stable where Stone arranged for horses for the four of them.

When the posse was mounted and prepared to leave San Jose for the long trip back to Pekin, another twenty miles, Stone thanked the railroad workmen for their help and sent them and their handy little car on their way back to Delavan.

During the long ride back to Pekin, the lawmen found that Britton was not at all the tough, troublesome man they had expected, but rather timid and somewhat nervous. He talked almost without pause until they reached Pekin.

14

As evening approached and the liquor flowed in the saloons along Pekin's main street, the angry mood of the men continued to build. Shouts were heard of lynching the entire Berry gang, now in custody, to rid themselves of these outlaws once and for all.

They used the example of an incident printed in the local newspapers that had occurred less than a month earlier in Indiana, about a gang of bank robbers who were lynched just outside Indianapolis. Two other members of that gang of bank robbers had managed to escape into Illinois only to be caught by lawmen in Mattoon, Illinois. They were held for Indiana authorities. When the Indiana lawmen got them back across the line and in the Indianapolis area, a huge mob of masked men had snatched them from the posse, interrogated them, and promptly hung them in the same tree the rest of their gang had been hung. Nothing had happened to the mob because no one knew who they were, and, besides, no one really cared anyway. The instigators brought up the new law that had been recently passed by the State of Illinois making it almost impossible to execute a person, even one convicted of murder. It had been nicknamed "the Lynch Law," They reasoned that if the people of Indiana could get away with lynching outlaws, they could too.

Fired by such talk, the saloons emptied into the street where the shouting continued as the men filled Court Street outside the jail.

From the jail window, Sheriff Pratt had watched the crowd gather in the street. He was determined to protect his prisoners even though they had killed his own brother whose body lay in the very next room. It had to be a hard decision - one that required much discipline. A lesser man would have simple sat back and let the mob have their way. No one would have blamed him.

Edward Pratt was not a lesser man, however, and he watched the mob intently. They were getting louder. It was obvious to him that only a few men were the ringleaders and doing most of the shouting. After giving it much thought, he decided that if he could get one of those men into the jail, perhaps he could persuade them to stop the nonsense and let the law handle the Berry gang. If so, they could, in turn, convince the crowd of angry citizens to disburse, thereby ending the threat of an assault upon his jail.

With that in mind, Pratt picked his man. He would grab a Delavan farmer named Flemming. This man was leading the pack in volume with his shouting and threatening, and had just been involved in a fistfight with another man who had disagreed with him.

There were a three or four men inside the jail who had came to pay their respects. They had volunteered to assist Sheriff Pratt. Now he sent two of them out to snatch up

Flemming. He watched from the window as they approached Flemming and walked him back to the jail.

The mob also watched. They watched in silence as Flemming was lead up the steps and through the door of the jail that had quickly opened, just long enough to allow a hasty entry. The door slammed closed and, almost instantly, there was a great uproar from the crowd as it finally sunk in that Flemming had been arrested. The roar grew to fill the small hallway of the jail.

Inside the jail, it was immediately obvious to Pratt that his plan was not going to work, because Flemming absolutely refused to cooperate. Pratt however, continued his attempt to persuade Flemming to come around to his way of thinking. He was sure that if he did, Flemming could calm the angry mob.

The mob's demands that Flemming be released grew louder and louder, then a large mob stormed the jail. They surrounded the building, threatening to attack the doors if Flemming was not released immediately.

Seeing that his plan had failed, Pratt tried to reason with the mob, but to no avail, as they seemed set on breaking down the doors. Pratt consulted with two other men in the jail - Pekin City Mayor, William T. Edds, and General Edwin McCook.

General McCook was well known among the local citizens as being a man of honor. Many of the men in the mob had served under his command in the Civil War, fighting along side him in many battles. Mayor Edds knew this and knew the men would listen to the man. The Mayor enlisted McCook to act on his behalf and tell the mob that Flemming would be released.

McCook went to the window of the jail and shouted for the mob to quiet down so that he might talk. He waited until they had quieted enough to be heard, then told them he was acting on behalf of Mayor Edds, and that Flemming was not under arrest and would be released when the crowd disbursed.

McCook concluded that the doors of the jail would remain locked with Flemming inside until the crowd left the area.

A hush settled over the people as they pondered what this man had said. They had not yet broken the law. They were just angry citizens who wanted justice. No one could blame them for that. Perhaps McCook was right. Besides, they could always appear to leave the area, but remain close by until Flemming was released, then return. They decided this was the best way to handle the matter, and soon they began disappearing around the corners, behind buildings, and into saloons where they drank and continued their encouragement of others to join the attack.

With the majority of the crowd gone, Pratt and Edds felt it was safe to release Flemming. Opening the door quickly, they let him walk out a free man.

Whether or not he had actually been under arrest was academic, but the actions of the crowd surely had such an effect on the Sheriff that he felt it necessary to submit to their demands. Saying Flemming was not under arrest would ease the impact of having to back down.

Flemming had refused to cooperate with Pratt, and now that he was free, they knew the situation could only worsen. With that in mind, Pratt and Edds decided more men had to be sworn in to protect the jail. Both men were equal to the task. With the situation temporarily defused, additional men were located and sworn in to protect the jail.

Forty men were sworn in by Pratt and stationed directly around the jail itself. Edds swore in twenty "special" policemen and positioned them at various locations on grounds adjoining the jail. These sixty makeshift special police officers were of questionable loyalty and greatly outnumbered by the crowd, but they would at least make the jail appear to be a more difficult target. Both Edds and Pratt felt they had done all in their power to hold off an attack. Surely the mob would not go up against this larger force.

Satisfied with the security of additional men, the Mayor decided he could go home. This left Sheriff Pratt and General McCook to control the situation. McCook was quite capable for he was also an officer of the law, only on the Federal level. He was an Internal Revenue Service Agent, appointed to collect local federal taxes, and was most recently working in the great whiskey ring that was operating locally. This may have also had an impact on the crowd, causing them to disperse, as they were not sure just where they stood should they go up against a Federal Agent.

Federal Agents were something new to the people of the County. Only this past January, John Berry, owner of the Sennett Saloon where many of the men were now drinking, had been named in an indictment for burglary, sworn to by Federal Agent McCook. It was for breaking into a warehouse owned by James L. Briggs and removing twenty five casks containing fifteen hundred gallons of wine, stored there by McCook himself. The wine had been confiscated from the local area, including some from John Berry himself.

The confiscation was done because the wine was being illegally sold. It was not bonded or taxed by the Federal Government, but was home made, and sold throughout the county in staggering amounts.

Through an informant, it was learned that the stolen wine was hidden in the fire cisterns located in the 200 block of Court Street. Someone had pumped all the water from the public cisterns, built for water storage after the great fire of 1860, and refilled them with the wine.

Hundreds of gallons of wine in the cisterns might not have been good for fighting fires, but when it was being recovered, there were a lot of happy fire fighters and many, many volunteers.

Though it is unknown if John Berry, who was Chief Engineer of the Pekin Fire Department, had anything to do with filling the cisterns with wine, he was, however, named in the indictment for burglary and the theft of the wine from the warehouse. The case was still pending in local court on July 30, 1869.

Although he was a Federal agent, McCook was a local man and had been for many years. He no doubt had ill feelings about the possibly of having to shoot men who had fought with him just a few years before. However, he was committed by duty as well as honor to helping his friend, Sheriff Pratt defend the jail against attack.

By any standard, the release of Flemming was an act of appeasement. The mob had challenged the authorities and Flemming was released. Disbursement of the mob appeared to have been successful. It looked like the swift actions of Edward Pratt and W.T. Edds, not to mention the timely intercession of General McCook, had staved off a calamity. Nevertheless, the situation remained critical. Pratt and McCook knew they had a long night facing them.

Meanwhile, the mob had slowly edged away until there were only a few men visible on the streets. Inside the saloons, however, the crowds were growing stronger, and it did not take the mob long to once again begin refueling the issue. With the body of Henry Pratt lying in state, the memory of George Pepper, and a cellblock full of Berrys believed to be responsible for both deaths, there was no lack of potential issues. The County Jail was full of them. It only required convincing everyone present that they had to lynch the Berrys.

Many in the mob had earlier, upon hearing of the shooting of Deputy Pratt, eagerly grabbed a firearm and rushed into action in a honest attempt to dispense justice to the guilty parties. But now they were being asked to attack the jail and confront armed men who were equally disposed to justice, and who were acting to uphold a sworn oath, wearing badges no less.

It was one thing to demand the release of an individual whose expressed ideals are sympathetic to one's own, and quite another to violently defy the law to murder, in cold blood, individuals who have had no judgements against them.

The aggressive leaders of this outraged mob, therefore, could not be assured of the same loyalty as before. The men had to have a reason for a direct assault upon the jail, and some did. The men from Delavan had always believed that justice for Pepper's murder had not been exacted, and no legal recourse existed. George Pepper was their reason.

The men of Tremont had the killing of their friend and neighbor, Henry Pratt.

To those from other parts of the county, a slain deputy, no matter who he was, was a cause for action. The lines were clearly drawn. The system had failed and corrective measures were necessary. If these murders were to be avenged, the citizenry would have to provide the means themselves. The decision to demand retribution of Bill Berry, by whatever means necessary, was the moral issue. .

Yet there were those who believed that drastic action seemed premature, and many surely had to wrestle with their conscience while contemplating the type of action being proposed. Edward Pratt himself presented yet another dilemma for the good men of Tremont. Even though they were trying to avenge the death of his brother, Sheriff Edward Pratt was sworn to protect the jail and its prisoners. Any move against the jail would have to be met by him. How could outrage and vindication of Henry Pratt's death be used as valid motives for such an assault, with Ed Pratt standing there to resist?

Edward Pratt would surely attempt to protect the jail, and none were more aware of this fact than the contingent from Tremont who had lived with and known the Pratt family all of their lives.

107

The Pratts, Edward and Werner, had been elected officials in the village of Tremont for years, and an assault on the jail would put the mob squarely in opposition to Edward. Additionally, such a confrontation would come on the eve of Henry's funeral, while his body was lying in the very living quarters of the man who would have to meet their assault. How could such acts be justified?

As temporary residents, Edward and Henry Pratt had become familiar figures about the streets of Pekin. They had come to know and be known by the citizens of the city, and were well respected and liked. These factors and the presence of the special police were just enough to make it unpopular for an immediate assault on the jail. Things were at a standstill, with a core of irate citizens demanding immediate street-justice, and a nearly equivalent number of dedicated citizens hoping for justice of a different sort.

Meanwhile, out on the streets of Pekin, Ed Pratt and W.T. Edds were pleased with their handling of the Flemming affair and reinforcement of the jail that evening. The streets became quiet, and observers noted that on this Saturday night, there was far less activity on the streets of Pekin than usual.

Earlier in the evening, the reporter for the Peoria Daly Transcript had wired the home office that, "there was every prospect that an attempt to force the jail doors would be made that night." By 11:00, the Peoria Daly Democrat reporter noted that; "there was less moving about on the streets than usual", and that, "it was so quiet as to excite remark."

In his last dispatch to the home office, the reporter left word that, "no verdict had been reached by the Coroner's jury, no further arrests made, and no further particulars." He concluded that, "no apparent preparation was making for an assault upon the jail."

All was quiet, disaster had been averted, the situation was finally under control, but not surprisingly, things changed quickly.

15

Faced with the increased police force around and about the jail, the mob needed something to tip the balance and at 11:00 that night they got it. The coroner's inquest into the death of Henry Pratt adjourned with no verdict. Testimony was to be continued the next day, and no immediate assignment of guilt for Henry Pratt's murder would be forthcoming. This was no doubt the breaking point for the mob. Upon hearing this, the leaders of the mob, in places out of sight, out of earshot, and out of mind of the law, began setting in motion a plan for the attack.

It was in one such place, a restaurant below the Sennett Saloon on Capitol Street, due west of the courthouse, that the most aggressive leaders of the mob became active.

Ed Pratt, in mourning, fatigued by the events of the last two days, distracted with the funeral arrangements for his brother, and overwhelmed by the level and intensity of activity generated by Henry's death, was oblivious to the signs because there was no discernable activity on the street. It was well past the hour in which most decent citizens would ordinarily be in bed. There had been very little street activity since the swearing in of the special police force, and tomorrow would be Sunday - a day most of the population would be expected to be found in church.

With the lateness of the hour, Ed Pratt mistakenly believed that the crisis was over. He felt it would serve no purpose to require the special police force to stand guard all night when there was no apparent need, so around midnight, he sent the bulk of the special police force home. Only a skeleton force was retained to keep vigil around the jail the remainder of the night. All he wanted was to retire to his bed for some much needed sleep.

Throughout the evening, the special police had maintained a precarious balance of strength between the mob and those wishing to protect the jail. The dispersal of this force made the jail vulnerable once again. This was what the mob had been quietly watching and waiting for.

The attack would have to take place immediately. It must be made while the police force was weakened and the jail was assailable. With all conditions favorable for the mob of angry men, a final plan was laid out. The time had came to make their move.

Shortly after midnight about twenty men, "numbering some of the best in the country," assembled near the Sennett Saloon, due west of the courthouse. Marching "with military precision," as witnesses would later remark, they crossed the square, passing north of the courthouse, and stopped on the south side of Court Street, directly in front of the jail's front door.

Someone in the crowd went to the door and began to pound on it, demanding to be let inside. Ed Pratt appeared in a second story window as members of the mob demanded the keys to the jail.

What he saw was a small group of men, a remnant of the force that had caused such concern earlier in the day, probably the only ones interested and only because they were now drunk.

For the second time that day, Ed Pratt would have to address and attempt to disperse a group of men who claimed to be infuriated by and demanding justice for Henry's death. He would have to, out of duty and some perverse twist of fate, plead mercy for those accused of killing his own brother.

What was left of the special police force still remained, so there was no apparent cause for concern. A few harsh words might dispel them, and the day's excitement might at last come to an end.

Pratt shouted to the men below, telling them he refused to relinquish control of the keys to the jail, and ordered the group to disburse.

The mob again demanded the jail keys and vowed to "burst in" if the keys were denied them.

Pratt told the crowd the keys were not in his possession, that even if he did have the keys he would not relinquish them, and that those wishing to attack the jail would do so "at their peril."

Neither Pratt nor the remainder of his temporary police force was prepared for what happened next. From somewhere in the crowd a signal was given; and out of the businesses, the restaurants, and the saloons, out of the hotels, and the private residences, and from the alleyways, men emerged. Hundreds of men swarmed into the streets around the jail.

Fear crept into the very souls of the lawmen watching the mob as it "sprang out from the alleys and the shadows of buildings as if by magic."

Samuel Watson was seated on a fence near the jail that night and witnessed a crowd of 200 to 300 men swarm around the jail.

John Griffith, a tavern owner from Groveland, was "stopping at the jail" that night. He had been in bed, but was awakened by a commotion outside. Griffith got out of bed and went to the stairway to see what would occur next. He cursed himself for not having gone on home earlier.

Meanwhile, George Hinman, head bandaged, right arm useless, also saw the crowd from his quarters in the jail. Realizing there was little he could do in the face of such a throng, Hinman remained in his quarters, but grabbed his pistol with his good arm and waited for the onslaught.

Ed Pratt, from his second story window, clearly saw the angry hoard which confronted him.

Grandville Edwards, a member of the special police, had been dismissed around midnight. All was quiet around the square when Edwards began his walk home, but only minutes after arriving at his residence on Court Street, two doors west of Campbell, Edwards observed a crowd forming around the jail. He immediately returned to the square, but the crowd had the way to the jail blocked.

Other special police returned as well, but it was too late. Momentum now belonged to the mob.

With the jail hopelessly besieged and the level of excitement greatly increased, many of the fence-straddlers in the group now may have been willing to take a more active role in the confrontation. Many in the throng who before would never consider challenging a sworn officer alone, and in the light of day, now eagerly did so in the dark, amidst a crowd. Darkness, along with the size of the crowd, provided anonymity.

There were others who just wanted to say they were a part of such a momentos undertaking. Such individuals, at a later date over the supper table, in the saloons, over the merchant's counter, or amidst virtually any gathering, could later awe their audience with vivid eye-witness accounts of the incident. After all, they were part of it. In all probability, they would not take part in the actual assault on the jail, but their mere appearance made the mob much more impressive and no doubt was a deciding factor in the later actions of the special police.

If, for the good of the cause, these persons could do nothing else, they could at least hold the remnant of the special police force at bay, and evoke in them a sense of fear and hopelessness, while the sincere members of the mob did their work. They would also provide an excuse for the force when they later tried to explain why they had failed to take any action to protect the jail.

Grandville Edwards realized this much on his return to the jail. As he neared the jail, he encountered a man named Smith, whom he knew to be a member of the special police force, confronted by a member of the mob.

The mob member demanded the keys for the jail from Smith who replied, "we are here to defend the jail."

Edwards tried to intervene, but was thwarted. Later he would complain that the mob "set us aside," and the only assistance he was able to offer was to plead with the crowd to be quiet, "on Pratt's account."

With the jail security force rendered useless, his jailer wounded, and the best Pekin Police Officers away in the field searching for the two remaining fugitives, Edward Pratt had no recourse but to attempt to reason with the mob. He knew no help would be forthcoming, and no attempt to engage this mob in meaningful dialogue would prevail. With the mob at the very doors of the jail, the situation seemed hopeless.

Griffith heard Pratt's pleas from the stairway inside the jail. Grandville Edwards, from his position in the crowd, heard Pratt beg the mob "to be quiet and let the jail alone."

Sam Watson, from his fence top perch, could hear Pratt asking the mob to disperse, and imploring the crowd "for assistance to protect the jail."

Ed Pratt appealed to those in the crowd who might still be willing to let the justice system take its course. Pratt appealed to the crowd below, "every man who is willing to help me defend the jail, step out." Not a man came forth.

With that last appeal by Pratt, true to their word, the mob assailed the front door of the jail - a simple wooden door on metal hinges, designed only to separate the sheriff's office from the general population. It would offer little resistance. Members of the mob began to busy themselves by attempting to cut through the hinges with hammer and chisel, and though finally succeeding in cutting through one, decided this method was far too slow for the more anxious members of the group and a sledge hammer was procured. A few blows with this instrument were all that was needed. In seconds, the door splintered and dislodged.

Seeing the mob begin to work on the jail's outer door, Edward Pratt had rushed downstairs to the front hall and stationed himself directly behind the besieged door. From this position he watched as with each successive blow, another fractured panel gave way and more of the throng outside became visible.

The fragmented door finally gave way, and the mob began to pour through. The jail's front hall was "instantly packed solid with human flesh," causing Pratt to retreat to the stairway.

Edward Pratt stood alone, a prisoner in his own jail. His own special police force, powerless to intercede, had left him to face his fate. His jailer was wounded and unable to offer assistance.

John Griffith, as well as all others in the jail, had been quickly surrounded by the mob and greatly outnumbered, forced to remain silent.

Alone, Pratt stood face to face with his opposition. He knew the situation was hopeless. There is no doubt he was sympathetic to the mob's cause, yet opposed to them by ethics, morals, and sworn oath. Ed Pratt was now at their mercy.

Two locked doors still separated the mob from the recipients of their wrath. An iron door, hung upon jambs of solid limestone, now separated the mob's advance contingent from the cellblock. A grated, lattice work door with "bar and chinck" lock secured the cells in which the individual prisoners were confined. Both would have to be unsealed for the mob to gain access to its prey, and acquiring the keys would certainly be a great help.

Ed Pratt was again ordered to turn over the keys to the jail and again he told the crowd the keys were not in his possession. Refusing to believe the county sheriff did not possess the keys, the mob fell upon Pratt.

Pratt, assailed from all sides, stood motionless, silently bearing the humiliation and infringement, as what must have seemed to be a score of hands searched every crease and crevice of his clothing in a futile attempt to locate the keys.

Finding no keys on Pratt's person, one mob member "seized him by the throat and began to handle him harshly."

Pratt could tolerate no more. In scarcely a day, his brother, a sworn law officer, had been murdered; he had been forced to release a prisoner in order to placate a mob; his jail had been twice assaulted and once violated; and now he was being subjected to bodily search and physical attack. When Edward Pratt felt the man's hand on his throat and found his own personal safety jeopardized, he was determined not to lose his life. Pratt reached down, drew his revolver, stuck it into the stomach of the attacker, and told him and the rest of the mob, "to keep their hands off or there would be trouble."

The man, as well as the mob, took Ed Pratt at his word and desisted, and Pratt would suffer no further indignities, at least physically, the remainder of the evening. Finding no keys on Pratt's person, mob members ordered Pratt to go get them.

Pratt ascended the stairs to his quarters and disappeared. Ed Pratt failed to return with the keys, and that sturdy, impressive iron door still separated the mob from the prisoners confined in the north hall. Successfully overcoming such a structure would be no easy task. The keys must be found. If Pratt did not have the keys on his person, then they must be hidden somewhere in his living quarters on the second floor.

The mob decided that Pratt's residence would be searched, but, out of some belated respect to Pratt, or perhaps to his gun, it was decided that only three persons would be allowed inside his living quarters. An impromptu election was held and a search committee was selected.

The three individuals made their way to the upstairs living quarters, where they explored and rummaged through the personal belongings of the sheriff. They found a variety of clothing and personal articles as they gingerly felt their way through dressers, chests, and closets. But they found no keys.

Why they didn't search George Hinman's room in the back is unknown. Perhaps it was because they knew Henry's body, neatly attired, and lying in a handsome linen-lined coffin, fully prepared for the grave, was lying in state there. They would have also found George, pistol at the ready, waiting for them to enter. All of this they would have found, but they would have found no keys.

The return of the search committee bearing the news of their fruitless search mattered little. No barrier would prevent them from fulfilling their mission, not even the iron door. The door was of solid iron, with hinges sunk in limestone, and presented a far more serious obstacle than the outside door with its fragile wooden panels. The previously successful strategy of blindly flailing away at the doors would be senseless. The services of a blacksmith were needed.

Within minutes, the blacksmith arrived and the attack upon the door leading to the north cellblock began.

For an hour and a half the blacksmith worked at cutting the door hinges with a sledge and chisel. The bleak, rhythmic sound of metal striking metal rang out throughout the courthouse square. Finally, the second of two hinges fell and the door was pushed open. Access to the cellblock had been gained.

The jail's north cell block was nothing more than a narrow hallway, bordered on one side by a white stone wall and on the other side by a row of small cells where the prisoners were housed. Although designed to accommodate twenty prisoners, the exact number of inmates confined there in the early hours of that Sunday morning is unknown. The only ones that mattered were those individuals who were brought in as the so-called "Circleville gang."

These prisoners were certainly aware of the commotion going on outside the north wall and realized that they were the reason for it. From the opposite side of the solid iron door, they heard Sheriff Pratt's last futile attempt to reason with the mob. Cringing in their cells, as far from the door as possible, the prisoners heard each blow of the sledge hammer as the blacksmith worked to separate the door from it's hinges. They could not block out the irate cries of vengeance and threats of violence resounding throughout the narrow hallway. Each heard his name shouted, and cringed still further from the door.

Bill Berry's name certainly echoed through the hallway many times that night, for he was to be the first target. When the massive iron door, the last significant barrier separating them from the angry mob, gave way and the raging wave of humanity poured into the north hallway, each must have feared his life was over.

As the mob pushed into the narrow hallway, they searched by lantern light for the cell containing Bill Berry. McFarland and

Daly huddled together in a dark corner of their cell. It was hard to distinguish sweat from the tears that ran freely down their terrified faces.

In the next cell, the light-struck Emanuel and Simeon Berry as they sat motionlessly and terrified on their cots. The mob pushed past them.

Finally, in the very last cell he was spotted. A member of the mob held a lantern to provide light.

A few scattered rays of light found their way into the darkness of the cell, revealing the form of Bill Berry crouched in a corner, glaring at the mob. Attention was drawn to the movement of his hand, and in it they could see that he was drawing a knife across the stone floor, sharpening it to a razor's edge. The knife was "a clasp-knife with a four and a half inch blade," as one newspaper would later print.

16

Berry was still protected by yet another iron door. This one was of latticework design, and would also require the services of the blacksmith. Employing the same strategy as on the previous door, the Blacksmith commenced work with his sledge and chisel.

Throughout the lengthy assault upon the cell door, Bill Berry continued to slide his knife over the stone, its long blade gleaming in the light of the lantern. Berry had time to contemplate his situation. He knew what this mob wanted. He knew he was the target and was going to be killed if he did not do something and do it fast. Although it appeared hopeless, he had no intentions of making it easy for them. Perhaps the mere sight of him with a knife would cause them to think twice before entering the cell. Perhaps they might even change their minds about getting him out, and leave the jail altogether. If that failed, with his sharpened knife he might be able to wound enough of them to cause a hasty retreat, giving him enough time that someone - anyone - might come to his aid.

How Berry came to possess a knife while in custody in the jail, is unknown. It may have been left on his person when he was locked in the cell, but that would be unlikely, because the deputies knew his reputation with a knife from the Pepper incident and would surely have searched him thoroughly. It was later rumored upon the streets that John Orrel, a strong member of the gang and an "escape artist" himself, was seen among the crowd, watching for a chance to help Berry escape. It is possible he threw Berry the knife while in the darkness of the hallway. Another very distinct possibility was that the knife may have been passed through the bars by another inmate, probably one of his own brothers, who were witnessing the crazed mob's attack upon him from just a few feet away, while no doubt praying the mob was not after them.

Regardless of the manner in which Berry obtained the knife, he apparently made no attempt to hide it, and in fact displayed it openly and boldly so that the mob could clearly see it. The mere sight of Berry dragging steel against stone and knowing his reputation with the knife sent some of the attackers to the rear of the crowd. However, it had no discernible effect on other men so intent on exacting payment for the crime of which he was accused. No, the mob had came too far and excitement was too great for them to turn back now.

A few more blows of the sledgehammer, and the door gave way. Broken loose from its supports, the heavy door swung open into the hallway, blocking general access to the cell, but leaving a passageway barely wide enough for one individual to pass at a time. In its fever pitch mad rush, the mob did not take the time to secure a larger passage as they tried to get at Berry through the narrow opening.

When the door finally swung open, Bill Berry exploded forward from his crouched position in the corner, kicking the lantern from the hands of a mob member and extinguishing the north hallway's only source of light. Berry leaped from his cell into the small area formed by the open door just as two men, a man from Delavan named Livingston, and a Pekin man named Mosher, entered it.

Berry swung his knife purposefully, and the blade found its mark. The sharp blade struck Mosher, cutting through his thigh and "severing the main artery," causing a wound that was thought to be fatal. Blood shot from his leg in fast, short spurts, in perfect rhythm with his heartbeat. The floor became wet and sticky almost immediately as Mosher fell back crying out in pain and disbelief.

Within seconds, Livingston was also struck with the blade. Before he could retreat from the cramped area, he was sliced across the side, the breast and the thigh, thus adding much of his blood to that still spilling from Mosher. All this was in darkness, with the screaming of the injured men, the spraying of blood from both victims, and the slippery floor. It was here that they almost lost Berry.

In the near total darkness, Berry sidestepped his two fallen victims and feeling his way toward the partial barricade created by the dislodged door, Berry came face to face with the huge mob packing the hallway.

Swinging his knife wildly, Berry attacked the crowd and actually forced them to retreat. Amid exclamations of surprise and fear, Berry followed and slashed out savagely as his would be assassins hastily retreated toward the outer hall.

Upon reaching the passageway at the barricade, Berry, to the surprise of the crowd, stopped. He stood alone blocking the entry leading to his cell. Such a turn of events came as a shock to many present, because had he continued through the doorway he may have been able to successfully escape the startled mob. In the dark hallway, they could not see who was coming at them. It could well have been one of their own people.

There was total confusion for a while. The newspapers would later claim that Berry's "courage failed him," and, to an extent, this was probably true. It is, however, far more likely that upon attaining this vantage point from the passageway, Berry realized the magnitude of the mob and the hopelessness of his situation. From this position, Berry was able to glance into the front hall. Finding this hallway to be well lighted and packed solid by the mob, many of they carrying firearms, Berry realized escape was impossible. He must return to his cell, where, protected by the narrow entry created by the disengaged latticework door, he might be able to deal with the mob one on one.

Berry quickly dashed back to his cell and the relative safety that it afforded. He had won one round and he knew the darkened cell was his only hope for survival. Here he would make his last stand against the mob.

Bill had taken the mob by surprise. No one in the crowd had expected the rabbit to turn on the hound. They had been forced to suffer an inglorious retreat, and two of their number lay wounded in the jail's north hall behind the barricade. A host of the county's best men, 300 strong, had been humiliated by a single man wielding a knife. It seemed they had under estimated Berry, who had not uttered a single word during the entire time.

Berry's retreat again emboldened many in the mob that vigorously pursued him into the north hall. But, again encountering near total darkness, they stopped short of actually entering the cell.

That dangerous passage between the brick wall and the broken lattice work door must again be bridged. Someone in the group must enter the corridor and confront Berry, who was still in possession of the knife. He had already demonstrated his intention of "selling his life as dearly as possible."

Berry remained cornered and could not escape, yet someone would have to enter the cell and disarm him if the mob's stated intention of hanging Bill Berry was to be accomplished.

In the darkness and confusion, a call for more light was given. A lantern was moved to the front. Someone in the mob yelled out that they should shoot Berry.

Berry heard this remark and retreated further into the darkness of his cell to make a less clear target for a shooter.

Amidst it all stood a man named Brownley, who was a saloon-keeper from Delavan, and a friend of George Pepper's. He decided to try his luck and slowly entered Berry's cell.

As Berry retreated further into his cell, where darkness would make him a difficult target, Brownley followed him. A great struggle ensued between the two men.

A lantern was passed from hand to hand down the narrow corridor to get more light. The juggling and jarring of the lantern created an eerie effect, as the dim glow of light it provided found its way into the cell.

The dull orange glow revealed the shadow-like images of Berry and Brownley engaged in deadly hand to hand combat. Brownley was bleeding. He had suffered repeated slashes from Berry's knife. Later it was learned that he had been stabbed seven times. He still refused to give way.

When light was finally procured, those in the north hall could see Berry. He had somehow managed to slip the death grip of Brownley and was crouched once again in a corner of his cell, slashing out blindly with his knife in an attempt to inflict yet another wound on his relentless opponent.

Finally, one such thrust, missing its target completely, struck one of the cell's brick walls. The knife blade was broken off near the handle. Bill Berry was finally at the mercy of his foes.

Fatigued, in pain, and bleeding from his several wounds, Brownley refused to give ground. Standing over the crouched Bill Berry, Brownley exclaimed, "Now we have you, you son of a bitch. Stand up like a man."

Berry knew his last hope for survival had vanished with the broken knife blade. His only hope of escape was now gone. No longer able to protect himself from the mob, he would be subject to their whims. Knowing all of this, Berry, who had "fought like a tiger" and "uttered not a single word" during the entire ordeal, perhaps in obedience to Brownley's challenge or perhaps merely to change his fighting tactics, rose slowly from his somewhat protected position on the floor of his cell.

Berry's vigorous defense of his life must have made a frightening impression on someone in the crowd, for at the precise moment that Bill Berry rose from the floor, some very foolish person in the crowd felt it necessary, perhaps out of fear, to render him totally incapable of resistance. From somewhere in the north hall, among all the citizens and with all the stone and iron about the cell block area, five shots, all of which were directed at Bill Berry, rang out.

One shot struck Berry near the left temple, passed cleanly through the brain, and exited the skull on the opposite side. Another struck Berry in the left arm, passed through, and lodged in his left side. The other three shots failed to find their mark, but caused considerable apprehension for those in the immediate vicinity of being struck by the ricochet from one of the rounds.

The reports of the shots echoed throughout the jail and town square. John Griffith heard the shots from the jail's outer hall.

R. Bradley, from inside the north hall, actually witnessed the shooting, but later, under oath, would testify that he could not identify the man who fired the fatal shots.

Sam Watson and Grandville Edwards heard them from the jail yard.

George Hinman, from his quarters in the jail, heard the shots below; as did Ed Pratt, who by this time must have felt that the sanctity of his oath and his office had suffered the final blow.

As Bill Berry fell to the floor, mortally wounded and bleeding from the wounds to the arm, side, and head, the crowd rushed upon him. He was beaten "nearly senseless" and dragged from his cell into the north hall. He was still not totally subdued.

In the hallway, Berry continued to defend himself and even to act on the offensive. The bullet wound to the head had not stopped his struggle for life, only slowed it somewhat. Persisting in the struggle, he continued to lash out at his assailants, until someone in the crowd took it upon himself to strike Berry in the head with a hammer that had been used to remove the cell door. The hammer rained down upon Berry's head until he was finally still.

With Berry incapable of resistance, several men carried the wounded men out of the jail and to a doctor. It was later announced that one of the men might have sustained a fatal wound.

Things had not gone exactly as the mob had planned. Impediments such as the special police force, Pratt's impassioned plea, and that stubborn iron door had not been expected. And, after overcoming these obstacles, the mob had certainly not anticipated Bill Berry's fierce resistance. If they had expected to encounter a passive penitent criminal, meekly pleading for his life while being led to his execution, they had certainly been wrong.

As they stood over his lifeless body, many in the crowd were apparently uncertain of what to do next. A hanging had been planned, but Berry's bloody body on the floor of the jail's north hall, made that object pointless.

There were those in the crowd who demanded that the mission be fully completed. It was argued that Berry should be hung even though he was dead. Someone in the crowd reminded the rest that "we came here to hang him and let's hang him."

There was a call "for a vote," and being decent people who believed that it was the democratic thing to do, they put the issue to a vote. Only three persons in the whole mob raised their hands in favor of a hanging, but the motion was declared to have "carried."

A rope was secured around Berry's neck and his lifeless body was dragged through cellblock, across the outer hall, through the front door. and out into the yard.

In the east yard of the jail property, near the fence and less than twenty feet from the spot where John Ott had been executed eight years before, stood a huge tree. It was a tall, spreading oak tree with large limbs, one of which extended at "nearly a right angle from the trunk" and was about ten feet above the ground.

As one reporter later wrote, "it looked as though a hole had been bored in the trunk, and a branch stuck to it."

It is doubtful that the mob considered the special attributes of this particular tree, for according to one reporter, "the mob then dragged him to the nearest tree and swung him up." In adding further details, that same reporter wrote, "a rope was thrown over a tree, and one end of it fastened around Berry's neck and the other held by determined men. He was swung up."

As they "swung him up," much to the surprise of the excited mob, Bill Berry, struck in the hand, side, and head by pistol shot, then kicked and beaten senseless and stunned by blows to the head with a hammer, continued to struggle for life.

He began moaning and grabbing for the rope. Cheers went through the mob as they realized he was still alive and they would get their hanging.

Two men were obliged to rush forward and pull down Berry's hands as he reached up and grabbed hold of the limb above his head in an attempt to forestall the inevitable. As soon as they let go of his hands, he attempted to loosen the rope around his neck. The same two men ran to him and clung to his legs, pulling them down. Finally, the last bit of life ebbed from Bills body.

The mob, pleased with their accomplishment, stood cheering as the body of Bill Berry swayed silently in the breeze. They began calling for the lynching of the rest of the gang.

Meanwhile, Stone's small posse had arrived in Pekin. They certainly were not prepared for what they found. During their chase across the prairie after Britton, they had no way of knowing the trouble that had been brewing in Pekin. Upon entering the outskirts of Pekin, they could see a lot of activity in town. Hundreds of men were gathered around the town square, completely filling the jail yard and streets around it.

Quitely, the small group of men rode forward. It was not long before Stone and the other men saw what they were excited about. Hanging from the limb of a tree in the jail yard was Bill Berry. It was apparent he was dead, yet two men still hung drunkenly onto his legs. One of them spat upon the body several times.

A lynching! It was the one thing an officer of the law dreaded most, because lynch parties were mostly made up of local town people who mean well, but were out of control. What lawman in his right mind would want to shoot some of the better people of his town over an outlaw? Perhaps he would have to shoot close friends or even relatives.

Seeing this, Stone knew that Britton's life was in danger, and perhaps even their own. Their presence had not yet been discovered, but he had to act fast. Skirting the court yard square by one block, Stone took Britton to Height's Livery Stable, located on the northeast corner of Court and Fifth street, a full city block to the east of the jail. There he secreted him away in the hayloft, under the protective eyes of Lewis Cass and John Berry.

Though Britton had talked constantly on the way to Pekin, he had arrogantly refused to tell them anything about the ambush. He was sure Bill Berry would "swear him clear." When he saw Bill swinging from the tree, he was not so tough and cocksure. He was crying. He begged officers for protection. He told them he would turn state's evidence against all the Berrys and tell them who had killed Pratt. He shouted that it had been all the gang. They had planned it. Bill Berry supplied the guns, and McFarland, the ammunition. Britton was frightened beyond belief.

Stone assured the prisoner that his posse would protect him while he went to talk with the mob. He would try to convince them to let the courts judge the rest of the gang.

With that, he took a double-barreled shotgun and walked the block to the jail. The mob parted as he passed through, showing no sign fear.

When he reached the front steps of the jail, he turned and held up his hands. He waited until the crowd settled down.

Almost everyone in the mob knew Alfred Stone. They respected him as a lawman and also knew that they could not do to him what they had just done to Sheriff Pratt. They knew Stone would use that shotgun on anyone who tried to get past him.

Stone told them the lynching was over. There would be no more attacks on the jail.

Out of fear, respect, or whatever, the mob remained silent. They listened to what he had to say.

Stone told them he had captured Britton, but would not bring him forward until they promised they would not harm him. Stone knew most of the men, and knew that once they gave their word, it would be safe to bring Britton forward.

After much debate among themselves, most of the men gave Stone their word that they would not harm Britton.

Confident they would keep their word, Stone signaled for Cass and Berry to bring Britton to him. He had decided to take him to the American House Hotel and place him in a window for the entire crowd to see. He had promised them that they would be able to see this man Britton, who had been responsible for the death of Henry Pratt, and they would.

As they brought Britton forth, they had to walk him through the crowd. Shouldering their way through the crowd, they reached the steps of the hotel, and just as they did, someone in the crowd yelled, "There's the man we want." As his words echoed, the end of a rope was thrown at Britton.

Cass deflected the rope with his arm and Britton fainted away and had to be carried to the hotel by the officers. Even there, he had trouble standing as they placed him in the window to be viewed by the crowd.

Britton later gained his composure somewhat and yelled to the crowd that they should not feel remorse for what they had done as Bill Berry was nothing but a cutthroat and a murderer. He promised to tell them all about the entire gang.

During his stay with the officers, he told them of his first encounter with Isaac Berry, and that they had in fact planned the theft of the horses with Shaw. He said they all had been involved in the attack against the posse. He added that Bill was the responsible person behind the resistance. Again he said he would tell it all to the state attorney.

Britton rattled on, telling how he had been involved in the shooting incident, how he had jumped a fence and lay down. Later he had run off into the darkness. He said he had stayed at

Bill's house that night, ate breakfast, and then headed out for Delavan.

Much later, when Stone was satisfied that the mob had settled down for the night, he transferred Britton from the American House to the same jail from which just a few hours ago, Bill Berry had been dragged. His body still swung back and forth on the rope as the small group of officers walked Britton past him. Britton was very thankful to be safely locked in his cell.

Now there was only Ike left roaming free in the wilderness, but with hundreds of men searching for him, his days of freedom were numbered.

17

On the first day of August, as the cool gray dawn broke over Pekin, all was quiet at the jail. The crowd had slowly, one by one, disappeared into the night, until only a handful of men remained.

Alva Culver, who had just last April been elected coroner, got word of the lynching and rode in from Delavan. He made his way along Court Street to the jail and stopped.

Berry's body was still hanging from the tree, swaying gently in the early morning breeze. Culver could see that Berry had struggled desperately with death by the brownish stain of blood on the rope, much of it no doubt from his hands as he gripped the rope during the final moments of his life.

Culver motioned for several men to lend a hand with the removal of the Berry's body. After cutting the rope and lowering the body to the ground, he ordered a rough box built for it.

As the town slowly came alive again, Coroner Culver, along with other members of the community, decided the body of Bill Berry should be placed on display for the rest of the people to see (a practice quite common around the country in those days). It would be a warning to all criminals that the people would tolerate no more.

The crude coffin was carried into the courthouse where it was placed in the lobby with the lid off, exposing the bloody body of Bill Berry, who would never again terrorize the people.

As Coroner Culver walked away, the "other towns people," the ones who had slept through it all, were already gathering to see the bloody results of the fight and lynching. They would have something to talk about for a long time to come.

Before the day was over, many people, some from miles away, would move in a steady stream through the doors of the courthouse to get a close look at the lifeless form that lay in the plain wooden box with the open lid.

He still wore the same clothing of the previous night, and most of his body was covered with dried blood from the wounds inflicted by the out of control mob, just hours earlier. He had a gaping hole in his left temple where the bullet had ripped through his skull. There were sunken areas on his skull where blood had dried and where unnamed men had struck him repeatedly with a hammer after he was already shot. His face and upper body were discolored, his neck was twisted and stretched beyond belief as a result of the rope which had finally taken "the last struggles of nature" from his body, leaving his bulging, unseeing eyes staring at the people who were parading past his coffin.

No doubt some jeered, some sneered, and others cursed at the body for all the crimes he had committed in the past, but there were the silent ones as well. The silent ones, who had been in the mob the night before, were grim. They seemed to be in deep thought, perhaps thinking about what they had done during the wild night only a few hours past. They had committed atrocities on this man that they had never dreamed themselves capable of until yesterday.

Some would never forget, some would manage to live with their deed, but there were those who would not be able to cope with this terrible thing in their minds. As would be evident in the next few days, the peaceful farmers who had been roused to such violent, gruesome acts would suffer twinges of consciousness. Some would become mentally torn apart by the memories of the terrible injuries inflicted upon Berry, such as him being beaten with fists, shot through the head, and struck with a hammer to quiet his struggles. Memories of holding his arms down as he attempted to grab the limb above his head and holding his leg when he tried to loosen the rope would haunt them as well.

There would be memories of the terrified looks, the crying, and perhaps even the pitiful pleadings of mercy for Bill Berry by his brothers, Emanuel and young Simeon, who cringed just a matter of feet, perhaps inches, from where these horrible deeds were committed. Blood from his wounds may well have splashed into the very cells in which they were confined.

Watching their brother being brutally murdered must have compounded the fear of the same happening to them. A person can only imagine the relief that must have engulfed the prisoners when Marshal Stone arrived and put an end to the lynching.

The majority of the townspeople would be sorry for what they had done, but none would be more sorrowful than the lonely woman and the two small children who quitely pulled a team and wagon up to the courthouse to claim the body for burial. The sad faced, teary-eyed woman was Nancy Welch Berry.

The children, a boy about twelve years old, named Albert and a ten year old girl named Ellen, understood none of this, but knew only that their father was dead, and that they had come with their mother to take his body home.

They came alone. No other family members accompanied them, not even to help carry the body. Perhaps the fear of the mob still being in town had been the reason. Perhaps there was no one left who could help, for most of the family was in jail.

Without help from family or friends, she and the children somehow managed to get the coffin loaded. They then began the long, lonely trip home. It would be the longest eight miles Nancy and her children would travel, as the wagon bounced over the rough road on the way to their Circleville home. Here they would lay to rest the man who they not only dearly loved, but was also their only means of support.

Meanwhile, the Coroner's jury on Henry Pratt had reached a verdict, and the Peoria National Democrat reported on August 8, 1869 that:

> The Coroners inquest in the case of the murder
> of Pratt, [Henry Pratt] returned the following
> verdict: came to his death by a wound in his
> right breast, made by two shots discharged from
> a two barreled shotgun in the hands of Isaac Berry,
> in the County of Tazewell, on the 30thday of July,
> 1869, and that Simeon Berry, William Berry,
> Emanuel Berry, Mathew McFarland, Robert
> Britton and C. Daly alias the Peddler, were
> accessories before the fact of such killing, and that
> in manner aforesaid the said Henry Pratt was, by
> the said Isaac Berry, William Berry, Emanuel
> Berry, Mathew McFarland, Robert Britton and
> C. Daly alias the peddler, unlawfully killed and
> murdered.

Later that same morning, the Coroner convened another jury to hear testimony of the events of Berry's death.

As he was doing this, Sheriff Pratt was making final arrangements for Henry's funeral with D. W. Umdenstock, owner of the local funeral parlor. From Umdenstock, he had purchased a coffin with handles for $38.00, an engraved plate for the coffin for $3.00, a rough box for $3.00, and obtained the use of ice bags for $5.00. Use of the hearse and extra ice was another $13.50.

He had already purchased Henry's burial clothes from W.A. Delany's store, consisting of a pair of pants, which cost $12.00, a $9.00 vest, and a tie and collar for $.75.

The total cost for these arrangements was $62.50, which was placed on an account for the time being.

The services were to be held in Tremont in the Baptist church, built in 1842. There would also be Masonic ceremonies, for Henry had been a member of that fraternity. The Reverend W.M. Steele would officiate the services, delivering a sermon which all but said outright that the men who had stormed the jail and lynched Berry had done nothing more than what was expected of them.

Finally, the time came for Edward Pratt to go to the funeral parlor and begin the trip to the church. After making sure the jail was left with plenty of security, he walked down the street to his waiting buggy where he found "a long line of friends and acquaintances" already waiting in wagons, buggies and on horse back, to make the nine mile trip to Tremont. As sad an occasion as it was, he must have felt touched to know that so many people cared.

Slowly the funeral procession moved eastward along Court street and out of town. No doubt there were many people waiting along its route to bid the deputy farewell.

It took nearly two hours to reach the church and carry the coffin inside. As the people entered, the tiny building soon filled and over-flowed with people.

The Masonic ceremonies were given first, then Reverend Steele delivered a stinging sermon so directed at the recent happenings, that it must have been a great relief for the men involved in the lynching to hear approval coming from a man of God. His sermon hinted very strongly that the men in this county had done nothing more than what they should have, due to the corruption in the judicial system.

The Tazewell County Register, on August 2nd, 1869 printed his sermon in full:

> HABAKKUK I: 1,2,3,4 The burden which
> Habakkuk the prophet did see, O Lord, how long
> shall I cry, and thou wilt not hear, even cry out unto
> thee of violence, and thou wilt not save ! Why dost
> thou show me iniquity and cause me to behold
> grievance?
>
> For spoiling and violence are before me; and there
> are that rise up strife and contention. There
> fore the law is slacked; and judgement doth never
> go forth, for the wicked doth compass about the
> righteous; therefore wrong judgement proceedeth.
>
> The writer of these words lived in the reign of
> the impious and tyrannical Mannassah, King of
> Judah, about 700 years before Christ. In the
> words which I have read to you, the Prophet gives
> a succinct but graphic description of the wickedness
> and corruption which prevail under the rule of
> this wicked King. I avail myself of a brief
> description given by another, of this wickedness

and corruption.

In these verses the Prophet sadly laments the
INIQUITY OF THE LAW, as one sensibly touched
with grief for the lamentable decay of religion and
righteousness. First he informs us that violence was
in the land. No man could call what he had his own
but in defiance of the most sacred laws of property
and equity he that had power and money on his side,
had what he had a mind to, though he had no
right...the land was full of violence.

In families and among relations in neighborhoods
and among friends, in commerce and in court of law
everything was carried on with a high hand and no
man made any scruple of doing wrong to his
neighbor so that he could make a good thing out of
it for himself and evade the law either by trickery or
bribery.

He complained that the wicked doth compass about
the righteous. One honest man, one honest cause,
have enemies besetting them on every side, many
wicked men, in confederacy against it run, them
down; nay, one wicked man with so many various
arts of mischief sets upon a righteous man, that
he perfectly besets him.

He states that the kingdom was broken into parties
and factions that were continually biting and
devouring one another...There are that raise up
strife and contention, that foment division, widen
breeches, incense men against another, and sow
discord among brethren. Strifes and contentions

that have been laid asleep and begun to be forgotten
they awake and industriously raise up again and
blow up the sparks that were hidden in the embers...
men warming their hands at those flames which are
devouring all that is good in the nation and
stirring up the fire also.

He asserts that the torrent of violence and strife
ran so strong as to bid defiance to the restraints
and requirements of laws and administration of
justice. Because God did not visibly appear
against them nobody else would, therefore the law
is slacked, is silent, it breathes not, its pulse
beats not, it intermitts and judgement fores not go
forth as it should; no cognizance is taken of those
crimes, nay, wrong judgements proceed. If appeals
be made to the courts of equity, the righteous shall
be condemned and the wicked justified, so that the
remedy is worse than the disease.
The legislative power takes no care to supply the
deficiencies of the law for obviating those growing,
threatening mischiefs. The executive power takes
no care to answer the good intentions of the laws
that are made. The stream of justice is dried up by
violence bribery, and corruption, and has not its free
course.

And all this was open and public, and impudently
avowed; it was barefaced. The Prophet complains
that this iniquity was shown him, he beheld which
soever he turned his eyes, nor could be looked off
it, "spoiling and violence are before me". Are they
not now before us? With what truth the description
of the Prophet's own time and nation applies to us,

and out time and nation I leave for you to determine.

Take an impartial survey, though brief it may be, of
our social condition. Of much, very much of good
that is among us, I gladly speak. Of individuals of
societies, of government, there is much to commend
and be thankful for. Of progress in knowledge, in
arts and science, in useful machinery, in works of
benevolence progress had been made and is
progressing. We are alive, vigorous and active to
advance every prospective scheme for benefitting
the material interests of the community, developing
the resources of wealth, fostering the old facilities
of the safe, speedy and cheap transit of the products
of the earth, the workshop and the loom to the
markets if the world. We are increasing in wealth
and power as a people. We are rising high in the
scale of nations...high in intelligence, in social
position, in wealth in power. We have very much in
these matters to be thankful for. But with all this
advancement this prosperity, in this high social
position, is there not a corruption widespread,
deep seated and growing, that is gnawing at the
very vitals of society and threatening, unless
checked, ultimately to destroy in wild confusion
and fierce anarchy the proud fabric of liberty
society and morality erected in this western
continent?
It becomes us, men of today, to give this question an
impartial hearing, to judge it accordingly to its real
merits, to look calmly to the issues of the present, as
they will inevitably effect our future interests, the
interests if our children and children's children.

It becomes us as men, as patriots, as fathers and bothers to gird up our loins to meet these issues fairly and fully.

That lawlessness and corruption are widespread deepseated and increasing among us, needs no proof, every reading and reflecting man knows it. It is trumpeted from one end to the other of our vast Republic, by the Daly and weekly press.

That a great number of individual crimes may now be brought to our notice by the multiplication of obtaining information is very true. But this cannot satisfactorily account for the immensely increased number of crimes....of all grades, hues and shapes...in all classes of society, in all parts of the country, that are published. It is sickening to read merely the headings of the crimes and immoralities in any city Daly paper. It cannot be that this is simply the result of facility and publication

It must be that crime and corruption are on the increase among us at a fearful rate. We must know this by what we see around us, the increase of vice and immorality in our own society, the slight regard that is given to one's pledged word, the trickery in trades, the falsehood and cheating in bargaining the artifices used avoid payment of just debts, the increase of drunkenness and gambling, of theft and of arson, of murder and suicide and the frequent perpetuation of other infamous crimes.

It has come to that pass that the law of the land
affords no safe protection to life and property. A
man possessed today of abundant visible property,
borrows your money to be paid twenty days hense,
ten days hense, he makes a sham sale of all his
property and you are powerless to force him to
repay you.

If a crime is committed, the law seems powerless
in the hands of its administrators to punish the
criminal, IF HE HAD MONEY. It was publicly
asserted in the Court House yard yesterday morning
and uncontradicted, that "but one murderer has
been hung in Tazewell County for twenty years, and
he was a POOR FOOL." Have there been no other
murders committed in the county during that time
by men who were neither poor no fools?

The truth is, as I was told several days ago by your
District Attorney, that the present legislation of the
country is all in favor of the criminal. It
throws around him a net work of protection,
guarding him, as far as possible from conviction, and
money secures the quibbles and technicalities of law
to insure his safety. And too often, when but a
slight punishment is inflicted, the executive
power interferes and an unpunished murderer
hardened by crime and embolden by immunity from
punishment, is turned loose to prey upon society.

I am fully aware that it is better for a guilty
man to escape than for an innocent one to be
punished. I know that the law must provide safe
guards for the innocent. I am fully aware that it

may be expedient for the executive to exercise his
clemency in the pardoning of a criminal. It is not
against the proper exercise of legitimate privileges
that I object. But it is against corruption, in
the use of money to override the law and justice
screen the guilty from deserved punishment, and
pardon the murderer, that on behalf of myself
and family, you and your families, of this outraged
community, of MY COUNTRY AND MY GOD, I
do object, and such things I must and will condemn.
They are proof of the deepseated corruption in our
midst.

I am not here today to cast reflections on
individuals and especially upon those in authority
over us, I am taught but a law, not a man's enacting,
"to speak evil to no man" and to "honor" those in
authority. I but deal in facts...facts given to
me...and, probably better known to you than to
myself. And facts are stubborn things. I but
give you the facts, draw your own conclusions.

There are facts connected with the sad cause for
our present assembling, which if anything will,
must deeply impress your minds and rouse you to
action. To action that will counteract the vice
and immorality abounding among us. There lies
the conservator of your laws, the protector of
your property, shot down like a dog, while in the
lawful discharge of his duty under the authority
given him by you. The Deputy Sheriff of your
county murdered by HORSE THIEVES! And who
was the harborer of the thieves? Who gave them
information that

your officers sought to arrest them? Who
urged them to resist them with murderous
intent? Who was the prime mover and
instigator in this atrocious murder? A
PARDONED CRIMINAL, himself a murderer, who
served but a day of his inadequate term of
one year's imprisonment in your State
Penitentiary!

How are the demands of justice complied with; how
is the executive clemency abuse; when the first act
of a pardoned murderer is openly to resist the law,
to defy its execution, and openly instigate others to
murder its own office when in the lawful discharge
of his sworn duty?

Let these facts appeal to you as men, as citizens, as
heads of families. The remedy for them, the only
remedy I know of, is in your hands, in the hands of
substantial farmers of the country, the property
holders, the fathers of families.

But I came not here to add fuel to the flame
of your neighbor's indignation against the vile
perpetrators and abettors of this atrocious deed.
I am not here, an isolated individual, to plead
my private cause before you. I am not here to
obtrude upon you my own opinions of State, of
Church, or of Religion. Nor did I come to express
to you the deep feelings of my heart for the loss
of my friend and brother. I came not to eulogize
him. You knew him better than I, and to know him
was to respect and love him. The highest tribute
that can be paid to his memory is.....that he died

144

in the brave and conscientious discharge of his duty as the conservator of law and protector of property. And the highest I can pronounce over him is, that his kind-hearted landlady, a comparative stranger to him, shed tears over his corpse, while she told me of his noble traits of character that in so short of a time had won her regard and affection. She loved him as a son. He deserved that love; he deserves the love of us all; we mourn for him, but not as those with out hope. He is not beyond the reach of our eulogy, and we turn to the live issues before us.

I am here today to erect for him an imperishable monument IN THE GOOD THAT YOU MAY EFFECT. I plead YOUR OWN CAUSE before yourselves, and the cause of your children.

This vice, wickedness and corruption must be stayed, or else its swollen stream, in time, will engulf us all in ruin irretrievable. What security have you now in law against fraud and swindling; what hope have you of obtaining justice by an appeal of law; how many of you actually suffer loss rather than trust to the uncertainties of the law? What is the state of morality among us; of temperance and sobriety; of liberality and unselfishness; of purity and uncorrupted in the discharge of public duty? If the standard of these are now low, and falling lower year by year, what will be the harvest of crime and corruption that your children and grand-children will have to reap? It is your cause and their cause that I plead before you to-day, in the presence of that sad evidence that vice and

immorality are rampant in your midst, and I call
upon you MEN AND WOMEN OF TAZEWELL
COUNTY, as you love your country, as you love
your children, as you value the peaceful possession
and quiet enjoyment of your property, and desire to
transmit this unimpaired to your posterity, to use our
individual influence and example to crush out the
drunkenness, the vice, the immorality, the corruption
which so widely prevails. That is the one remedy
that I know of. IT WILL BEGIN WITH
INDIVIDUALS, and enlarge the circle of its
benefits as individuals as the influence of their
example in a sober, righteous and godly life.

With all our knowledge, with all our social
advancement, with all our progress in arts and
science in discoveries and inventions can we read the
SIGNS OF THE TIMES? Are we blind to the
issues that are Daly pressing upon us with
accumulating force? Shall we learn nothing from the
lesson taught us by the history of the past?

The Prophet who was so graphically depicted the
vice and wickedness of Judah in the reign of
Manassah foretold a fearful punishment upon that
God forsaking people, and it came. Where are the
proud empire of old, of Egypt and Assyria, of
Greece and Rome, exalted in wealth, in learning, in
Arts and science, but debased in the vice and
debauchery?

Can we read no analogy between thirteen colonies
On the Atlantic Coast and a colony of Trojans
Landing upon the shores of Italy and form this small

146

beginning, by indomitable perseverance, heroic courage and stern integrity expanded into Imperial Rome, mistress of the world, yet bearing within her the seeds of her own destruction? As her power increased, her ambitions grew, and stretched out her arms, embraced the world and made it tributary to her prosperity. As that prosperity increased, vice and corruption and debauchery advanced till the en came, in the wildest anarchy and a deluge of blood. It is all for the men and women of to-day to stay the tide of vice in our land, or else the end may be similar.

You raise monuments to commemorate the patriotic dead, who fall in defense of their country, and emblazon the cold marble with the record of their names and heroic deeds. And you do well. Raise a monument to him, who, eminently worthy of your respect and affection, fell in defense of your law and your property. But I will ask no marble monument for him. Let his name and his worth be engraved upon your hearts. Raise for him an imperishable monument in the example and influence of a sober, pure, and virtuous life.
One set of lawless violence never justifies another, One revengeful deed, never justifies retaliation in kind. It is for you, the men and women of to-day to change the state of society among us, to raise the standard of virtue and morality by the example you dare to set to all around you. It is for you to secure for your posterity, peace and prosperity, and the enjoyment of happiness in a virtuous and well spent life, or a heritage of crime and misery.

In corroboration of the view taken in the discourse
of the prevailing INIQUITY OF THE TIMES, I
desire to append the following extract from a city
paper published on the same day the discourse was
delivered. it is a fact frequently deplored by all
good citizens, that the public morals are bad.

Vice and crime, of every name, were never
heretofore so common in American society as now;
fraud riots in high places, theft flourishes in
unprecedented abundance; licentiousness, brutality,
violence, and assassination have become so
prevalent, as scarcely to excite a passing wonder.

The poison has affected even the tribunals of justice,
And the public now rarely anticipate conviction,
Much less punishment for the crime of murder.
Instances in proof of those facts need not be cited.
They will recur to the mind of every person in this,
or almost any other community. What was once
called majesty of the law has lost its majesty in the
general corruption of public morals.

Silence befell the tiny church for awhile, perhaps many of
those present were evaluating the words of Reverend Steele. If
they were, they must have been able to read between the lines,
for in essence, Reverend Steele had just told them, they were
justified in what they did. They were justified according to the
scripture of the Bible, and he was trying to relieve their minds
of the heavy burden of guilt in executing William Berry before
he could be judged.

Perhaps this sermon did help relieve the minds of some
who were tormented by the sights and events of that night.

With the funeral over, Sheriff Pratt and Marshal Stone could take up the search for Isaac Berry in earnest. They returned to Pekin, where the coroner's jury soon issued a verdict in the killing of Bill Berry. It was as reported in the Peoria Daly National Democrat on August 8, 1969:

> The jury in the case of WM. Berry, brought in a verdict to the support that he came to his death from a wound to the head received from a shot from a revolver, in the hands of some person unknown.

Bill Berry's last futile attempts at grabbing the rope while being hanged would later be discounted as "the struggles of expiring nature."

The lawmen also found that Nancy Berry and her two children, Albert and Ellen, had already left town with the body of her husband and their father.

Meanwhile, rumors abounded about Isaac Berry, with people seeing him everywhere. Many searches were made on Sunday afternoon, but he was not located. It was on this day that he was reportedly seen in Hawley's Grove where fourteen shots were fired at him.

Many other rumors floated about, including one that he had been shot and killed in the shoot-out with Deputy Pratt, and had been dragged away, by his friends. Others said he had been shot, dragged himself away and died somewhere in the thickets and may never be found. These rumors may have been started by his family to get the posses off his trail, but it failed to work as evidenced by a report in a Peoria newspaper:

> About five hundred men were on the hunting path on Monday, of which one hundred and fifty were from Pekin, and the remainder,

principally from Tremont, Delavan, Dillon and Circleville.

And the search for Isaac Berry continued.

18

In a small room at the American House Hotel, a man, heavy with thought, sat alone on his bed. The man had not attended the services of Henry Pratt, for if he had, perhaps he would have felt differently about his participation in the lynching.

It was August 1, 1869, and Felix Knott sat in the room, troubled by the events of the past few nights. He stole nervous glances at the revolver on the table beside his chair. He trembled and his sweat flowed like water, but he took no notice for he had reached the point of no return.

Lately he had been nervous, much more than usual, and had difficulty controlling his anxieties. Felix had been depressed over losing the election of City Clerk of Pekin. A year before, on April 20th, he had been elected City Clerk by receiving five votes to his opponent's, W.F. Henry, three. He had enjoyed a full year in office as City Clerk, which was an important

151

position on the city council. He had felt important. Then came the yearly election of April 19, 1869, however, much to his dismay, he lost the election to William Mallingford. Mallingford had received a majority of the votes, with ninety-two cast in his favor.

Felix was out. He became depressed, spending most of his time to himself. Then along came the "great excitement" of the Berry gang. He had been caught up in it and unable to get out. He had something to do - something exciting. It took his mind off the election and gave him a way to release his anxieties.

He was in the mob on Saturday and, undoubtedly, like everyone else, had been encouraging anyone who would listen to join them in attacking the jail to lynch all the Berrys. He had been in the attack on the front door of the jail and on the door securing the hallway to the cellblock. He had watched the hinges of the door give way and had seen the frightened expressions on the faces of the prisoners, who knew they were going to be lynched.

Felix had been fired up when the door of Bill Berry's cell swung open. There, however, he was not a forerunner. He had left that up to the others, perhaps because he had seen the knife in Bill's hand as he applied it to the stone. Felix had watched as the men tried to drag him from his cell, only to come away with severe wounds inflicted by the knife he wielded. There had been blood everywhere, with men crying out in pain - something Felix was not accustomed to. It was a gruesome sight, what little could be seen in the darkness of the hallway, and Felix had seen it all. He had watched Brownley jump into the cell and give Berry a "great battle."

It was then that the deafening roar of a pistol discharging rebounded off the solid stone walls of the cell. Felix heard five shots and watched Berry fall to the floor of the cell.

The shooter had disregarded the safety of everyone by firing a gun inside the cell, but, by some fluke, no one other than Berry had been hit by the ricocheting bullets.

Although no one ever stepped forward and identified the shooter, it was common knowledge that Felix had fired those shots.

Outside, Felix had watched as the "last struggles of nature" left Bill's body. Only when it was all over and there had been complete silence, as the mob stood watching the results of their deed, had Felix realized what he had been a part of. Perhaps he had been one of the two men who had pulled Berry's arms down when he had tried so desperately to grab the limb above his head. Perhaps he was one of those men clinging to Berry's legs, or perhaps had been one of those men who had spat upon Berry's body as it finally hung still at the end of the rope.

Whatever he had done, it was completely out of character for him, and had tormented him constantly since. He had always been a decent man, but now he had helped kill a human being. He knew Berry had been a criminal, but he was still a human being.

Besides, there was the law to worry about. The mob had broken the law and surely they would all be punished. For a while he thought it would just blow over because Berry was lynched and no one had mentioned the shooting. Maybe things would be a little brighter when the coroner's jury came back with its verdict. Things might look a little brighter, for he would then see what they found as the cause of death and what action the law would take against the people for the lynching. He would learn then if anyone had seen the shooter.

Then came word that the coroner's jury had issued a verdict in the death of Bill Berry. They found that Berry had "died from a bullet fired from a revolver into his head, by a person not known."

Felix knew who that person was. And he knew someone in the crowd had seen him fire the shots and would surely tell Marshal Stone. He also knew that he could not be locked up.

His mind could handle the anxieties no longer, and he picked up the pistol. Felix had made a decision, and raised the pistol to his head. Without hesitation, he pulled the trigger.

A shot rang out. His anxieties were gone. Felix fell to the floor unconscious and bleeding profusely from a small hole in his temple. The blood gushed from the hole and formed a pool on the carpet as his hand still gripped the pistol. This was the way he was found when friends rushed to his room to investigate the shot.

A doctor was quickly summoned, but seeing the head wound, knew it was hopeless. The doctor knew Felix would die, he just did not know when. He applied large bandages around his head to stem the flow of blood. With this done, all he could do was wait.

The Doctor waited, but Felix clung to life. Hour after hour passed and he still lived. Finally, the Doctor, unable to stay longer, summoned a nurse to attend the injured man until he expired. The nurse and friends set about cleaning the room. The blood stained carpet had to be sent out for cleaning and the costs were charged to Felix, as he was still alive.

Although the doctor had been sure it would not be long, Felix lived for two days, but on August 3, 1869, Felix Knott, ex-steam boat clerk and ex-city clerk, died. At ten o'clock that same morning, because prior arrangements had been made, he was buried.

On August 5, 1869, one newspaper would print:

> We understand that Knott, one of
> the young men concerned with the
> late excitement in Pekin, died in that city
> yesterday. He is spoken of as a promising

young man, and some persons say the
excitement of the scenes there, brought about
his death.

The same paper on the day before had printed:

He was a young man who had no enemy
but himself.

For the rest of the citizens who were involved in the
lynching, the general consensus of the public could not have
been better put than was printed in a "Law vs Justice" editorial
in the Jacksonville Daly Journal on August 10, 1869. It read:

A few days since the deputy sheriff of Tazewell
County was murdered by a desperado who was
connected with a gang of horse thieves and
scoundrels in that county. The excited populace
took the murderer, or his confederate, out of the
hands of the officers and hung him without even a
drun-head trial.

The reason for such a proceeding on the part of the
peaceful citizens of Tazewell County is obvious.
This gang of reprobates had been making its
headquarters in the county for years plundering the
citizens, and even taking life when they found it
necessary in the prosecution, time and time again
members of the band, had been arrested, but always
managed to escape through some loop-hole in the
law, as much as we abhor lynch law, we cannot
blame them; their lives and property needs must be
rendered secure in some manner, they had no other
recourse.

The writer likens the law to a machine:

> Like a grand and complicated machine which will
> not work it answers the purpose of show, and often
> amounts to but little more. Law is not necessarily
> opposed to justice, though frequently there is not
> enough law, or what there is, is not of such
> character as to insure justice. Either justice should
> be whittled down to suit the narrow dimensions of
> the law, or the law should be remolded as to insure
> punishment of the guilty.

Perhaps this article was written to help the people of
Tazewell County cope with the bloody lynching, and perhaps it
did save others from the same fate as Felix Knott. There were
other suicides reported during those few days after the incident,
but it is unknown if they were due to the lynching. Unlike the
sermon of the Reverend Steele, it tells of the great need for
reform in the justice system to block such loop-holes in the law
that may cause such actions on the part of the people.

19

During all this time, Isaac Berry had been hiding out in Hawley's Grove, just trying to stay alive. He had hidden there soon after firing the fatal shot that had killed Deputy Pratt.

Reflecting back as he lay there in the thickets, he could still hear ringing in his ears from the loud blasts of the shotgun, and still had visions of the deputy as he staggered backward as if in slow motion, clutching his chest. He could still see Constable Copes kneeling behind one rail of the fence, reloading his revolver. He had expected to be shot at any second, however, after what seemed an eternity, with nothing happening and the officers paying no notice of him, he had turned and ran into the woods along the creek.

He had followed the strip of woods to Bill's house, a quarter of a mile to the west, where he rushed in and hurriedly told Bill what he had done.

Before Bill could have reacted, Frank Britton ran in with a frightened look on his face. He was shocked when he saw Ike, for he thought Ike had been killed.

Ike quickly related to Bill how he shot Marshal Stone. He actually thought it was Stone that was chasing him. Stone would be laid up with his wounds for a long time. Best of all, no one would be able to prove who had pulled the trigger and fired those shots because of darkness.

Bill appeared to be happy. He was glad the men had done his bidding and fought back. This would show the people of this county that they had fooled with the Berrys long enough. Because the law would be hesitant to come after them fearing a repeat of that night, they would now have the run of the county.

For a few minutes, Ike was without question a hero in the eyes of Bill and Britton. His jubilation fizzled fast, however, when someone ran in with the news that it was Henry Pratt and George Hinman who had been shot, and that Pratt was dying at the widow McKasson's house. The messenger did not know how badly Hinman was injured, but said everyone knew it was Ike that did the shooting.

This came as a shock to Ike. It certainly put a new light on the subject, and, for the first time, Isaac realized he was in real trouble. He had just killed the brother of the County Sheriff and wounded his jailer. The other members of the posse had ridden back to Pekin to get some reinforcements, and would be back before daylight. The real problem was that Alfred Stone was alive and well and would be after him for sure.

There was no doubt in Ike's mind that he would never get a fair trial in Tazewell County. Stone may very well just kill him outright. He had to get away as soon as possible, and, as usual, he looked to Bill for help in his plight.

By the time the excitement had died down and Bill had double-checked what the messenger had said, it was nearing dawn. Bill's wife, Nancy, prepared breakfast for the men

Britton decided he would slip away before daylight and head south, by way of Delavan, then on to Mason County, where he belonged. He could hide out with relatives there.

Ike decided that he would hide out in the woods until Attorney Cohrs could straighten the mess out. He would be able to slip home at night, and if anyone came snooping around, he could ease out the back way into the woods again until they left.

With this in agreement, Ike had said his good-byes to the family and Britton, and headed for the woods known as Hawley's Grove, which started just behind Bill's house.

Hawley's Grove was a strip of woods, one mile wide and six miles long, composed mainly hardwood trees, with thickets so dense it was almost humanly impossible to penetrate. The land had been named after its owner, Norman Hawley, who developed one of the first coal mines in that grove.

It had been almost daylight when Ike left the house and headed into the woods. He walked a few hundred feet into the woods and found a place where he had a good view of the clearing. Both Bill's house and the home of his mother were visible. The road leading from Pekin could be seen winding through the short corn in the fields to the north. He sat down against a tree to begin the long, hot wait for nightfall. Ike had been up for two days and nights now, and was tired, but not nearly so as to fall asleep and let the coming posse catch him.

When the posse finally arrived a short time later, Ike was shocked by the size of it. Instead of the usual four or six men, there were fifty or more, with none other than Marshal Stone in the lead. The very sight of this huge posse must have sent chills over him.

From his vantage point, he watched as they rode up to Bill's house and began searching every place large enough to conceal a man. His confidence was further shaken when he saw the men drag Bill from the house in shackles and put him on a horse. He heard Bill's shouts of protest that reached across the fields to his location, for Bill had always been vocal. Ike watched as the mass of horsemen then rode to his mother's house.

They dismounted and searched her place. He could even see her standing in the yard in her long gray dress with her arms folded across her breasts, shaking her head, perhaps wondering where she had gone wrong, and maybe blaming her husband, James, for departing this earth so early in life. He watched as the posse, finding no one there, mounted and rode away.

Ike was devastated. With Bill arrested and locked up, who would see that they got a fair trial? Cohrs would have no reason to help, for Bill himself had been arrested for killing a deputy. Cohrs was the only lawyer around that had the political connections to get them "sworn clear."

Really scared for the first time in his life, Ike knew he had to get better hidden or be caught. He decided he had to be in the largest, thickest section of the grove. He slipped across the narrow town line road and into the woods.

He stumbled through blackberry briers so thick that they were nearly impossible to penetrate. The thorns on the briers tore at his clothes and skin as he desperately pushed his way through. Before long, his clothes were ripped and blood seeped into the fabric, crusting as it dried.

Little did Ike know that very soon three enormous posses with as many as five hundred men would be constantly combing the woods, fields, hills and hollows for him.

Two huge posses, each with over a hundred men, arrived in the area and dismounted at the edge of Hawley's Grove. Carrying rifles and shotguns, they spread out through the woods, forming a line across the entire mile wide strip. This was the only way they knew to cover the thickets in their search for Ike. A man could walk right past another laying or standing still in the dense under brush. They walked slowly and paced some twenty paces apart, so as to cover as much area as possible on the first pass.

Ike was forced deeper and deeper into the thickets, and at times would be so close to capture that he would hear the clang of the cold steel of the shackles as they bumped together while hanging from a saddle horn of a member of the posse.

Ike must have felt like a fox surrounded by hounds, and driven ever forward, or face the sights of the hunters' guns. All day he managed to stay just ahead of the searchers, but late in the afternoon, he was spotted by one of the hunters and fired upon.

Fortunately, the shot missed its mark, striking the under brush and deflecting to the side. Off in the distance, a volley of shots followed, indicating the men were shooting at anything that moved, or perhaps just firing so they might later be able to tell that they had fired at the killer of the deputy sheriff.

Trying to escape the shots, Ike took to the ground, crawling through the briars on hands and knees. This afforded the hunters a much smaller target as he moved forward through the grove.

In the late afternoon of the first day in the woods, he heard another sound that sent shivers up his spine and fear rushing over him.. This fear was brought on by the baying of bloodhounds that had been. put on his track after he was spotted in the thicket. His mind raced to plan his next move. He knew he had to hide his scent from the dogs. He looked around. There was only one way to do that - take to the tree tops.

Ike climbed high into a tree, then went from limb to limb until he reached another tree. The thickness of the grove had enabled him to climb from limb to limb and tree to tree through the woods, putting quite a distance between him and the hounds. After what seemed like hours, he stopped and listened. He could heard the hounds far off in the distance He had been successful. He had outfoxed the bloodhounds.

Unbelievably exhausted, he waited in the branches of a tree. The sound of the baying hounds died out. Ike was sure his plan had worked.

When he could no longer hear the baying of the bloodhounds, Ike dropped to the ground, slid up against a tree and leaned his head against its rough bark to rest. He was totally exhausted from exerting so much energy during the crawl through the treetops. He closed his eyes and, weary as he was, drifted off into blissful sleep.

The loud report of gunfire jerked him back to reality just as a bullet tore into the tree inches above his head. Exhausted as he was, he had little trouble summoning up the energy to dive headlong into the brush and quickly crawl away. He had no idea how long he had been asleep or how close the man was that had shot at him. He only knew that he had to put some distance between them. He heard a lot of shouting, but managed again to slip away.

It is unknown what Ike did with the double barrel shotgun, but if he had been carrying it when he heard the dogs, he would surely have thrown it away as he climbed the trees. Perhaps he knew the gun would have been useless to him unless he wanted to die, for if he fired it, he would surely have fallen under hundreds of rounds fired by the posse.

Ike had nothing to protect himself with. For that matter, he had nothing to use to get food. He was reduced to gathering a few blackberries, some not quite ripe yet, to eat.

It had been a while since he had seen anything of the posse. He found a concealed spot and sat down. Nightfall was near. Perhaps the posse would give up and go home for the night. He could slip out of the woods to his mother's for some food and water. He would be able to get more clothes, as his were hanging in shreds already, and he had only been running a day.

However, he was not to be that fortunate, because the posse did not give up. They knew he was in the woods. They had seen him, even shot at him. They were not about to give up now. They hounded him all night. He was forced to change his position constantly. He fought against sleep, as he was exhausted. He had been up for three days and nights without sleep, but knew that if he fell asleep, he would be captured.

Resting only for a few minutes at a time, he managed to last out the night. He could hear the men talking as they stood guard around the thicket. He could hear the anger in their voices when they spoke of the death of Pratt. He knew they would search until they caught him, or he gave up. But Ike knew his life wasn't worth a nickel if he tried to give up. Someone would shoot him on sight, or they would lynch him in one of the huge oaks.

As dawn broke, he thought things might be a little better, but soon found the posse was once again stamping through the brush, brandishing their guns, and hoping to get a shot at him.

Hunger pains struck his stomach, and he tried to relieve them by eating a few blackberries gathered as he crawled from one location to another. He was forced to drink whatever water he could find. Sometimes he found it in the tiny springs that seeped from the banks of the creek. At other times, he drank from the sunken holes left by animals in the dry creek bed. Lately, water had been very scarce due the lack of rain, but enough remained to at least partially satisfy his thirst.

The day was proving to be an image of the day before. He was nearing total exhaustion as the hot, humid, miserable day wore on, and he kept just out of sight of the posse. Several shots had already been fired at him, but none of them had found their mark. He could be thankful that the men had either made poor aim, or that the trees and bushes had deflected the bullets. He would later remark to a reporter that he "figured he was just not destined to be shot."

Ike lay in the bushes while the searchers walked within an arms reach of him. At times, he had to hold his breath, and hope they would not hear the pounding of his heart as he lay there. He had seen the boots of the men as they passed, close enough to touch, yet he went undiscovered.

Finally, he got a break. For the first time, he found himself between the searchers and his mother's house. They were to the north of him now, still beating the bushes. If they continued, he would be able to crawl back the way he came and get home. Darkness arrived to find him tired, dirty, hungry, and thirsty. The posse was far enough away that they could not hear his movements, so he crawled out of the woods and into the cornfields surrounding the grove.

20

Using the shoulder high corn for cover, Ike decided to go to a cousin's house that was a mile closer than his mother's farm. He would go there first and get some water and food. Cautiously, Ike made his way there.

Although the shock was evident on Mrs. Larimore's face as she opened the door, she invited him in. Mrs. Larimore gave him a pitcher of water that he quickly gulped down. She set about preparing him something to eat. Sanford joined him at the table but never discussed anything other than how thirsty and hungry he was. Sanford left when Mrs. Larimore placed the food on the table and Ike began stuffing it down. He was starving.

When he finished eating, Ike asked Mrs. Larimore to go to his mother's and "fetch him a change of clothes."

This she refused to do. She suggested that he go there himself and get some clothing.

He replied that he was "too pressed" to go himself. He said good-bye to her and left the house.

Once in the cornfield, he changed his mind and decided to go see his mother. Again using the corn for cover, he made his way there.

His delight at being at the house of his mother vanished quickly, for it was here that he learned for the first time that Bill had been lynched during the early morning hours of Sunday. It was now Monday and the family was preparing for Bill's funeral. This was a crushing blow to him, for he and Bill were very close. Bill had always been his advisor, his savior, and now he was gone. Ike did not know what he was going to do.

To top off this grief, Mary Hamilton, a neighbor lady who was a friend of his mother's, reprimanded him for causing the shootings that had resulted in the death of two men. She blamed him for his own brother's death.

Ike told her he had killed no one. She told him that he should be afraid for his own life now, for the posse was out to get him.

He, perhaps to flex his masculinity, told her he was afraid of no one... except Alfred Stone.

It was here that he also learned of the $500 reward placed on his head by Sheriff Pratt. With 500 trigger happy men riding in the posses, many who cared little for him and might use this as an excuse to get even, he would have to be very careful. Besides, $500 was a lot of money, and there were many who would like to collect it.

Bill's death tore at his very soul, but he had no time for tears. While at his mother's house, a huge posse of men rode past, pushing hard in the direction of Stanford's house. Ike remembered that he had not seen Stanford when he left the Larimore house. Stanford must have slipped out of the house while he was eating and went to the law. Even his own kin had turned against him for the $500 reward. He knew the posse would come to his mother's place next. Mrs. Larimore would tell them of his request to go there to fetch him some clothes.

Ike ran from his mother's house, crossed the road and ran back into the woods. He had been afforded no time to get clothes or food and water to take with him. Once again he had to live off the land or die.

At Sanford Larimore's place, the posse found that Ike had already left. They decided he might be in the cornfield by the house and began a search that lasted most of the night. One can only imagine what fifty or a hundred horses would do to the young corn. The field would be ruined.

A shot rang out. A man yelled that he had just shot Ike. Fortunately for someone, the bullet had not found its mark, because Ike was not in the field but deep in the woods a mile away. Yet he was still close enough to hear the shot that sent chills over his spine.

Just before dawn, another man yelled from the other side of the field, "here he is." The posse immediately rode across the now destroyed cornfield, only to find it was a false alarm and no one knew who had shouted. They had decided it had been a friend of Ike's who wanted to draw the posse away so he could escape if he was still be in the field.

Back in the woods, with the searchers once again on his trail, Ike managed somehow to slip through every search pattern of the posse without getting caught. One reason, according to a news article in the Peoria Daly National Democrat was:

> The posse searching for Ike Berry was divided
> into three corps or divisions, but was not well
> disciplined as some of the old veteran corps of the
> army that put down the rebellion.

The posse was actually three separate posses led by A.U. Stone, Benjamin Stickney, and Ben F. Towner, all well experienced in commanding large forces of men. Still, Ike managed to elude the searchers time and time again.

During the late afternoon of the third day, members of the posses searching Hawley's Grove began drifting away. They were near exhaustion and headed home. By late afternoon most of the men were gone. A silence fell upon the woods. Ike cocked his head to listen. Hearing nothing, he thought the posse may have left. He had to find out.

Ike eased to the edge of the woods. With great caution he stepped out into a clearing. Several shots rang out. Dirt kicked up around his feet even though he was already running hard for cover.

Some diehard, trigger-happy men had quietly staked out the grove after most of the posse left. When Ike tried to leave, they spotted him and opened fire. They were still out there, and for the next two days, they kept Ike busy dodging bullets.

How many times he tried to return to his mother's place is unknown. But after five long miserable days and nights in the woods without food, water, or sleep, he was finally able to slip past the few remaining armed men. He made his way to the old homestead.

While Rachel stood watch, Ike managed to get some much needed rest. Rachel knew Ike had to leave the county immediately or be killed. When he was rested, Rachel gave him a bedroll with clothing, food, and water. Rachel gave Ike what little money she had on hand and one of her best horses, then sent him on his way to Champaign County, Illinois, where other relatives would take him in for a few days.

During this time, Rachel was not idle. She made several trips into Pekin to consult with Attorney Cohrs about Sim and Man, who were still in jail. Rachel did not have the money it would required to hire Cohrs to represent her sons. If she sold the homestead it would take time, and time was short.

It is believed that during one of these meetings with Cohrs they came up with an idea for a defense fund. Should Ike be captured by a certain attorney, that attorney would use the reward money as payment to defend not only Ike, but Sim, Man, Daly, Britton, and McFarland as well. For Ike's safety, the capture could not be anywhere near Pekin.

Ike remained on the farm with an uncle under a different name. He helped in the fields for a few days, but then left unexpectedly. Perhaps word had reached him of his mother's plan, for he headed for Circleville.

In a later report to lawmen, Ike confirmed that he made his way to Circleville to see his family, and to try to arrange for more money to live on while he was on the run.

It is believed that he spent only one night with his mother, who laid out certain plans for him. He then headed for Bath, Illinois, located in Mason County near the Illinois River.

According to Ike in an interview with reporters later:

> he went to find a way across in order to go to
> Peoria and turn himself in to authorities there,
> believing he would at least be safe from lynching
> and get a fair trial.

Arriving in Bath, Ike hid out in a thicket near the train depot. He had been away for two weeks, and this seemed like an eternity for him. He was fifty miles from home with no money or place to sleep. He was hungry, tired, and in need of clothing. He had been sleeping in the woods, eating whatever he could find suitable, and his clothes were filthy, torn, and bedraggled. He needed a shave, for now he had two weeks' growth of whiskers on his face.

Ike was not used to being in this condition. He may have been a criminal, but he did practice personal hygiene as well as the next man. Of late it had slipped by the wayside.

On August 23, Ike walked on the platform at the train depot in Bath. No one knew him here, at least not by sight. Ike felt the other people at the depot staring at him with disgust thinking he was a bum. Perhaps if they had known there was a $500 reward for him, many of these same people would have risked contamination to grab him. As it was, they merely looked, turned their noses up, and walked on down the platform to get further away from him.

No one knows for sure if Ike was going to catch a train to Peoria as he would later tell, or if this was where he was supposed to "be captured" by the attorney, but a young attorney from Pekin, named Mark Bassett spotted Ike and began pointing at him.

Ironically, Bassett was one of Cohr's assistants and handled the Berry family's legal needs at times. He had run for the position of City Attorney just last year.

Ike was immediately surrounded by armed lawmen on all sides. They had been waiting for him and were prepared to deal out their type of justice, evident by the number of gun barrels he was staring at, should he try anything foolish. Seeing this, Ike surrendered, but denied he was Isaac Berry for fear he would suffer the same fate as his brother.

When Bassett stepped forward and properly identified him, Ike knew he was captured. He confessed his true identity. Thus ended the most massive manhunt in the history of Tazewell County, Illinois.

He was taken to the local lockup where he would be held until authorities from Tazewell County could be notified and arrived to take custody of him. The plan Rachel and Cohrs cooked up had worked.

21

A telegraph was sent to Sheriff Edward Pratt announcing the capture of Isaac Berry. The news spread like wildfire throughout the town and on to Delavan and Circleville that Isaac Berry had been captured by Attorney Mark M. Bassett while he was on a business trip to Bath.

Sheriff Pratt was almost beside himself with anticipation. Ike Berry was finally in custody and would now pay for killing his brother. Pratt knew he had to control himself. He knew he might not be able to hold back all the anger and hate he felt for this man. He knew he and the other officers would like nothing better than to take this man out and hang him from the nearest tree. But as much as he hated Ike, and would like to do just that, he was sworn to protect him until he had his day in court, just as he had tried to do for Bill.

Knowing his feelings toward the man, and perhaps those of the people of Tazewell County, Pratt decided that he would have to take Isaac to the Peoria county jail, where there would be greater protection. He also believed the people would not be willing to travel across the river among people they did not know, to attack that jail. He would have to leave Ike in the Peoria County Jail until he was sure it was safe for him to return to Tazewell County.

Pratt sent for Alfred Stone. Together they determined which deputies they would take to Bath to safely transfer Isaac to Peoria. They would need men who they knew would not lose control, who could not be influenced by others, and who would not only protect Isaac from any angry mob, but would also kill him if he tried to escape. This last part Pratt was not too concerned about. He was confident Isaac Berry would not attempt to escape with Marshal Stone there, for he knew that Ike had a great fear of him.

Stone and Pratt both felt that assistant Marshal Rudolph Kessler should be allowed to go along. Even though he had been shot at by Ike, they were sure he could control himself, and besides, he was as fine a lawman as could be found. John Berry was the second man chosen by Pratt and Stone. He was a tough fighting man and one not to mess with as he had proven when Britton was arrested. He could take orders well and no one could influence him to do something he did not want to do.

Pratt, Stone, Kessler and Berry, would be an impressive sight, and only a fool would have challenged them for Isaac Berry.

After making arrangements for Isaac's stay at the Peoria County Jail with that county's sheriff, Pratt gathered his deputies and caught the train for Bath.

* * *

The fifty-mile trip from Pekin to Bath must have seemed to take forever for Pratt, who was very anxious to meet up with

Isaac Berry, but it actually took only a short time. They arrived to find a crowd of people gathered around the train depot. At first, Pratt was concerned that the prisoner had been snatched from the hands of the local law, but that concern was soon eased when the local constable boarded the train and assured them Berry was safely tucked away in their jail.

With Stone at his side, Pratt stepped down from the train, and perhaps had to brace himself for the confrontation with Berry for the first time since Henry's death.

The crowd parted for this impressive group of men as they walked along, shotguns, handguns, and shackles plainly visible so as to discourage any fool who might be among them. It seemed the people were just curiosity seekers. Bath was a small town and this was undoubtedly the biggest thing that had happened there since Abraham Lincoln dedicated the town years before.

At the jail, all four lawmen, Sheriff Pratt, Marshal Stone, Marshal Kessler, and Deputy Berry, stopped at the cell bars and stared through them at Ike Berry perched on his cot. The hatred for the man was plain to see in all eyes. For Sheriff Pratt, here was the very man who had taken the life of his brother.

Seeing this hate must have sent a sudden sense of fear over Berry that he had never felt before. Here was the brother of the man he had murdered. The very man who he was to be entrusted to for the trip to Peoria. A fear that he might not complete the trip settled in his mind. It was a fear so real that he could see the scene in which his brother had been lynched by the mob, only this time the man hanging was him.

For Stone, Ike represented an evil that had taken away a close friend - a career criminal who had boasted that it was Stone that he had shot.

Ike knew he was looking into the eyes of a man who could kill him within the blinking of an eye. He dropped his eyes to stare at the floor.

Stone motioned Pratt and the others back. When he cell door was opened, he stepped inside and secured the shackles on Ike. Ike gave no resistance.

The walk to the train depot became a parade as local people followed behind. They had never seen so many lawmen together at one time.

Stone pushed Ike up the steps to the passenger car of the train. It would be he who would have to watch that their prisoner made it to Peoria. He not only had to watch Ike, but Pratt, Kessler, and John Berry as well, to see that they stayed within the limits of the law while handling Berry. There was the same hatred in their eyes for this man. Henry had been a good friend and a fellow lawman. He had served three years in the Civil War safely, only to return and be gunned down by the likes of him.

Even being the dedicated lawmen they were, it was possible something just might set them off into a rage so out of control that nothing could stop them from doing the proper justice on this fellow. Stone kept his vigil of the group and Berry was not harmed on the trip to Peoria.

This is not to say the deputies did not tell Ike what they felt. In fact, each lawman managed to tell him what they would do to him under other circumstances.

John Berry slipped into the seat behind Ike, leaned over close and quietly said, "We should just blow your brains out."

Rudolph Kessler told him something to the same effect.

Then Sheriff Pratt walked close, leaned against the seat across the isle and stared down at Ike. Finally, he said, "If I were not in the position I am in, I would kill you."

These men showed extreme control over their feelings, and Berry, even though he may have rode out the trip in fear of his life, soon arrived at the Peoria County Jail safe and sound. He was so relieved when the great iron door finally slammed behind him that he grabbed hold of the bars and jerked them testily, remarking, "I think these are strong enough to hold me and keep the others out! "

* * *

Sheriff Edward Pratt and his deputies returned to Pekin to feel out the people as to their intentions of lynching Ike Berry. Only after he was completely satisfied that the people would not harm him, did he make the decision to bring Ike back to Pekin where he would await trial.

The people had had their fill of killing after the terrible death of Bill Berry. Perhaps the sight of the damage done by the bullets, hammer, and rope had satisfied their thirst for blood. They assured the sheriff they would now be content to let the court system handle the rest of the Berry gang. The people had once again become decent law- abiding citizens.

During his stay in the Peoria County Jail, Ike Berry was interviewed by newspaper reporters from the Peoria Transcript. According to their story filed with the newspaper on August 8, 1869, they had found:

> not an animal as they has expected, but rather
> a mild mannered, likeable man who was not
> at all unattractive.

He spoke softly to the reporters, telling them of some of his activities while he was on the run. He told them how he had been chased by the posse, hounded by dogs for days at a time in the thicket known as Hawley's Grove and how he had been shot at several times. On the first day alone, as many as fourteen shots has been fired at him, with none finding their mark. He spoke of how he had heard the bloodhounds after him, and how he climbed up and went from tree to tree attempting to fool the dogs. The plan had worked, but he was still in the grove for five days before he could break through the circle and make his way to relatives living in the area. The reporter wrote:

> Berry tells his story in a simple manner,
> without any affection of sorrow or any seeming
> fear for the future. He says he is innocent of the
> murder of Pratt, and all he wants is a fair and
> impartial trial. He expressed his gratification of
> having been removed to Peoria, and in this showed
> the only symptoms of fear that we saw him express.

> Once he caught hold of the iron door to his cell and
> remarked that it appeared to be strong enough to
> keep him in the cell, and to keep others out of it. He
> seemed pleased when we informed him that before a
> mob could get him, four locks on as many doors
> would have to be broken.

The reporter went on to say:

> He seems to be a firm fatalist, and said that he felt
> that if he was born to be shot, he would not be hung
> and vice verse.

The reporter found Ike entertaining and spent almost four hours in the cellblock talking with him.

* * *

On September 14, 1869, Isaac Berry was transported to the Tazewell County Jail in Pekin, where he was locked in a cell only a few feet from where his brother Bill had fought so desperately before being shot, beaten, dragged out, and hung.

Still in jail, were the rest of the gang, including Emanuel and Simeon. There had been no bail set for them. Whatever Ike's plans were of discussing the gang's defense with the others was interrupted when Pekin Police Officer James Milner was placed inside of the cell block, right next to Ike's cell and in full view of the prisoners.

A meeting had been held between States Attorney Whitney and Sheriff Pratt, and it was decided that James Milner would go into the cell block for the purpose of preventing the prisoners from whispering their plans.

For what length of time he remained is unknown, but he was there for at least two days, for in his testimony later, he said Ike was excited but the rest of the gang members were crying while he was there. It seems they were not over the attack on the jail, and were still unsure of their chances of survival.

On September 15, 1869, during a conversation between the two, James Milner was told by Ike that he had been there when Henry Pratt was killed and that he did do the shooting. He told him that they did not know who was shooting at them, however he had expected Stone and Milner to be the officers after him that day. He said that he heard the man shout to stop and that he had a warrant.

During the next few days, a change of venue was filed in the Berry case, and although a "powerful attempt" had been put up to prevent the Berrys from getting that change of venue, on September 16, 1869, the gang succeeded in getting the trial changed to Jacksonville in Morgan County. The Peoria Transcript reported on September 16, 1869:

> The Berry gang succeeded in procuring
> change of venue from Pekin to Jacksonville.
> Even if they had stood their chances here, we
> think it would have been a hard matter to

have impaneled a jury. It is hoped that the
whole gang may be sent to the 'State Hotel'
at Joliet, and thus rid the county of the pest with
which it has been afflicted for the past ten years.

22

For whatever wrong an individual felt he may have incurred, the potential remedy lay in one of the three branches of the Circuit Court. A disputed land deed might be resolved in chancery court. An unhappy wife may find relief in civil court. And, of course there was criminal court, where cases involving everything from a $2.00 theft to murder were heard. Any and all problems might find solution in Circuit Court.

A casual examination of the court dockets from the 1860's would astound the modern reader because of the trivial nature of many of the cases, and the number of seemingly frivolous cases that were filed. It must be remembered that the theft of a wagon wheel or a pair of boots might represent a significant loss to a citizen of this semi-frontier region of central Illinois, nearly one and a quarter centuries ago.

So, the cases were filed, long journeys were made, and for a brief season, at regular intervals throughout the year, the county seat became the center of all meaningful activity. So it was throughout the state of Illinois at the time.

And so it was in Jacksonville in late November of 1869. Characteristically, the population of the county seat would swell at such times, and would experience a virtual whirlwind of activity as citizens of every walk of life converged on the county seat to have their cases heard. Hundreds of cases would routinely be filed, and the principal parties had to make an appearance. Moreover, warrants were issued and witnesses were subpoenaed. The sheriff and his deputies were kept in constant motion by the demands of the court as a steady stream of humanity kept gravitating toward the county seat.

In addition, there were the idly curious, who were determined to show up, perhaps just to keep themselves abreast of interesting gossip.

This swirl of activity was pleasing to many. Certainly the merchants, the restauranteurs, and of course the local saloonkeepers were elated. Happiest of all, were the hotel keepers, who must have anticipated an overflow crowd during these times.

One such happy hotel proprietor at the Mansion House in Jacksonville, observed the lanky figure of Edward Pratt enter his establishment nearly one week before the scheduled opening of the November term of court.

The reason for Pratt's visit to Jacksonville was three fold: he had papers to deliver and subpoenas to serve, he was also scouting potential hotel accommodations for those from Tazewell County who he knew were soon to follow, and last but not least, Ed Pratt was in Jacksonville to arrange for the orderly transfer of six prisoners from his custody to the custody of Morgan County Sheriff Sieso.

After arrangements were made, Pratt returned to Tazewell to await the date of the trial. The trial would be the first criminal trial to be held in the new Morgan County Court House, due to be completed within a week. Constructed in the gothic architectural style, this beautiful three story structure with its wide arched gables and brilliantly painted gold roof was quite a showplace. What better way to break in a new and impressive temple of justice than with a murder trial? Impressive as the new structure was inside and out, some delay in acquiring the necessary furnishings had been experienced. The building was therefore not yet fully prepared to meet the demands that would soon be placed upon it. The local newspaper in Jacksonville wrote:

> The new courthouse is not yet completely fitted
> up with the new furniture being prepared for it,
> but as it stands now, in outside ornate appearance
> and in the commodious and tasteful inside
> arrangements it presents a striking contrast to the
> old dilapidated temple of justice.

Nevertheless, the new courthouse was a source of pride to the citizens of Morgan County.

On Monday, November 22, 1869, court was convened. Judge Hodges, the presiding judge, impaneled a grand jury, and some preliminary business was transacted. Then, a few important cases were called, but most of them were continued or dismissed. The court, attorneys, and their associates seem to have been more interested in exploring their new arena than in dispensing justice that day, for court was adjourned after a morning sessions so they could tour their new surroundings. With obvious sarcasm, one Jacksonville reporter noted:

> In time, the court and lawyers had to take one
> afternoon to accustom themselves to their new
> quarters and view the place where they will shortly

lie. Fresh paint, shining varnish, white wall, and clean floors are novelties to the practitioners at the Jacksonville bar. So long have they drawn their inspiration from the cracked walls, broken windows, and crazy furniture of the old temple of justice that very naturally, the change is rather hard on them at first. For a few days their eyes will probably be attracted to John Dos vs Richard Roe et al, and other sublunary matters.

If this reporter's disdain for the legal profession was missed or overlooked in the preceding sentences, he left no doubt about his feelings with this ending:

No one can blame them, we used to feel just so when in possession of a new top.

By far, the most exciting case on the court docket during this term would be criminal court case #51, the Isaac Berry murder trial. The case had been transferred to Morgan County on a change of venue, presumably because of the publicity received in Tazewell and the surrounding area.

However, no informed reader of the Jacksonville press could have been ignorant of the case or unfamiliar with the facts as presented by the Pekin and Peoria newspapers. The case attracted statewide publicity, and both Jacksonville papers printed verbatim published accounts from Pekin and Peoria.

In Jacksonville, anticipation of the trial was great almost from the instant it was learned that the case would be heard in Morgan County. It was evidenced by the following newspaper article published two months before the trial was to begin:

The Peoria Transcript says that Ike Berry who is charged with the murder of Deputy Sheriff

Pratt, of Tazewell County, is to be brought to
Jacksonville for trial. So it seems another
Murder trial excitement awaits the citizens
of our staid city.

Those Morgan County citizens who had not read the
accounts in the Jacksonville press learned something of the
case, simply through casual conversation. The task of
impaneling an impartial jury, even 80 miles away, would not be
an easy one. Pekin and Jacksonville were, after all, "sister
cities" and with all the coming and going between the two
areas, what was known to have occurred in one area would,
more than likely be known in the other as well.

So the Jacksonville Weekly Sentinel, in beginning its
coverage of the trial, needed no synopsis, and concluded simply
that the details of the case were "perhaps fresh in the minds of
our readers." It was to this distant battleground that the legal
combatants made their journey, followed or accompanied by a
host of witnesses under subpoena, and other interested parties.

Of those Tazewell County residents directly connected
with the upcoming trial, Mark Bassett, the young attorney who
had seen Isaac Berry in Bath, Illinois and turned him in to the
law, was defending Isaac and the rest of the gang. Many
thought it strange that he would represent the gang, but then
there was that matter of the $500 reward offered for Ike's
capture. Could there have been a deal cooked up between
Bassett and the Berrys? Money was something the gang of
horse thieves did not have. Perhaps the $500 reward was just
enough for Bassett to defend all six gang members.

Whatever his reasons, Bassett was defending them, and he
was the first to arrive in Jacksonville on November 22, and
entering an appearance at the courthouse that morning. He, in
fact, had been part of the organized tour of the courthouse
facilities that afternoon. Afterward, he checked into the Dunlap

House, an imposing three-story wood frame structure located on State Street, a short walk from the courthouse. Even as Mark Bassett was settling into his temporary home, anticipation of the upcoming trial was mounting. One paper wrote:

> We understand that the case of Ike Berry will
> probably be called up very soon, perhaps today.
> It is the most important criminal case on the
> docket.

Finally, on November 24, 1869, the six defendants, under heavy guard, were brought to Jacksonville by Sheriff Pratt by means of the Peoria, Pekin, and Jacksonville Railroad, where they were turned over to Morgan County authorities. Following delivery of the prisoners, Sheriff Pratt scrawled the following note on the back of the warrant:

> Delivered the within named persons to the
> Sheriff of Morgan Co. by virtue of an order of
> the Taz. Co. Court - for Change of Venue
> Nov. 24, 1869
>
> Ed Pratt
> Sheriff TC

By this time, all parties were present. The stage was set. If, on the eve of the trial the prosecution possessed an ace in the hole, it had to be the youthfulness and inexperience of the defense attorneys, Bassett and Rodecker. Mark M. Bassett, although associated briefly with the law practice of the wealthy, powerful, and extremely influential Benjamin S. Prettyman, had been practicing law himself for less than a year.

Alfred W. Rodecker, having been admitted to the bar less than six weeks earlier, was even less experienced. This trial would in fact be Rodecker's first before a jury.

If, however, Whitney and Roberts took any comfort from the youth and inexperience of their courtroom adversaries it went unnoticed.

As Bassett and Rodecker prepared to enter the courtroom that morning, they were approached by William H. Barnes, an able and articulate Jacksonville attorney who had become interested in the case. Barnes offered to assist in the defense of the "Berry Gang" and apparently offered the services of his law partner, G.H. Lacey, as an advisor.

Barnes' offer may have been motivated by a selfish desire to gain publicity for his own law partnership, or he may have had a feeling of sympathy for the pair of young, inexperienced, and overmatched colleagues trying what might well be the most important case of their careers. Perhaps he was motivated by a genuine concern that the ends of justice and fair play be met.

Whatever his motives, Barnes' offer was quickly accepted. The young law partners from Tazewell County knew they needed help, and Barnes' offer was the only one forthcoming. The motive hardly mattered.

Case #51, "The People vs Isaac Berry et al", was called on Wednesday, November 24, 1869, and to the surprise and concern of the prosecution, six attorneys, three for the prosecution and three for the defense, would argue the case.

The impact of Barnes' assistance was felt immediately, for with a gallery full of representatives from the press and a multitude of curious onlookers, the defense moved that the case be continued, "through some informality in the record." The "informality" was that the defense had not received a complete copy of the record.

The judge ordered a complete copy be given to the defense and continued the case until the following day. The newly formed defense team had bought a little time. Before court convened the following morning, Bassett and Rodecker would have time to discuss the merits of the case with their new found ally.

That evening, Caesar A. Roberts, Cassius G. Whitney (and wife), Edward Pratt, Rudolph Kessler, James Milner, and George S. Hinman all checked into the Dunlap House.

Also taking a room at the Dunlap House was Warner L. Pratt, brother of Edward and Henry Pratt.

Although a resident of Jacksonville, William H. Barnes quietly secured a room at the Dunlap House where he would be able to spend every waking hour, when not in court, with Bassett and Rodecker. Rodecker, a bachelor at the time, shared a room with Bassett, so that they might have the time to better prepare the case.

23

At nine o'clock on the morning of November 25, 1869, case # 51, "The People vs Isaac Berry et al," was again called, but, this time it was for real.

Six heavily shackled prisoners were led into the courthouse by Morgan County Sheriff Sieso and Deputy Fay, and each took a seat at the counsel table in front of and slightly to the left of Judge Hodges.

The trial opened with C.G. Whitney reading the indictment against the defendants. The indictment charged that on the thirtieth day of July, 1869, each of the defendants did:

> unlawfully, felonious, willfully and of their
> malice aforethought did with a certain shotgun
> loaded and charged with divers leaden shot make
> an assault on Henry Pratt by discharging said shot
> gun with the intent to kill and murder. Said shotgun

they the said Isaac Berry, Simeon Berry, Emanuel Berry, Matthew McFarland, Robert Britton and Cornelius Daly, then and there had and held.

All six defendants promptly pled "not guilty" to the charge. After the pleas were entered, the business of the court immediately turned to the selection of a jury, and it is here that we get a hint of what the prosecution considered to be the weaknesses in their case and an inkling of the type of trial it was to be.

We do not know what questions were asked of the prospective jurors, but we do know that several veniremen were rejected by the prosecution "in consequence of their belief in circumstantial evidence."

The bulk of the prosecution's case then, would rely solely on circumstantial evidence. Apparently, those who had little faith in such evidence would be excluded from jury duty in this particular case. The emphasis placed on jury selection by the prosecution illustrates the fact that C.G. Whitney was taking nothing for granted.

To the casual observer, his case was a sure winner. The notoriety the case had received, the "facts" as published in newspapers across the state, and the public outrage would seem to make this an open and shut case. Most believed this trial would probably be nothing more than a rubber stamp of public opinion.

Whitney knew better. Six men were alleged to be responsible for the murder of Henry Pratt. Each defendant was alleged to have taken part in the killing. Whitney knew, however, that out of his score of witnesses, only one could identify Isaac Berry as firing the fatal shot from a shotgun that had never been recovered. This was shaky enough, but so far as the other defendants were concerned, it was worse.

Of the witnesses to the events preceding the murder of Henry Pratt, none had viewed the entire sequence of events. The terms of time and location, and much of the testimony, might seem contradictory. Worse yet, some of those thought to possess pertinent information were blood relatives of the Berrys. Others considered themselves friends. Still others were neighbors of the Berry's and their associates, who fearing retribution upon acquittal, might tend to soften their testimony.

C.G. Whitney knew that he might have a good case against Isaac Berry, but to convict the other defendants, he would have to present some mighty convincing testimony. By presenting bits and pieces of information, he would have to construct this jigsaw puzzle right before the eyes of the jury, showing that six, not just one, were guilty of the death of Henry Pratt. Obtaining a conviction in the press was one thing, receiving a conviction in a court of law was another. The unexpected intervention of William Barnes presented yet another problem, but he could not blame young Bassett for doing the same thing he had done.

From the beginning, C.G. Whitney realized he himself might need help, and to this end he had enlisted the aid of his democratic predecessor in the office of the State's Attorney, C.A. Roberts.

Mr. S.H. Reed was the first jury member agreed upon. In spite of the delays incurred by the prosecution and defense in rejecting potential jurors, ten members of the jury had been selected by the time court adjourned for dinner. After dinner, jury selection was completed.

Upon completion of jury selection, all subpoenaed witnesses from the rolls of both the prosecution and defense were called into the courtroom and sworn in.

Twenty-six witnesses stood before Judge Hodges who administered the witness's oath. Twenty-five of these witnesses had been subpoenaed by the prosecution. Twenty-two of them would testify in the trial. All were excluded from the courtroom upon motion of the defense.

The motion to exclude witnesses is a standard motion used in almost all criminal cases. This, of course, is to prevent the testimony of one witness from coloring or influencing the testimony of others, thereby eliciting them to speak the truth as they personally know it. By this method, prosecution witnesses might discredit other prosecution witnesses in the eyes of the jury. Of course, the same was true for the defense witnesses.

Each witness would be asked questions pertaining to the over all chain of events. Each witness, at the time of the occurrence of the events, was probably involved in some routine and insignificant aspect of their daily ritual and had given little consideration to the details to which months later they would be asked to recall.

Most importantly, and what many defense lawyers count on, was the well demonstrated fact that human perception is variable and inconsistent. It had been proven time and again, that any number of human beings, shown an identical set of objects, in an identical sequence of events, would give varied and conflicting accounts of what they had seen. Several months had elapsed since the occurrence of the events to which these witnesses would be asked to testify and memory can be a fragile and fickle thing.

Mistakes would be made and inconsistencies in testimony would surface. The strategies of both the defense and prosecution were then clear. The prosecution would attempt to construct a delicate fabric of second hand, circumstantial, and yes, maybe even present a bit of physical evidence. The defense would attempt to tear it all down.

By mid afternoon all the jurors had been seated and the trial began. Opening arguments in the case were presented by C. G. Whitney for the prosecution, and Mark M. Bassett for the defense. The remarks of both were brief.

Whitney "briefly and clearly" stated his case. Whitney informed the jury that Henry Pratt was a sworn deputy sheriff of Tazewell County and in the performance of his duty when he was murdered by a shotgun blast. In addition, he told them that Ike Berry had been the one that fired the fatal shot. He briefed the jury about Ike Berry and Robert Britton approaching William Shaw with a plan to steal Wilbur Clary's horses; and of their subsequent arrest, and release; of William Berry's conversation with Shaw and Whitney; of the gathering at McFarland's saloon; of armed men parading the streets of Circleville; and of the arrival of the posse and the resulting tragedy.

Whitney also told of Robert Britton's incriminating statements to Stone, Milner, and John Berry when they had arrived back in Pekin on the night of the lynching. C.G. Whitney accused Ike Berry of murdering Henry Pratt, and accused Emanuel Berry, Simeon Berry, Robert Britton, Matthew McFarland and Cornelius Daly of being "accessories before the fact" and therefore equally responsible.

Mark M. Bassett's opening address was short, and he made some introductory remarks in favor of the prisoners which seem not to have been particularly inspiring. On the part of Simeon Berry and Robert Britton, he spoke of youth and inexperience. The others he portrayed as industrious family men with wives and young children to support. Alcohol was cited as an explanation for the lamentable and forgivable conduct of his clients.

As he spoke, Bassett became more aggressive, fired on by his feeling of grandeur in front of the captive audience. He insisted that no crime had been committed by his clients. He told the jury that no plot, plan, or conspiracy existed and that some of the defendants were not even present at the time of the shooting. He also said that some of those who were present had no idea what would transpire, and made no effort to resist the

191

officers. He completed his opening statements, saying that Ike Berry acted alone in what he perceived to be self-defense.

It was time to hear testimony.

24

The first witness called by the prosecution was Dr. Richard C. Charlton. Under direct examination, Dr. Charlton testified that he knew Henry Pratt and had last seen him in Circleville on the 30th of July, 1869. Charlton testified that when he examined Henry Pratt that night, Pratt had been dead approximately fifteen minutes. That several shots had penetrated Pratt's right breast, just above the nipple and that the tattered remnants of a pocket book remained, torn with shot, in Pratt's right breast pocket. Dr. Charlton further testified that the shot that killed Henry Pratt had been fired from his right side, and that the shot "passed through his lungs."

Unwilling to concede the doctor's statement that Henry Pratt had been shot from the right side, Bassett quickly objected.

Judge Hodges overruled the objection.

Bassett took exception.

Judge Hodges so noted.

On cross-examination, Bassett questioned the type of clothing Henry Pratt was wearing on the night he was killed.

Dr. Charlton testified that when examined by him, Henry Pratt was attired in a coat and vest.

With Bassett still questioning the logistics of the fatal blast, Charlton repeated his earlier testimony and added, "the wounds were just above the right nipple," and the fatal wounds "ranged toward the lungs."

Dr. Charlton was excused.

Charlton's testimony established that a death had occurred and that the victim, Henry Pratt, had been killed by a shotgun blast.

Overcoming defense objections and cross-examination, the state had established, through expert testimony, that the fatal shot had entered Henry Pratt's body from the right side. The direction Pratt was facing and his position relative to the source of the blast which killed him would become a bone of contention between state and defense as the trial moved quickly into it's most significant phase...examination of the three eye-witnesses.

Finally, after an interval of three and a half months, a time during which rumors ran rampant, the first eye-witness account of Henry Pratt's death became a matter of public record.

The first such witness to be called was Rudolph Kessler. Whitney asked him a few questions designed to elicit introductory information concerning his familiarity with Henry Pratt, his occupation, and the reasons for his presence in Circleville on July 30, 1869.

Kessler responded to a series of questions taking the jury and other listeners through the events of that fatal evening step by step:

I knew Henry Pratt and last saw him 30th day of July last. I went to Circleville with Henry to arrest Isaac Berry and Frank Britton. we left town, around seven o'clock in the evening. We stopped to get William Copes at his farm about six miles south of Pekin. The four of us proceeded on to Circleville, stopping at Mrs. McKasson's house just out side of Circleville. We hitched our horses behind her barn. As we were going toward the gate, Esquire Larimore said, "There go the men you want"!

Bassett, unwilling to concede the identity of any of the defendants, promptly entered an objection.
The objection was overruled.
Exception was taken by Bassett.
Rudolph Kessler continued:

We went out the gate. Pratt pulled a warrant & said to them 'Hold on boys. I have business with you.' They went on...There were three men He went towards them and they went faster. Pratt said to us 'Come on'. We passed two men who had stopped...One with a gun ran on and we after him. Pratt was just ahead of me. At twenty yards across a bridge Pratt hollered halt or I will fire and fired in the air... Copes fired also rapidly ten or fifteen shots in all...I then heard a loud report and saw Pratt whirl. Caught hold of him. He said 'I am shot.' I said where. He said through the heart. We carried him to the house of Mrs. McKasson's. And I went for the Dr. Pratt never spoke after the above.

Whitney asked how far away from the man Pratt was when he yelled.

Kessler replied, "Pratt was forty yards off from the man when he called `halt`. We were 75 to 100 yards from Mrs. McKasson's when Pratt fired."

"What did you see?" asked Whitney.

Kessler replied that he, "saw the man running while Pratt was firing...We ran 50 yards after Pratt's first fire before we heard the loud report...Then found that Pratt was shot."

Whitney interrupted, asking if he knew which direction the shot came from.

Kessler replied, "The shot came from the west side of the road."

Whitney asked how far away from the fence Pratt was when he was shot.

Kessler said, "Pratt was eight feet from the fence."

"Did you know any of the men?" asked Whitney.

Kessler answered that he "did not know who the men were we passed."

"Did you see that person or any one dressed like him afterward?"

Kessler said he "never saw the same persons afterwards to my knowledge...nor the same clothes."

From the defense point of view, Kessler's testimony up to this point had done little to undermine their case. The scene had been described. Four armed men had pursued three men, only one of whom was armed, and two of the pursuers had opened fire on one of the pursued. None of the suspects had been positively identified, nor was any evidence given indicating the pursuers to be lawmen. Therefore, the argument for self-defense remained intact.

The prosecutor asked Rudolph Kessler what Henry Pratt's position was when they went to Circleville that night.

Kessler replied, "Pratt was acting as deputy sheriff."

"Did Pratt have a warrant?" Whitney inquired.

Kessler said he "saw the warrant after they left Pekin."

Again Bassett objected.

Again the objection was overruled.

Exception was taken by Bassett.

"What was Deputy's Pratt physical condition when you last saw him that night?" Whitney asked.

"Pratt was alive when I went after the Dr. [I]was gone about three hours and when I got back he was dead."

Whitney concluded his direct examination of Kessler.

Circumstances under which the warrant was obtained and the posse's ride to Circleville were of no concern, and the less said about these issues the better. What the defense needed to show was that the posse never identified themselves as such or that Ike Berry and the others were not aware that the four armed men who confronted then that night were lawmen. The defense's only concern was with occurrences from the time the posse first observed Ike Berry and his friends, to the time Henry Pratt was shot. They would try to press upon the jury that the defendants had acted in self-defense.

In cross-examination of Rudolph Kessler, Bassett asked where he was when the men were first spotted.

Kessler replied, "I was inside the gate when I saw those parties coming up the lane."

"How many were there?"

"There were three of them; they had passed the gate when we told them to stop."

"Who fired first?"

"Pratt first said, 'Halt or I will fire'. Copes fired first."

"Did the man return any fire?"

"The man did not return the fire."

"What happened next?"

"Pratt kept on firing."

"Do you know where he was firing?"

"Pratt fired in the air."

"How many times?" Bassett asked.

"[I] don't know how many shots were fired."

"How long was it after Pratt fired that the man fired the shotgun?"

"It was some fifteen seconds before Berry returned the fire."

"How many loud reports did you hear?"

"[I] heard two loud reports."

Bassett changed his line of questioning by asking, "Do you know how many people reside in Circleville?"

"Circleville has one hundred to two hundred inhabitants."

"Where is Mrs. McKasson's house located?"

"McKasson's house is about a quarter of a mile from the town and is two hundred feet from the fence."

"When did you last see the man that fired the shotgun?"

"The last time I saw the man that fired the gun he was running down the road with the gun in his hand; didn't see him after he fired the shots."

Bassett had only a couple more questions, He asked, "How long were you at Constable Copes' house?"

"We stopped at Copes' four or five minutes on the way to Circleville."

Apparently in an attempt to confuse Kessler, with all the switching of his lines of questioning, Bassett asked, "How far from you was Pratt when you heard the loud report?"

"Pratt was fifteen or twenty feet ahead of me when I heard the loud report, he turned around and I run up and caught him," Kessler replied.

Bassett had no more questions.

Kessler was excused from the witness seat.

Bassett had been pleased with Kessler's testimony. For their point seemingly had been driven home: a man with a shotgun and two others had been pursued by three or four armed men, who fired ten to fifteen shots at them. The man with the shotgun had even waited approximately fifteen seconds before he returned fire. Kessler had testified that he had seen the warrant after he left Pekin and that Henry Pratt pulled the warrant out of his pocket as he attempted to halt the three men passing McKasson's gate. His testimony, however, provided no assurance that he or other members of the posse, Henry Pratt in particular, had identified themselves as, or could be recognized as lawmen.

William Fletcher Copes was the next witness to testify. Whitney went through the usual process of identification and occupation by asking Copes the introductory questions. Then he drew Copes attention the events of July 30, 1869.

"How did you come to be with Deputy Henry Pratt on the day of August 30, 1869?" asked Whitney.

"[I] saw Henry Pratt about half an hour before sundown on that night. He asked me to go with him as he had a little job to do. He wanted to arrest Ike Berry and a stranger. Pratt said he had a warrant."

Copes' statement concerning the warrant launched a vigorous debate between Bassett and Whitney over the admissibility of the hearsay testimony.

Bassett, apparently not willing to concede the existence of the warrant, refused to let second hand reference to its existence pass into the record.

Whitney, aware that the actual warrant had somehow been lost, needed every such reference included.

Judge Hodges eventually ruled in favor of the prosecution, and Copes' testimony concerning the existence of the warrant, as well as Henry Pratt's status as deputy sheriff, was allowed to stand.

Bassett took exception to Judge Hodges' ruling.

Copes continued:

Mr. Pratt, Hinman, Kessler and myself were in the wagon. We stopped at McKasson's. There were several men about 250 yards from town. Someone said `there they are'. We saw three men going past the gate. Pratt, Hinman and myself went out. Pratt said to the men 'Hold on. I have some business with you' They were Ike Berry, Matthew McFarland, and Emanuel Berry. I have known the Berry's for a long time. Isaac Berry had a gun. They started running. Pratt yelled and Emanuel Berry and Matthew McFarland stopped. Isaac Berry kept running. Pratt said 'Copes these ain't the men we want'. I heard no mention about officers. Pratt and I went on after the third man. Pratt got ahead of me and called to him to stop and said 'Halt or I'll fire` Pratt then did fire up in the air. He then fired toward him. We were gaining on Berry rapidly. By the time we got to where the road runs near the fence, we were in twenty feet of Berry. Then he ran into the fence and laid his gun on the fence and fired. Pratt was at that moment facing the northwest, turned and holding his piece toward Berry, trying to fire it. Berry fired. The first shot struck Pratt, the second struck Hinman. Pratt slapped his hand on his breast and said 'Oh boys, I'm shot." I saw Berry standing by the fence. My piece was empty and I did not feel like rushing up to Ike. I did not know at the time that Hinman was shot. I think it was a double barreled shotgun that Berry had. Mr. Pratt made several steps antiverse into the road, when someone caught him. I found Pratt afterwards. He was sinking backwards. He did not speak after that time. We took him to McKasson's and laid him on the floor, on some blankets I was there not over ten minutes after that.

Copes' vivid description of the murder must have had an enormous effect on the jury. But what must have been most pleasing for the prosecution, and most distressing to the defense was the last few sentences of Copes' testimony where the existence of arrest warrants for Ike Berry and Robert Britton again became an issue.

Cope concluded:

Pratt was shot in the right breast pocket, above the nipple. I saw the warrants. The shot struck the book in his right breast pocket, and tore the warrant. Isaac Berry's name was on the back of the warrant.

Bassett was silent.

An objection on grounds of heresay did not apply in this instance, for unlike the earlier reference in which Copes testified that Pratt told him he had a warrant, Copes had now testified that he actually saw the warrant, tattered and torn with shot. This was unimpeachable testimony that was very damaging to the defense's case. Worst of all, Isaac Berry had been positively identified by a man who had known him all of his life and was distantly related by marriage. Copes' testimony had left one lawman dead, one lawman wounded, and a smoking shotgun in Ike Berry's hands.

Bassett's tactics changed slightly in cross-examination. Henry Pratt's status as deputy sheriff had been established as had the existence of arrest warrants for Ike Berry and Britton. Ike Berry had been positively identified as having fired the fatal blast. The best line of defense now seemed to be the claim that Ike Berry and the others were not aware of the identify of the four armed men who first confronted, then fired at them that night.

Therefore, in cross-examination of Copes, Bassett was concerned primarily with lighting conditions and distances between the various parties.

"What time did the men pass down the road?" asked Bassett.

"It was near dark when the men passed down [the] road."

"How many were there?"

"There were three of them."

"What were they wearing?"

"Berry had on a dark suit."

"Did anyone say anything?"

"Pratt said `Hold on boys, I want to see you. They made no reply. We ran after them."

Bassett, pacing the courtroom, asked, "Who fired the first shot?"

Copes answered,"Pratt shot first."

"Did he tell them he was an officer?"

"Don't know whether he told them he was an officer or not."

"When did the first men stop?"

"McFarland and Emanuel Berry stopped after running twenty or thirty yards."

"Did you warn the running men to stop?"

"Before Pratt shot, Pratt said `Halt or I'll fire."

"When did you fire your weapon?"

"I fired the second shot," Copes replied, "Pratt fired five shots, I think. I don't know how many shots were fired before Berry ran to the fence, but it was eight or nine."

"Did you see anyone else running at this point?"

"I saw none of the other boys at that time."

"How far away were you when the shot was fired?" asked Bassett, almost as an after thought.

"I was eighteen feet distant when the shotgun fired from behind the corner."

Bassett had no more questions.

Copes was excused and the afternoon session of circuit court was adjourned for supper.

Judge Hodges informed those present that court would reconvene later that evening.

The attorneys left the courthouse and reassembled around supper tables in nearby restaurants.

It seemed there was much to talk about. Copes had been a great witness for the state. He had been unbreakable under the heavy cross-examination by the defense, and that, no doubt, was the topic of conversation around the table at which Brown, Whitney, and Roberts gathered.

The trial was still in its early stages but things seemed to be going the prosecution's way. One issue remained unresolved. That issue would torment the prosecution, while at the same time, provide the only source of hope and comfort the defense would know during the trial. Did the posse identify themselves as such, or were they recognizable as such?

Attorney Bassett, Rodecker, Barnes and Lacey certainly considered these questions while pondering strategy around their supper table. Certainly, every reference to the existence of a warrant that could not be produced in court would be objected to.

Judge Hodges had already demonstrated his intention of admitting such testimony, but the objections must be made to preserve the basis for a later appeal if for no other reason.

For the defense, what must be avoided at any cost was any reference indicating that Ike Berry and the others recognized Kessler, Copes, Hinman, and Henry Pratt as lawmen. As long as this recognition was not established, a self-defense strategy remained plausible.

* * *

Within the dimly lighted confines of the Morgan county jail, six prisoners also took their evening meal. The surroundings were not nearly as sumptuous as those of the seven legal minds who argued their fate, but the mental energy of those six prisoners was certainly focused on the same issues that occupied those intent on defending them.

Each of the prisoners considered the testimony already heard and considered how it affected him.

Simeon Berry and Cornelius Daly never heard their names mentioned and must have felt somewhat relieved.

Emanuel Berry and Matthew McFarland were also relieved for even though they had been identified as accompanying Isaac Berry as he walked past McKasson's place, no evidence linking them to the murder had been given.

Robert Britton breathed a little deeper for he had been named as the object of an arrest warrant Henry Pratt was attempting to serve at the time of his murder. Still, no hard evidence had been presented to link him to the murder.

Isaac Berry sat alone in his cell, fully conscious of the fact that he had been acknowledged as the murderer of Deputy Sheriff Henry Pratt. He had been identified at short distance, by a lawman, who had known him all of his life. Isaac knew that barring a miracle he would be convicted of murdering Henry Pratt.

25

The winter sun set early and the Morgan County Courthouse was veiled in darkness. Lamps were lighted throughout the building to accommodate the needs of the evening session of the circuit court, and eerie shadows were cast upon the walls of the newly painted building as attorneys, defendants, and spectators filed into the arena.

Following the call to order, George Hinman was called to the witness stand and the standard introductory questions were put to him.

The basic examination revealed that Hinman resided in Pekin and was a jailer. He knew Henry Pratt, and went with him to Circleville on July 30th, to arrest Ike Berry & Frank. That Pratt said he had a warrant for them, but he did not see it.

Following the pattern established in earlier testimony, Bassett objected.

The objection was over-ruled.

Bassett took exception.

The Judge so noted.

Hinman continued. "While I was hitching the team Mr. Larrimore said `There go your men' and that he knew Ike's Berry's voice."

Copes' recognition of one of the defendants was damaging enough. Bassett would not concede another. Again he entered an objection.

It was over-ruled.

Again Bassett took exception.

Hinman was allowed to proceed.

> Copes, Kessler and Pratt went out; Pratt said to them, `boys I want to talk with you.' I think there were five or six men besides our crowd. When we got out we passed two or three men. I did not know them. We overtook two of the men seventy-five or one hundred yards from McKasson's gate Pratt said `Stop or I will shoot'. He did shoot. They ran on and there were several shots fired. We ran several panels of fence, when I received a shot. Saw no gun. When I was shot, Copes was one or two panels before me. The report was loud when I was shot. Should think it was a gun; heard the report of no other guns after that. Was shot over the right eye, and in the right shoulder. Was near the fence. Think it was a large size duck shot. When I went to Pratt, Kessler was with him and said he was `gone up', meaning Pratt. As soon as I went to Pratt he was taken to McKasson's house. I was not badly hurt. It was only twenty or thirty minutes till I left. The shot with which he was shot were about the size of those shot I was shot

with. Some were larger, there was a hole shot through his coat and vest some two inches in diameter, the middle of it was all shot out.

Hinman had been busy caring for the horses as the other members of the posse were conversing with the crowd gathered in front of McKasson's house. Being further from the road than the others and late in joining the chase, Hinman's perspective differed from that of the others. Hinman testified that five or six persons had passed McKasson's gate, and that only two or three of them had been passed by the posse just prior to the shooting. His testimony left several subjects unaccounted for.

Up to this point, the defense had been given little to be optimistic about, but Hinman's testimony offered a ray of hope. There might be something here that the defense could use. Where were they? Who were they? Were they armed? Could it be that one of these unknown, unnamed men was really responsible for killing Henry Pratt? Could it be that Ike Berry did not fire the fatal shot?

In cross-examination of George Hinman, Bassett was even more concerned with identification of the defendants and logistics than it had been in previous testimony. From Hinman he hoped to gain a better footing for the defense.

Hinman testified:

> Kessler and Copes were with me. Copes was with Pratt when shooting began. I was fifteen or twenty steps behind them when the shooting began. There were five or six men. The first thing Pratt said was `hold on boys; I want to talk with you.' I did not know the parties. I think there were five men going down the lane. Copes was with Pratt, right ahead of me. After Pratt called to them, two of the men stopped. We

passed them, and said nothing to them. I saw no guns with those who stopped. There were two or three went on. I was sixty or seventy yards behind the two that were furthest ahead. It was dusk. I don't think I could tell who a man was at the time, sixty or seventy paces distant. It was dusk. Pratt called to the parties to stop, four or five times before he fired. The three parties who stopped were behind when the shooting begun. The men in front did not fire when Pratt and Copes fired their first shots. They ran probably seventy-five yards before they fired. I did not hear Pratt tell them he had a warrant for them. I was twenty or thirty feet from Pratt when he was shot. Copes was right ahead of me; I was putting my hand upon my revolver when I was shot; I did not see anyone when I was shot. The first men I saw were Pratt and Copes and Kessler. The men who ran ahead had on dark clothing; I don't know who they were. Just before they fired, those men were running up the road. I could see them as they ran.

Following this testimony, the defense had some reason for optimism. In most respects, Hinman's testimony corroborated the earlier testimony of Kessler and Copes. However, glaring discrepancies existed. Copes and Kessler testified that they initially saw three men pass McKasson's gate, and that one of them was armed. Hinman had just told the court that as many as five or six men had passed McKasson's gate just prior to Pratt's pursuit, when earlier, Kessler and Copes had testified that only one man ran on after being ordered to stop. Hinman's story was that he had seen two, and maybe three men running ahead of the posse. He had not heard Henry Pratt make mention of a warrant or identify himself as a lawman before the chase. Hinman had told the jury that he heard only one loud report, not two as described by the previous witness. He had went on to say that, although only thirty feet from Pratt at the time, he could not see who fired the shot which wounded himself, let alone the man who fired the shot which killed Henry Pratt. Furthermore, Hinman testified that, considering the lighting and distances involved, he did not think he could have identified anyone.

All of this must have left C.G. Whitney and his associates shaking their heads, for in one fell swoop, the prosecution's seemingly irresistible case had been damaged by one of it's own witnesses. The months between the event and court had taken its toll. A shadow of doubt had now been cast over the earlier testimony and the groundwork so painstakingly laid by examination of the first three witnesses had been compromised. Valuable ammunition had been supplied to the opposition, and some element of doubt may have crept into the minds of the jurors. A reasonable doubt was all that the defense required to force an acquittal, and George Hinman, himself a victim, may have just supplied it.

The prosecution pressed on. Hinman's testimony may have muddied the waters, but if Hinman believed he saw five or six men in the road that night, then so be it. There were, after all, six defendants, only one of whom had been previously identified, and the identity of all six defendants and the role they played in the murder must ultimately be established. Four issues still required fortification: the existence of a valid arrest warrant for Ike Berry and "Frank"; identification of the posse as being such; identification of the defendants; and delineation of the role each defendant played in the death of Henry Pratt.

The testimony of the next witness, William H.H. Larimore, would touch on all of these issues. Being a sworn Justice of the Peace, a U.S. Postmaster, and a relative of the

Berry's, Larimore's testimony would have credibility. Furthermore, Larimore had been witness to many of the events that had now become significant in this trial.

Larimore took the witness seat. From this vantage point, he was able to view the entire courtroom and look directly into the defendant's eyes as questioning began.

Larimore presented his testimony:

> Lived in Circleville, in Tazewell County last July. Am a justice of the peace and postmaster. Knew the Berry boys. Saw Daly some four or five days before Pratt was killed. Saw Ike Berry, McFarland, and Joe Combs, the Peddler, the night before. The saloon is about three hundred yards from McKasson's. It is south of McKasson's. Next day saw Berry in charge of the officers, on the 29th day of July, about midnight, Stone, Milner and Cass arrested them on that night. Stone is City Marshal of the City of Pekin. They arrested Ike Berry and Britton. Several others were present when those men were arrested. It was at William Berry's house in Circleville. "

Bassett objected. Any reference to the arrest of their clients in such proximity to the death of Henry Pratt must not be conceded.

The objection was over-ruled.

Exception was taken.

Larimore continued:

> Saw Ike Berry and Britton next morning in Pekin. It was after they got out of jail. It was eight or nine o'clock. Saw them about eleven

o'clock as I went home. they were sitting on the fence. Ike said, `I wish you had another horse, I would ride'. I told him Bill Berry would be along soon; next saw him about noon in Circleville. Saw them several times after that. Bill Berry came about two o'clock. when Bill came back he went to the saloon. I was at my office. There were Bill and Emanuel Berry, McFarland, Britton and Daly, and Ike Berry. About two o'clock they came out of the saloon. Bill told them the officers would be out after them and to stand their ground; that he had guns and revolvers."

Bassett objected again. Five of the defendants had been pictured listening to William Berry's incitement to resist and his promise to provide firearms.

The objection was over- ruled.

Exception was taken.

Larimore's testimony resumed:

They paraded the streets several times. I shut up and went to McKasson's. About half past two they passed by there going northwest. About thirty yards, and turned and went back. Don't know where they went. Knew Henry Pratt. Saw him when I went to Pekin that evening. Told sheriff what I heard Bill Berry say. Henry Pratt was standing at the corner of the square; understood there was a warrant.

Reference to the warrant was objected to by Bassett.

The objection was over-ruled.

Exception taken.

Direct examination of William H.H. Larimore went on:

> Went home about dark. Did not see the defendants till after the officers came. Was in the yard, and saw some persons coming. And someone said 'There are the men'. The officers then went out, and Pratt said, `Hold on boys I want to see you'. When I overtook McFarland and Britton, one of them said it was the officers. Saw Britton, Daly and McFarland as I passed the bridge. Heard some firing, and then I heard a loud report. Went over and found Pratt, who said `I am shot'. Britton was thirty or forty yards from McKasson's gate. Pratt was about one hundred yards from the gate when I found him. Heard McFarland tell him we were officers. The men ahead could not hear it. Don't know whether Ike Berry knew Pratt or not. Saw no firearms in possession of these men that day, but heard them shooting up at Bill Berry`s house. Bill Berry's was a kind of head quarters for them.

For the defense, Larimore's testimony had been extremely damaging. It was bad enough that Bill Berry's statements concerning the eminent arrival of Officers to arrest Ike and "Frank," and his incitement to resist them, had been allowed. Now, in apparent obedience to Bill Berry's plea, five defendants were portrayed as having paraded the streets of Circleville in a display of unity, determined to accomplish the task. Moreover, several defendants were said to have been present at the time Henry Pratt was murdered, including Britton and Daly, who had not been identified in earlier testimony. Five of the six defendants had now been placed in McFarland's saloon shortly before the murder and had been seen in the area at the time

Henry Pratt was killed. All this by competent witnesses, all sworn officials.

The report of gunfire from Bill Berry's farm had been heard the afternoon before Henry Pratt's murder, and Ike Berry had been positively identified as having fired the shotgun blast which killed Henry Pratt and wounded George Hinman. Only five of the multitude of sworn state witnesses had been heard, and already the case for the defense was in serious trouble.

Something had to be done to halt the prosecution's momentum. To do this, Larimore's testimony must be thoroughly probed and any discrepancy must be exposed to the jury. Failing in that, any statement made that might be beneficial to the defense must be highlighted. For the most part, under cross-examination, Larimore would be led through the same series of questions that had been asked by the state as the defense probed and prodded in a futile attempt to find a contradiction.

"Mr. Larimore, how long have you lived in Circleville?" Bassett asked.

"I have lived there fourteen years." replied Larimore.

"Have you ever seen the Berrys near McKasson's house before?"

"The Berry boys, all but Bill, go past McKasson's to go home."

"Did you go to McFarland's Saloon that day?"

"I was the first man there on Friday at McFarland's saloon."

"On Friday, the 29th day of July, were you present when Isaac Berry and Robert Britton were arrested?"

"I was there when they were arrested."

"Did the officers have a warrant for that arrest?"

"I don't know whether they had a warrant or not."

"Did the two men resist arrest that night?"

"There was no resistance on the part of the prisoners."

"Do you know where they were taken?"

"They were taken to Pekin."

"When did you next see them?"

"I next saw them in Pekin the next morning."

"What time did you leave Pekin?

"I left Pekin at 10 or 11 o'clock."

"Did you see the men again that day?"

"I saw Ike Berry and brother Bill about an hour after I got home and next saw them at the saloon; there were Ike Berry, Bill Berry, Emanuel Berry, Britton, and the peddler."

"Did you hear any conversation?"

"Bill said 'Stand your ground, boys, we have got guns and revolvers'," replied Larimore.

"How far away were you at the time?"

"I was twenty or thirty steps from them."

"Did you hear them talking about false imprisonment?"

"I heard nothing about false imprisonment."

"Were the men angry?" asked Bassett

"Bill was the only one that seemed angry."

"Do you know if they had been drinking?"

"I think they had been drinking."

"What time was that?"

"It was a little past 2 o'clock," Larimore answered.

Bassett had no more questions.

The witness was excused.

Far from finding a weakness, defense probing of Larimore's testimony may have highlighted the very elements the most damaging to the defendants. Bassett, in asking about the false imprisonment, may have been trying to throw some fault onto the lawmen and give the impression to the jury that the men were going to be falsely imprisoned again, thereby gaining a little sympathy for the defendants. Failing in that, he had, however, managed to pry from Larimore the fact that Ike Berry and Frank Britton, in Bill Berry's house and in his presence, had not resisted arrest on the night before Henry Pratt's death.

This might put a small doubt in the minds of the jury that these same men would have acted any differently on the very next night. With the next two witnesses the state hoped to put the "warrant issue" permanently to rest. In an unorthodox move, Tazewell County State's Attorney's chief prosecutor C.G. Whitney was called as a witness in his own case.

C.A. Roberts directed questions at Whitney, and began by asking, " Mr. Whitney where do you live?"

"[I] reside in Pekin."

"What was your occupation in July last?"

"[I] was state's attorney in the twenty-first judicial district in July last."

"Do you know the Berry brothers?"

"Knew William Berry and Isaac Berry."

"When did you last see William Berry, and what, if anything, happened?"

Whitney replied:

> [I] saw William Berry on the 30th of July last. It was about ten o'clock on the morning of the 30th. At the request of one Shaw, I went to Esquire Glasgow with him and he told Glasgow he wanted to make a complaint against Isaac Berry who had incited him to commit larceny. He wanted to get the warrant before Berry got out of jail, but did not get it in time. Saw William Berry and he asked if a warrant had been issued for the boys' arrest, told him yes he said the officers had better not go out there, that the boys had committed no crime and they had been fooled with long enough.

Bassett objected to any testimony concerning threats of violence toward sworn officers in the act of performing their duty, especially on the morning of Henry Pratt's murder.

The objection was again overruled.

Exception was again taken.

Direct examination of C.G. Whitney went on. He testified:

> [I] saw warrant after Pratt was killed, it was torn with shot. [I] think the warrant is lost have been unable to find it, it was against Isaac Berry and Frank, whose other name was not known, who I since learn was Robert Britton, it was for inciting one Shaw to commit larceny.

Roberts ended his direct examination.

The existence of the warrant could hardly be denied. In cross-examination, Bassett, hoping to find some irregularity, inconsistency, or possibly to confuse the opposition, took a shot in the dark. "Was there anything unusual about this particular warrant?"

Whitney replied, "The writ was in the usual form of a writ."

Bassett decided not to pursue his questioning of Whitney.

The prosecution prepared to call their next witness. If C.G. Whitney was the first man to view the arrest warrant for Ike Berry and Robert Britton, maybe W.W. Sellers was the last man to see it.

Sellers, editor of the Tazewell Republican, the most prominent newspaper in Tazewell county at the time, had served as foreman of the coroner's inquest into Henry Pratt's death. He was very familiar with the facts in the case and, as a lawyer himself, was fully aware of what the lost warrant meant from a legal standpoint. He must also have known that as the last identifiable person to have possession of the warrant, he might well become the scapegoat if the trial did not turn out as most Tazewell county residents expected. W.W. Sellers took the stand and told the court the following:

> I live in Pekin. I knew Henry Pratt. I saw him the morning after he was killed. I was foreman of the Coroner's jury. I took from his pocket a certain book.

Sellers produced the torn and bloody memo book he claimed he had taken from the body of Henry Pratt and displayed it to the court. Lacking the crucial item itself, the prosecution settled for the next best thing - a dramatic display of the memo book, complete with holes and blood. The very book he claimed held the indispensable item. He continued with his testimony:

> Saw the warrant. Showed it to the jury, then gave it to some party authorized to receive it. Read the warrant. It was testified to by Mr. Whitney. The shot went into the right breast, making a large hole in the coat, vest, and shirt. The warrant was loose on the inside of the book, and not within among the other papers.

Direct examination ended, leaving the defense with an obvious target. Incompetence existed somewhere. Whitney and Sellers were both prominent citizens who had been charged with specific responsibilities. Both were lawyers, and one had made a serious mistake. The defense wanted to discredit one or both of them.

Bassett asked several questions to which Sellers replied:

The warrant was as described by Mr.Whitney. Do not know where it is. The shot was duck shot in size. The last time I saw the warrant was at the adjournment of the Coroner's inquest. I gave it to some one authorized to take it. I don't know who it was.

"I gave it to someone authorized to take it. I don't know who it was." That statement must have given Bassett a little thrill. Now he had lost evidence - crucial evidence. He studied the jury, then dismissed Sellers.

W.W. Sellers had come off appearing a bit foolish, but his testimony certainly corroborated that of other witnesses. His display of the book and description of the shot-torn warrant extracted from the coat pocket of the slain deputy must surely have produced the effect upon the jury the prosecution desired.

How many people are authorized to take evidence from the foreman at a coroner's inquest? Not many. Usually only one - the coroner himself. This was interesting since Alva Culver, the coroner, was not subpoenaed to testify at the trial. Had Culver had lost the warrant or allowed it to be removed from his possession, or it had been disposed of intentionally by someone attempting to aid the Berrys in their defense?

State Attorney Whitney was laying out for the jury the events that had happened from the arrival of the posse in Circleville, to the moment of Henry Pratt's death. There had been some convincing testimony. He would add more fuel to the fire with a lengthy procession of witnesses to testify to the actions of the defendants the afternoon before Pratt's murder. It had been a long day, however, and the hour was growing late. There was only time enough for one more witness before court was adjourned for the day. He decided to call Andrew Ditmon, a Circleville shopkeeper and long time neighbor and acquaintance of the Berry family.

Ditmon took the stand and testified:

> I live in Circleville. I know the Berry boys. I have seen Britton and Daly and McFarland. I knew Shaw in Circleville. I saw the defendants on the 30th of July passing the street and singing songs. My store is on the opposite side of the street from McFarland's saloon. I saw Ike Berry the day before Pratt was killed passing my house. Don't know how far they went. They were loud and boisterous. On the 30th they came to my door and wanted to get in and get something to drink, and threatened to break the door in. I saw Ike Berry in the evening, going down the street with a gun. Ike Berry was coming from Bill Berry's and going toward McFarland's saloon. I did not see any of the defendants the day after that. While they were passing the streets I saw a pistol on Britton. It was between sundown and dark I saw Berry with the gun, and the shooting was between 8 and 9 o'clock.

Obviously, Ike Berry and Britton were both armed. Ike was seen carrying a shotgun from the direction of William Berry's house. Boisterous displays in town evoked imagery of a rowdy, defiant, and self-indulgent group, and Andrew Ditmon's characterization of the Berry gang on the afternoon of Henry Pratt's death entered the record unchallenged by the defense.

Much to Whitney's surprise, and perhaps as a show of the defense team's confidence, Bassett did not cross-examine Ditmon.

It was near midnight and Judge Hedges adjourned court until the following day. The lamps and candles were extinguished, as the spectators and parties retired to their respective accommodations to ponder the results of the day's testimony.

26

As court reconvened early the next morning, the state intended to expand upon the groundwork he had laid with Andrew Ditmon's testimony the night before. Several witnesses to the actions of the Berry gang on the afternoon preceding Pratt's death were slated to take the stand.

John Bailey was the first to be called. Under direct examination, Bailey stated that he knew four of the defendants: Ike Berry, Man Berry, Sim Berry, and Matthew McFarland; and had also known Bill Berry. Bailey told the court that he had seen all of these subjects on the evening of Henry Pratt's death and that Henry Pratt was killed sometime between 9 and 10 o'clock at night.

Bailey then described the circumstances of brief encounter with the defendants that night:

> They were sitting on the porch at McFarland's
> saloon. Bill wanted me to treat. Told him I didn't
> have time. Britton came up and took Ike to one
> side and talked to him in a low voice. I started
> on and stopped at McKasson's. There was a
> shotgun leaning against the door at McFarland's.

Direct examination of John Bailey had brought forth testimony that placed five defendants and a shotgun at McFarland's Saloon in Circleville the evening of the murder. The existence of a shotgun leaning against the door of the saloon was good evidence, but possession had not been established. Every farmer in the county had a shotgun, and there had been no testimony to connect this particular weapon to Henry Pratt's murder. Only that a shotgun was present.

Whitney turn the witness over to the defense for cross-examination.

While Bassett had no questions for Andrew Ditmon, there were many for John Bailey. Perhaps in Bailey he saw a man sympathetic to their own cause. After all it appeared he was close enough to the Berrys to drink with them. For his cross-examination, Bassett asked Bailey to tell him what he had observed on the day of the killing.

Bailey testified:

> I live one mile west of Circleville. It was dusk
> when I went to the saloon. I saw no revolvers. I
> saw a gun standing on the porch. I don't know
> how Bill Berry was dressed. Ike came up to me
> and shook hands with me. He had on a black hat,
> and so had Bill. I think they all but Emanuel
> Berry and McFarland had on dark clothes; I have
> seen other crowds there. I have seen other men
> drinking there. I saw Sam Miller there and old

man Lane. The Peddler was quarrelling with Lane about who treated last. There were eight left at the saloon. I heard some of them say they were going home. I saw no guns in their hands. They started the nearest way home. The normal route home for the Berry boys was past Mrs. McKasson's. The last time I saw Ike, he was with two others going towards Mrs. McKasson's about 75 or 100 yards from the saloon & about 200 yards from McKasson's. I heard none of them making any threats. I think they had been drinking. I stayed at McKasson's all night. I saw Pratt at McKasson's. "

Bassett was happy with his testimony and John Bailey was excused. His testimony had offered a ray of light for the defense.

Whitney would attempt to remedy this, however, with his next witness. Bailey had testified that he had seen Sam Miller with the defendants at McFarland's saloon shortly before the shooting, so Whitney called Sam Miller to the stand.

He testified:

I live in Circleville. Know the defendants. Saw them on the day Pratt was killed. It was late in the evening. They were at the Saloon. I was there ten or fifteen minutes. Saw Britton have a revolver. Ike Berry came there with a shotgun from Wm. Berrys. He called Britton out & talked to him. I went home when I left there. I heard the firing about three quarters of an hour after I left.

Sam Miller testified under oath that he observed Robert Britton in the possession of a revolver, and Ike Berry carrying a shotgun to the saloon from the direction of William Berry's house. He also observed the conversation between Ike and Britton but claimed it was Ike who called upon Britton.

Bassett had been looking forward to questioning this witness, but the optimism he had felt before he testified, was fading rapidly.

Under Bassett's questions, Sam Miller testified:

> It was after sundown when I went down town. I saw others in town that night at the grocery. I was there but ten minutes I did not see them drinking, they were on the porch. The saloon is across the way from the post office; there is another saloon there, I saw Britton with a revolver in a scabbard. I went home when I left there. It was one half to three-quarters of an hour after I left till I heard the firing. Bill Berry had on a black hat and gray coat and check pants. I did not drink with them that evening. I saw all these men there. Saw old man Lane there. He and the peddler were talking.

Samuel Miller's testimony had not been altered under cross-examination and it had the net effect of canceling the thinly veiled pro-defense testimony of John Bailey, yet it supported previous prosecution witnesses' accounts of the evening and helped to fill important gaps in the prosecution's case. The shotgun Bailey had seen at McFarland's saloon was, perhaps, the most important issue addressed by Samuel Miller's testimony. Miller had testified that he had viewed a pistol in the possession of Frank Britton. This supported Ditmon's earlier testimony. All of this seemed to support the earlier testimony of William Larimore, who claimed to have heard Bill Berry's declaration that "wc havc guns and pistols."

The case for the defense would deteriorate rapidly from here.

Joseph Miller owned a farm located about a mile east of Circleville and was apparently in the habit of taking his evening meal at Sarah McKasson's home. He would be the next witness called.

On the night in question, Joseph Miller, working in the fields all day and oblivious to the day's earlier events, had arrived at McKassons minutes before the shooting began.

Joseph Miller was called to the stand and sworn in. Whitney asked him to recall what he had observed that night.

Miller testified:

> I live in Circleville, Illinois. I know the Berry's. I have seen McFarland. I know Bill Berry. Henry Pratt was killed on the 30th of July. That day I was harvesting I came to McKasson's that evening. I had been there fifteen minutes when Pratt, Copes Kessler and Hinman came up in the wagon. I saw four men pass along the road, going north. Pratt, Copes and Hinman went out, and some one said, 'Hold one boys, I want to see you and then some one said `Halt!' directly I heard firing. In a few minutes I heard another report, and heard someone say 'I am shot`. I ran to where Pratt was. Heard one of defendants say `someone is shot let's get out of here'.

There seemed to be little in this account for the defense to work with. The only hope for the defense would be to continue its contention that the defendants did not recognize the officers as being officers and that the shooting was done in self-defense. Hoping to achieve this goal, Bassett asked, "How many shots did you hear?"

Joseph Miller answered. "I heard but two pistol shots at first but in all there were ten or fifteen shots."

Now Bassett had established that the posse had fired ten to fifteen times before Ike Berry had returned fire. If the defendants were not aware that the posse was indeed a posse, the self-defense argument remained valid and a chance for acquittal remained intact. He excused Miller.

The State's parade of witnesses rolled on relentlessly. Whitney called Sarah McKasson.

Sarah McKasson testified:

> I live in Circleville, Illinois. Know the Berry boys and the others by sight. Pratt was killed on the 30th of July. I saw the defendants in the afternoon. McFarland's saloon is on the south side of the street. The road runs north and south past my house. They were going toward Wm. Berry's. They stopped at Berry's house. There were five of them when I first saw them. Isaac Berry Britton, McFarland, Manuel Berry, & one other were together. William Berry was with them. All were together except Simeon Berry. Next saw them coming toward my house. It was near 4 o'clock. They were singing, then saw them late in the evening. There were seven of them. They passed my house. Saw no arms. Heard nothing said. The officers came about three-quarters of an hour after they passed the last time. It was after sundown. After the officers went out after them, I saw three men pass my gate.

Again, a rowdy, boisterous display which alarmed the people of Circleville, with Bill Berry leading the pack and all but Simeon Berry a part of the group. Cornelius Daly, while not mentioned by name, was of course assumed to have been the "one other" referred to in Sarah McKasson's testimony.

In cross-examination, Bassett would again concentrate on the witness' statements concerning the lighting conditions and the identity of the posse. "Was it light enough for you to determine who the officers were and who the other men were at that time?"

Sarah answered:

> The officers came out just after sunset. I saw three men pass after the officers went out. It was dark when they went out and I could not distinguish the officers while passing out of gate. This was just before I heard the pistol shots. The officers were in the barnyard. I did not know who the officers were, but was told they were officers. I heard none of their conversation while they were parading the streets.

It was after sunset, and therefore dark. Sarah McKasson did not recognize the officers as such but was told their identity. Her identification of the defendants parading the streets of Circleville went unchallenged. She was dismissed.

Undaunted by the testimony of Sarah McKasson, Whitney pressed on with his case. He called Anna McKasson, Sarah's teenage daughter, next. Perhaps the daughter would provide what the mother lacked.

People in the courtroom watched the young girl take the stand and heard her testimony:

I live in Circleville, Illinois. I know the defendants. Henry Pratt was killed the 30th of July last. I saw the defendants pass our home that afternoon. They passed several times. There were Bill and Ike and Sim and Emanuel Berry and McFarland and Britton and the Peddler.

She had presented further identification of the defendants. Strangely, Anna McKasson was the only witness to identify Simeon Berry as being a participant in the parade that passed thorough Circleville and McKasson's house. Perhaps it was because he was more her age than the rest, and she would have paid more attention to him.

The rest of her testimony was consistent with much of the previous testimony. She had heard nothing that was said and heard no threats. Nor has she seen any arms on the men who were passing during the day."

Mary Hamilton was a neighbor and apparently a close friend of Rachel Berry. On the Monday following the deaths of Henry Pratt and Bill Berry, a time when emotions were at a fever pitch and public opinion was virtually universal against the Berry family, Mary Hamilton was one of the few individuals willing to risk public scorn to attend Bill Berry's funeral.

Following the funeral, she had accompanied Rachel Berry to her home where she had the opportunity to talk with Ike Berry, who at the time was the object of a county wide manhunt. The only purpose in her presence at Rachel Berry's home that day had been apparently as a show of respect for her longtime friend and neighbor. While Mary Hamilton may have felt sympathy for Rachel Berry, she felt no such allegiance for her sons accused of such a horrendous deed.

The state called Mary Hamilton as a witness because she has spoken with him just three days after the murder and possessed information that might provide insight into Ike Berry's state of mind as he fired the fatal blast.

Mary Hamilton seated herself in the witness stand. She told the court what she knew of the issues in question:

> I live in Circleville. I know the defendants. I know when Henry Pratt was killed in Tazewell County. I saw Ike Berry, the Monday after Pratt was killed, at his mother's. I told him two men were killed. He said he killed nobody, and that he was not afraid of no one but Stone.

Bassett objected.

This one reference to Ike Berry's fear of A.U. Stone was the very remark the prosecution wished to hear, and probably the only reason Mary Hamilton had been called to testify. The implication was that Ike Berry believed that A.U. Stone would lead the posse sent to him. Ike's fear of Stone might account for the rather bizarre behavior exhibited by the Berrys and their associates that day. It seemed the justifiable fear the Berrys held for Stone might explain their perceived need for a show of force, including the use of firearms. Further implied was the possibility that, as Ike leveled his shotgun that July evening and fired the fatal blast, he believed his target to be the one man on earth whom he feared - Alfred Stone.

The objection was overruled.

Bassett took exception.

Cross-examination of Mary Hamilton was remarkably brief. Bassett asked, "When did you talk to Ike Berry and what did he say?"

Mary replied, "Ike Berry said he shot nobody. It was the day Bill Berry was buried."

Mary Hamilton was excused.

Had it not been for William Shaw, Ike Berry and Frank Britton would never had been arrested on July 30, 1869. If not for Shaw, there would have been no confrontation between the posse and the Berrys in Circleville that night, and Henry Pratt would not have been killed. If not for Shaw, Bill Berry would be alive and there would be no trial. This entire episode would never have occurred if not for Shaw. It was his word and his word alone that had set the entire sequence of tragic events in motion.

The outcome of the trial might well hinge on what Shaw had to say. The importance of Shaw's testimony was not underestimated by either set of counsel. Examination of Shaw would produce the trial's hottest moments as the defense tenaciously opposed the inclusion of much of his testimony under direct examination, and attempted to impeach his credibility under cross-examination.

Whitney called Shaw to the stand. After being sworn in, Whitney established his identity, where he lived, and what his connection to the Berrys was.

Shaw testified:

> I live in Circleville. Know the defendants, and know Bill Berry. Know Henry Pratt. Saw the defendants in Circleville on the day Pratt was killed. Saw Ike Berry and Britton in Pekin on that day. Before I saw them in Circleville, William Berry told me not to get the warrant out, and later said, after I got the warrant, it would have been better if I had not gotten it.

Bassett objected.
The objection was again overruled.
Bassett took exception.
William Shaw continued:

He wanted me to go with him. I told him I had
no horse. He again said `Shaw why did you get
that warrant for? I told you not to get it.' I told
him I did my duty.

Again Bassett objected, on the same grounds as the first
objection.

Again this one was also overruled.

And again Bassett took exception.

Whitney pressed on with his examination of Shaw. "What
else did Bill say to you?"

Shaw answered, "He said `I am your friend, but you must
watch them other boys'."

The testimony was interrupted again as Bassett objected.

Objection was overruled.

Bassett proceeded to take exception.

Whitney resumed his questioning.

Shaw testified:

When we arrived in Circleville, Ike Berry and
Britton were at the saloon. Wm. Berry got out
of the buggy on the side towards the saloon. I
jumped out on the other side. As I was leaving I
heard Bill Berry say `there goes the damned son
of a bitch who got the warrant'.

Objection.

Overruled.

Exception.

Shaw continued:

"I went over to Ditmon's. This was about
two o'clock in the afternoon. Saw Ike Berry,
McFarland and Britton go to William Berry's

231

house about three o'clock. Saw them afterwards parading the streets. Am not certain that Emanuel Berry was with them. Crowd was composed of Britton, Wm. Berry and Ike Berry and McFarland. Before I laid down heard several shots fired at Wm. Berry's after parties went up there. Saw Ike Berry and McFarland and Britton after the firing.

Whitney ended his direct examination. His was pleased. Testimony concerning the parade and those participating in it had been corroborated by William Shaw. He had seen several individuals walking toward William Berry's place and heard gunshots shortly thereafter. He had seen Ike Berry, Matthew McFarland, and Robert Britton together after target practice at William Berry's house at about the time previous witnesses claim to have seen Ike Berry carrying a shotgun from the same location. Bill Berry's presence was re-affirmed as was his apparently antagonistic frame of mind.

In cross-examination, Bassett's strategy was obvious. Information concerning William Shaw's unsavory background had undoubtedly been supplied to their attorneys by the defendants. It was this very background which had attracted Ike Berry to Shaw in the first place. At this point, Bassett would attempt to use this information to discredit Shaw and impeach his testimony. Bassett would try to show that William Shaw was a character far more sinister than any of the defendants, and that the entire unfortunate incident was initiated by Shaw as a result of some sort of hostility he bore for Ike Berry. If this could be accomplished, perhaps it would move the jury to believe that Ike Berry and Britton had been wronged by their arrest on July 29th and the outrage exhibited by the gang the next day was justified. The show of support, as evidenced by the so-called "parade," might seem understandable, and the claim of self-defense might yet remain possible.

Bassett began cross-examination with a few questions concerning Shaw's background.

Shaw testified:

> [I] live in Circleville. Have a farm in Circleville; have kept a saloon in Circleville some of the time since I came to live here; lived in Peoria a while, and then came back to Circleville; have been indicted for stealing.

Next Bassett touched on Shaw's relationship with Ike Berry and Robert Britton. He asked if Ike and Britton had been his friends.

Shaw answered, "Was not friendly to Ike and Britton on the day of Pratt's death. I had been instrumental in getting Ike and Britton on the day before."

Bassett had shown William Shaw to be a part-time saloonkeeper who had been indicted for theft and had for reasons of his own, found it necessary to leave Circleville for a while. Trying hard to discredit his testimony, Bassett asked Shaw to give his account of the events leading up to and including the night of the shooting.

Shaw continued his testimony:

> Saw Ike Berry and Britton in Pekin the day before their arrest. Did not see the Peddler with them the day Pratt was murdered. It was about three o'clock in the evening, there were several of them. The next time I saw these fellows they were marching back and forth.

Evidence of the parade and the presence of Ike Berry and Britton were reaffirmed. There was little help for the defense. Bassett asked Shaw to continue.

He said, "Britton came to the door to kick it down. Saw Bill and Emanuel Berry. Was asleep when they came to kick the door open. Did not hear the shots at night."

Shaw was home asleep when Britton attempted to kick the door. He identified Bill and Emanuel Berry as accompanying him, but could not positively identify the person actually doing the kicking.

Cross-examination ended. The defense had fought hard to discredit Shaw's testimony.

The prosecution had fought just as hard to preserve it. To that end, Shaw would become the only witness to be questioned under re-direct.

Questions concerning Shaw's background had really produced little controversy. Implications might be drawn from his role as part-time saloonkeeper and his disappearance from the area for a period of time, but defense questioning had unearthed only one issue that might impeach his testimony - his previous criminal record. It was this issue that the State addressed in re-direct. Whitney asked, "What was the actual charge the defense was trying to make us believe was so terrible?"

Shaw responded with, "[I] was indicted for larceny several years ago. Ten to twelve years ago. [I] was not convicted of the charge. Have been living there ever since."

William Shaw was excused.

Prosecution and defense had both done their utmost to present Shaw's testimony in a light best suited to their particular needs. Each hoped the twelve men seated in the jury box would consider his testimony in favor of their case.

The line of State witnesses continued. Joseph Barlow would be the first of three remaining Circleville residents to take

the stand. Barlow, like Larimore and Sam and Joseph Miller, had been at McKasson's house on the afternoon in question. He had viewed the Berrys parading the streets, witnessed the posse's arrival, and was near by when the shooting occurred.
Barlow testified:

> Live four miles from Circleville Knew defendants. Knew William Berry and Henry Pratt. Remember when Pratt was killed. Was at Mrs. McKasson's on that day came there the day before. Was there when Pratt, Copes and others came. While the officers were in the yard some one said, `There they go' Think Copes and Pratt went out of the yard first. Saw two men in the road. Think they were Sim Berry and the Peddler. Some had passed previously. Do not know who they were. Think there was three of them. Soon I head someone cry `Halt' and heard several shots fired and then Pratt was right back in a short time shot. Saw defendants in the afternoon. They went into McFarland's Saloon and were there when Bill Berry came from Pekin. Heard him tell them `To stand their ground'."

Mark Bassett objected to statements attributed to William Berry.

The objection was over-ruled.

Exception taken.

Whitney was then allowed to conclude his examination of Joseph Barlow.

He testified. "Saw them watching the streets after that. Saw no arms. They passed Mrs. McKasson's as many as eight times. All of the defendants were in the party the last two times about dark."

Joseph Barlow's testimony supported that of several previous witnesses. Nothing was to the contradictory. The gathering at McFarland's Saloon, the parade, and even Bill Berry's appeal to "stand your ground" was consistent with previous accounts. Barlow's description of the posse's arrival, the confrontation with the Berrys, and Pratt's death fit nicely with the statements Copes, Kessler, and Hinman had made under oath. The jury had heard it and would consider it, but the testimony of Joseph Barlow would later be stricken from the record.

Joseph W. Burnham would be the next witness. Burnham would also testify that he had seen the gang at McFarland's Saloon on the day in question, and that he was present at McKasson's place that night.

After being sworn in, he gave this testimony:

> Live in Tazewell County. Know the defendants. Knew Wm. berry. Never saw them more than once or twice. Henry Pratt was killed on the 30th of July. Was at McKassons the night he was killed. Kessler, Hinman, Copes and Pratt came to McKasson's that night they asked if I had seen the Berry boys, and others. They drove into the yard. One of them said, `Here they come'. Hinman and Kessler and Pratt and Copes went out. Two men were going down the road north, according to the best of my knowledge. The men were Sim Berry and the Peddler. Previous to that I saw three men pass. Did not know them. Soon after I went, I heard someone say, `Halt'. The next I heard was firing. A few minutes after met some men carrying Mr. Pratt. That day saw Ike Berry and Britton in the afternoon a short time, They came to Ditmon's

and went back. Bill Berry told them to stand their ground.

True to the pattern he had set earlier, Bassett objected to the remark purportedly made by William Berry.

Also true to the earlier pattern, Judge Hodges overruled the objection.

Exception was taken.

Burnham was allowed to continue.

> "Saw parties marching up and down in a violent tumultuous manner from time Bill Berry returned until dark. They appeared to be watching the woods for someone. Saw parties pass Mrs. McKasson's several times. From five to eight times. All the parties were together. Simeon and the Peddler joined the party late. He would stop and drink from a bottle they had occasionally. Heard Wm. Berry with anger, tell the boys to stand their ground.

Objection.

Over-ruled.

Exception.

The witness concluded direct examination:

> Never heard such conduct in Circleville before. People there are now very civil. Sometimes they were cursing & abusing citizens. Then singing vulgar low songs and religious songs. They were abusing Shaw particularly.

Bassett objected to the reference to Shaw.

He was over-ruled.

He took exception.

All of that hardly mattered to Whitney who had no further questions for the witness. Everything the State wished the jury to hear from Joseph W. Burnham had been heard, but the statement that may have most incriminated the Berrys was Burnham's declaration that `they appeared to be watching the woods for somebody'.

It was apparent from the threats made by Bill Berry, the presence of firearms and shots said to have been fired that an ambush had been planned.

Once again, Bassett had his opportunity at cross-examination. As before, a series of shot-in-the-dark questions produced unsatisfying results.

Burnham testified:

> First saw the parties sometime after dinner; there were three of them at the saloon. They were violent and boisterous the last time saw these parties together they had passed McKasson's house and turned and went back to Circleville, Sim Berry and the Peddler were behind. Neither of the defendants has ever done me an injury while parading the streets they were cursing and abusing the citizens and singing songs.

Burnham's testimony was not broken. There were no contradictions nor explanations why he would want to present false testimony against the Berrys, therefore his testimony would stand.

Amanda Reed would be the last of the Circleville residents to testify. She and her husband, Ephraim, lived within the village limits on East Street, directly across the road from McFarland's saloon.

Amanda was very familiar with the activity around the saloon. She knew the patrons who frequented the saloon and was very familiar with their riotous, sometimes violent brand of recreation. Living across the street from the saloon, Amanda Reed had seen it all, but the activities around the saloon on that day were even more curious than usual, and on that day a deputy sheriff had been murdered. The village of Circleville had never before seen such excitement.

Amanda Reed told the court what she had observed on that day:

> Knew Henry Pratt. Knew the defendants Henry Pratt was killed on the 30th of July. Saw the defendants on the streets that day. There were Ike and Wm. Berry, and the Peddler and Britton and McFarland. First saw them down at Berry and McFarland's Saloon. They went to Bill Berry's to supper and remained only long enough to get it. Then came out & paraded toward Mrs. McKassons Britton had a revolver in his belt. Saw them last sitting on porch of McFarland's Saloon. Then they scattered some going one way and some another. About 15 minutes after they left I heard firing. Saw Bill Berry and Shaw when they came from Pekin together.

Whitney had what he wanted. He finished his questioning.

In cross-examination, Bassett, as with previous witnesses, attempted to highlight the elements of the defendants behavior that evening:

To his questions, Amanda Reed testified:

> It was about four o'clock when I saw these men at the saloon when I met them in the evening Bill

Berry and McFarland were there. Saw no violence toward anyone. Saw no more of them after the shooting.

Amanda Reed had watched the parade and met Bill Berry and Matthew McFarland shortly thereafter. She testified that she had heard no threats.

Having elicited this statement from a hostile witness, Bassett apparently felt he could do no more, therefore the witness was excused.

Reed's statements concluded testimony from the citizens concerned, as well as that of a few lawmen. However, there were more witnesses to come. State's Attorney Whitney had been saving these witnesses for a dramatic conclusion to his case.

27

The parade of prosecution witnesses was winding to an end, but five Tazewell County lawmen were yet to be heard from. A. U. Stone, John Berry, James Milner, and Lewis Cass would be called to testify to the circumstances surrounding the arrest of Robert Britton, and more importantly, to subsequent conversations with Britton and Ike Berry. Edward Pratt would be called to again address the same issue of the lost or non-existent arrest warrant.

A. U. Stone was the first of the remaining witnesses to be called. Whitney asked Stone the usual introductory questions and for his account of Robert Britton's arrest.

Stone replied:

> Live in Pekin. Knew Henry Pratt know the defendants. Have been deputy sheriff for four years. Saw Robert Britton after the death of

Pratt. Saw him in San Jose Mason County. Lewis Cass and I found him at the hotel in bed about 9 o'clock went to the door & knocked. He said who is there. I said 'Landlord'. He opened the door and I went in and presented my revolver and said if you move I will kill you. He had a revolver under his pillow. On the way to Pekin in presence of myself & Cass, Britton said he and McFarland and one of two Berrys were passing a house when men came out of the house. And one of them said 'Stop boys I have a warrant for you. I jumped into the field and Ike Berry into a fence corner. Heard someone groan & thought Berry was shot'."

Bassett objected to second hand statements, supposedly made by Robert Britton, being used to incriminate Ike Berry.

The objection was over-ruled.

Exception was taken.

Examination of A.U. Stone continued. He testified:

He said that Ike Berry came into Mason County about a month before Pratt's death and got acquainted with him and asked him 'if he was business' and explained by telling him he wanted him to go home with him and go into horse stealing & said that Wm. Berry would get them out if they got into trouble. He said he went up with him and they were going to steal some horses but they were disappointed in finding the horses. They then commenced drinking.

Bassett yelled an objection, on the same grounds as the previous one. Stone was testifying on the basis of second hand information, to the statements and actions of two other people.

One of them a defendant in the case and the other deceased. Clearly hearsay.

The objection was overruled.

The defense took exception.

The judge so noted it.

No further questions pertaining to conversation between Robert Britton and Ike Berry prior to Henry Pratt's murder would be asked. Instead, Whitney shifted the focus of his examination to conversations with Ike Berry that A.U. Stone was party to, or overheard.

Stone replied:

> Saw Ike Berry & Britton the night before Henry Pratt was killed. After Ike Berry was arrested I heard him say that he had left his gun near Forest City, in a cornfield. That he had been through several counties & was afraid the mob would get him.

Again Bassett objected to statements attributed to Ike Berry. As Stone was now testifying to first hand comments he had heard Ike Berry make, there was less grounds for an objection now than there had been previously.

The objection was over-ruled.

Exception was taken.

The prosecution had drawn from Stone all that was intended. The defense would now get its chance to question the witness.

Stones' testimony had been extremely damaging to the defense. Previous witnesses had stated Robert Britton was in possession of a pistol shortly before Henry Pratt's murder. In addition, Stone testified that Britton had just such a weapon under his pillow at the time he was arrested. The substance of Stone's testimony was so damaging and the possibility of contradiction so remote, that Bassett could not argue its accuracy, only the manner in which the information was received.

Stone was asked how he acquired the information to which he had just testified.

He replied, "We were talking together about killing."

Bassett hadn't expected that answer. He decided to end his cross-examination before Stone could give any more damaging testimony.

Whitney had no further questions. Stone was excused.

The second police officer to testify was John Berry, the well known Pekin saloonkeeper and captain of the fire engine company.

He was called to testify at the Berry trial, since on July 30, 1869, he had participated in the arrest of Robert Britton. Following the arrest, John Berry was party to the conversation with Robert Britton in which Britton made certain incriminating statements concerning himself and the members of the Berry gang.

John Berry testified.

> Live in Tazewell county. Know defendants. Was with Stone when Britton was arrested. On the way from San Jose to Pekin, Britton said Ike Berry had persuaded him to go with him and steal some horses and cattle.

Bassett entered his usual objection.
He was over-ruled.
He took objection.
John Berry continued:

> Ike told him this when he was in Mason County almost a month before Pratt died. Ike said that

244

they could steal horses or cattle and his brother would have them sworn clear.

Again, the same objection.
Another over-ruled.
Another Exception.
John Berry continued:

Britton at this time said that he jumped over the fence the night of Pratt's death and laid down. All were present except Simeon. Thought Ike Berry was killed. Heard some one say "I am shot" Heard some one running out of McKasson's say hold on boys I have a warrant for you.

Another reference to the warrant was objected to by Bassett.

The objection was over-ruled .

Exception was taken.

Whitney needed no more from John Berry regarding the post-arrest conversations with Robert Britton. In that regard, John Berry had substantiated the earlier testimony of A.U. Stone. Whitney asked John Berry to tell the court of statements made by Ike Berry following his arrest.

John said, "[I] heard Ike Berry after he was arrested say that he thought that the mob was going to overtake him. Officers promised him protection."

Thinking the jury might interpret such a statement, attributed to Ike Berry, as an admission of guilt. Bassett objected.

The judge over-ruled it.

Exception was taken.

Whitney pressed on.

John answered:

> Ike said he had been roaming about over the
> country and was going to see his friends in
> Fulton county when he was arrested.

Another objection on the same grounds as the
previous one.
Objection was overruled.
Exception was taken.
John continued his testimony,

> On the way to Peoria one of the officers said to
> Ike Berry that he would kill him if he was not
> situated as he was. This was after Wm. Berry
> had been hung by the mob in Pekin and Ike knew
> of the hanging.

The direct examination of John Berry ended.

Upon conclusion of direct examination, Bassett entered
another objection. He moved that all testimony of John Berry
pertaining to conversations with Robert Britton and Ike Berry
after their arrests be stricken. Statements, contended the
defense, made by the defendants with the threat of lynching ever
present, and while surrounded by hostile lawmen, had been
coerced and were therefore inadmissible.

Judge Hodges briefly considered the motion and then
ruled that all of John Berry's testimony would stand.

The defense was in trouble. The statements made by
Robert Britton were ruled to have been made voluntarily
following his arrest. Statements attributed to Ike Berry were
ruled admissible, presumably because the witness had heard
these statements first hand, and coercion had not been shown to
be a factor. John Berry's testimony regarding statements made

by Ike Berry and Robert Britton would stand even though, in the contention of the defense attorneys, any man surrounded by lawmen and accused of the most horrendous of human crimes, might make statements which would later be misinterpreted, especially when the victim was a fellow lawman.

Additionally, to escort a prisoner into town at the precise moment one of his alleged confederates was being lynched would cause anyone to say anything to save his own life. The defense felt that such statements were meaningless and should not be admitted into evidence. And finally, there was Ike Berry, who, the object of a month long manhunt was arrested for murder. Aware that his own brother had been lynched by a mob for merely being suspected of complicity in the very murder of which he stood accused, surrounded by police officers while in transit from one jail to another, he might have just said anything.

Bassett would have to show that the statements of Robert Britton and Ike Berry were coerced. With these issues in mind, Bassett doggedly proceeded with its cross- examination of John Berry.

John Berry testified:

> Britton's statements were voluntary. Don't know of any questions that were asked him at the time of the conversation with Ike Berry on the way to Peoria. He knew Bill Berry had been hung in Pekin by a mob of citizens. Might have said to him if he was not in the position he was in they would blow his brains out. Pratt said to him 'If I was not in the position I am in I would kill you.` Berry was told he had been a thief all his life, and must not tell lies.

The defense had made its point with John Berry.

Whitney waived redirect and John Berry was excused.

Lewis Cass was the next witness to be called.

The Jacksonville Daily Journal, on November 27, 1869, stated:

> Little is known of Lewis Cass except that he
> was a sworn Pekin police officer and possibly,
> a part-time Tazewell County jailer.

On the ride back to Pekin from San Jose, Cass was party to the same conversation with Britton to which Stone had testified earlier. It was for this reason that he was now called to the stand. It was therefore no surprise that Whitney, in questioning Lewis Cass, followed much the same pattern as it had in questioning A.U. Stone.

Cass gave the following testimony:

> My name is Lewis Cass. I live in Pekin. Am a
> jailer of Tazewell county. Was present when
> Britton was arrested. It was in San Jose, Mason
> County, Illinois on the next night after Pratt was
> killed. Used no threats except I went to the
> door. I put my pistol to his face and told him if
> he resisted, he would get hurt. Britton had a six
> shooting revolver under his pillows. After his
> arrest and while on the way to Pekin he said he
> got acquainted with Ike Berry in Mason County.
> Britton said he first met Berry at Forest City,
> and that Berry asked him if he was business.
> Britton replied, 'I don't know what you mean by
> business.' Berry explained that he wanted him to
> go to Circleville and steal some horses. Britton
> at first refused, but afterwards got half tight and
> consented.

As with previous witnesses, Bassett objected to second hand testimony being admitted.

The judge over-ruled it.

Exception was taken.

Cass continued:

> He said they were all on a bender on the day of Pratt's death. That they were going to some place to stop that night, as the officers came after them. Wm. Berry said the officers were coming after them. Don't recollect that anything was said about Simeon.

The reference to William Berry brought another objection from Bassett.

The objection was quickly over-ruled.

The defense took exception.

The judge so noted.

Cass then completed his account of the conversation with Robert Britton, saying, "he heard someone say as they were running, 'halt I want to see you. I have a warrant for you'."

Another reference to the warrant. Another objection from Bassett.

Overruled.

Exception.

Direct examination of Lewis Cass ended.

In cross-examination, Bassett had two points he wished to address; the innocence of Simeon Berry and what was felt to be the coerced nature of the statements made by Robert Britton following his arrest. Thus far in the trial, there had been a glaring lack of evidence against Simeon Berry. In most of the testimony, his name was never mentioned. There had been no testimony to implicate Simeon in a conspiracy to murder Henry Pratt. There was nothing to connect him to a weapon, or even hint that he was present as Bill Berry's plan for resistance unfolded. Those few accounts which mention Simeon portray him, at worst, as a late arriving tag-along in one of the last parades past McKasson's house, but much of this testimony had been stricken. Lewis Cass had also just testified that, throughout Robert Britton's incriminating post arrest statements, Simeon's name was never mentioned. This was precisely the statement the defense wished to underscore and firmly implant in the minds of the juror.

Lewis Cass was asked these questions by Bassett.

Cass testified:

> Britton was arrested on Saturday night. Said to him, when door was opened, I would hurt him if he moved. After we got to Pekin the crowd tried to hang Britton and threw a rope at him. I caught it on my arm and took him to a hayloft and thus saved his life. was an officer and authorized to arrest him. He said nothing about Sim Berry that I know of.

During his cross, Bassett used Lewis Cass's second hand report of Robert Britton's statements as evidence of Simeon Berry's innocence. Cass was required to repeat his declaration of Simeon's innocence.

When he did, the jury heard it and would have to consider it in deliberation.

Following the cross-examination of Lewis Cass, Bassett moved to have all statements made by Robert Britton after his arrest excluded.

Judge Hodges, in a classic example of the no-decision, denied the motion, but advised the jury that they "ought not to consider the statements made by Britton in regards to any one but himself."

Bassett took exception to this half-measure.

The exception was noted by Judge Hodges.

The next state witness was called to the stand.

James Milner would be the last of the three Pekin police officers to testify. He had participated in the arrest of Robert Britton and Ike Berry in the early morning hours of July 30, 1869, and was certainly well acquainted with the two defendants.

In mid-August of 1869, he had been given an assignment in which he became familiar with the other defendants as well. Following Ike Berry's arrest and incarceration with his confederates, Tazewell county authorities were concerned that Ike might use the opportunity to influence the other prisoners to concoct a story believable enough to win an acquittal, or, for that matter, might convince them to attempt an escape. After all, every one of them faced the death penalty, or at the very least a lengthy prison term.

To guard against this possibility, C.G. Whitney wanted an officer stationed inside the jail close enough to hear their conversations. He knew it was also quite possible that Ike might discuss the details of the shooting with his brothers, therefore giving them what they needed most for a conviction. This task had been assigned to James Milner, who went into the cell area and remained there for an undetermined length of time.

Milner had been called to testify to the conversations he had heard.

He testified:

> Know Edward Pratt. Know defendants. Saw Ike Berry in jail in Pekin after his arrest during last August. Was sent in by Mr. Whitney, to keep him from talking to the other prisoners. He said we did not know who they were shooting at but I did the shooting-- heard the man say stop. I

have a warrant for you. Did not know who it
was. Thought Milner and Cass would be out.

Bassett objected. Statements made by Ike Berry after his
arrest, in the presence of a hostile guard, were not voluntary,
and were therefore inadmissible. Reference to the warrant was
also an issue. James Milner had, like so many witnesses before
him, referred to a document which could not be produced in
court. This testimony should be stricken as well.

Both issues had been raised and ruled upon numerous
times before. On each previous occasion Judge Hodges had
ruled against the defense and over-ruled the objection. He did
so again.

The defense took exception.

The judge again noted it.

James Milner continued his testimony, saying, "I was in
the jail to prevent Ike Berry from whispering to the other
prisoners."

Objection once again by Bassett.

The objection was over-ruled

Exception again taken.

Direct examination of James Milner ended.

Bassett had objected on two accounts to the admissibility
of James Milner's testimony. Both objections had been denied.

In cross-examination, if anything were to be gained for the
defense, evidence of coercion must be shown, or a contradiction
in the witness's testimony must be displayed and exploited. In
both attempts, the defense had apparently been unsuccessful.

Cross-examination of James Milner produced no
bombshells. Bassett, apparently, probing for some indication
that Ike Berry had been threatened, or for some inconsistency in
Milner's testimony, came up empty. Milner's direct testimony
seemed to have been reviewed by the defense in detail, except
that in cross-examination, Milner told the court that Ike Berry

"was excited in the jail" and "the other prisoners were crying in the jail." James Milner's testimony would stand and he was excused.

Only one prosecution witness remained to be heard and that was Edward Pratt, Tazewell County Sheriff and brother of the slain deputy. By waiting until now to call Edward Pratt to testify, it was apparent Whitney had saved the witness it believed would have the most powerful emotional impact on the jury for last.

Whitney would ask only very few questions of Edward Pratt. Those questions would deal with two issues: the existence of the arrest warrant for Ike Berry and Robert Britton, and the legitimacy of Henry Pratt's position as deputy sheriff. Both issues had been argued by counsel and ruled upon by Judge Hodges several witnesses ago.

As the courtroom of silent people watched, Edward Pratt walked in and seated himself in the witness chair. He stared directly into the eyes of each defendant.

The court room was silent. Finally, Ed Pratt was questioned. Whitney asked the usual preparatory questions. Pratt answered:

> My name is Edward Pratt. I have been for some time sheriff of Tazewell County. Knew Henry Pratt. He was a brother of mine. He was a regularly appointed deputy. I gave him a warrant to arrest Ike Berry and Britton on a charge of inciting a felony.

Edward Pratt's testimony offered no new revelations and added little weight to evidence presented previously, but what better way to end the case for the People than by displaying the noble, dedicated, lawman still mourning the death of his brother. The effect this display had on the jury cannot be underestimated.

The impact of Edward Pratt's testimony was most apparent in the defense's reaction to it. Given the opportunity to cross-examine, the defense declined.

Edward Pratt's testimony would be allowed to stand unchallenged even though, according to John Berry's testimony, Pratt had made statements to Ike Berry which might be considered intimidating. If that was the case, any testimony concerning statements made by Ike Berry following Pratt's remarks could be said to have been coerced, and would therefore be inadmissible.

The defense had a right, if not an obligation, to examine this possibility, but had chosen not to. Perhaps the defense considered cross- examination of Edward Pratt, in which they would no doubt try to discredit his testimony, to be more destructive in the eyes of the jury than anything he might have to say.

Edward Pratt was excused.

At this point, the State rested its case and the seemingly endless succession of prosecution witnesses finally came to an end.

It was late afternoon and the November sun was failing fast. The fading sunlight again necessitated the lighting of lamps, and again, grotesque shadows bounced and danced upon the courtroom's ceiling and walls.

Against this eerie background, spectators waited for the defense to begin the presentation of its case. They waited as attorneys Barnes, Bassett, and Rodecker huddled briefly to consider their alternatives.

Six defendants were on trial for murder and it was expected that each would be given an opportunity to testify in his own defense. In addition, three defense witnesses, Nancy Berry (William Berry's widow), Josiah Combs(co-defendant with Ike Berry in a horse theft case and incarcerated for refusing to testify against the Berry's at the coroner's inquest into the death of William Berry), and James W. Shay (suspected gang member and relative of William T. Shay) had all been subpoenaed and were expected to take the stand.

They too, waited as the three defense attorneys weighed the pros and cons of calling these people to testify.

The defense strategy thus far had been pinned on three issues: the existence of the warrant, Henry Pratt's status as deputy sheriff, and self defense - premised on the contention that Henry Pratt had not properly identified himself as an officer. The defense had argued these points incessantly during the presentation of the State's case and, by way of objections and cross-examination, may have made some headway with the jury. If properly driven home during closing arguments, any or all of these questions might raise a "reasonable doubt" in the mind of at least one juror, and that was all that was needed. All the defense needed was one juror, wrestling with the evidence and his conscience, to say, "I'm just not sure." Barnes, Bassett, and Rodecker knew that the matter would probably come down (as most trials do) to the simple issue of credibility of witnesses.

As the defense attorneys whispered to each other in that dark courtroom on that bleak November afternoon, it was apparent that they had discussed all issues previously, for their consultation was brief.

After the brief consultation, much to the surprise of the court, the spectators, and most definitely the defendants themselves, the defense announced to the court that they would present no witnesses or evidence on behalf of their clients and asked the court to proceed to closing arguments. Closing arguments would provide all six attorneys with an opportunity to address the court.

The defendants were not required to say anything or to present any evidence unless they desired. It was the state's obligation to prove the case against the defendants beyond a reasonable doubt.

The arguments began immediately and became lengthy and impassioned. Court was adjourned in the late afternoon, but re-convened at seven o'clock that evening to continue the closing arguments. Late that Friday night, the court had to adjourn for the day, even though the closing arguments were not complete.

* * *

As court reconvened Saturday morning, the galleries were filled with spectators anxious to hear the rest of the final arguments. They were even more anxious to be among the first to learn the fate of the accused.

The trial was nearing conclusion with only the final addresses of attorneys Barnes and Roberts left to be heard before the case was given to the jury. It was possible a verdict could be returned before sundown.

28

Caesar A. Roberts rose to deliver the prosecution's closing remarks. Roberts opened by saying:

> The time and patience of the jury has already been sufficiently taxed, but I am required to speak now, in vindication of the law and in the name of justice, and to assist the jury in maintaining the honor and dignity of the law.

Roberts told the jury that it was not his fault that the defendants stood before the court. It was the fault of the defendants themselves. Then, in a style reminiscent of Anthony's eulogy of Caesar, C.A. Roberts told the jury, "I am not here to hold up the bloody carcass of Henry Pratt. I am here to ask you to mete out justice to the prisoners."

He then launched a lengthy discourse in which he attacked defense positions point by point and in concluding, called the jury's attention to the testimony and the law in the case.

Throughout the trial, Simeon Berry's participation in the events of July 31, 1869, had been an issue, and testimony concerning his involvement had been inconclusive and contradictory. None of the witnesses could place him at the tavern at the time Bill Berry appealed for resistance. Some witnesses claim Simeon Berry had later paraded the streets with the rest of the gang while other witnesses testified they had not seen him. Simeon's presence at or near the scene of Pratt's murder had never been conclusively established.

Before ending his remarks, much to the surprise of the court, C.A. Roberts told the jury that the testimony had not shown Simeon to have been involved in the crime, and that he hoped Simeon would be acquitted.

At various times during the trial, the State had held up the bloody carcass of Henry Pratt, the noble lawman, mercilessly cut down in the prime of his life by a band of outlaws. The defense had a stained body to exhibit as well - that of William Berry.

His grisly murder was used by Barnes to his clients' advantage. By reminding the jury of Bill Berry's gruesome death, he attempted to use this hideous incident to divert the jury's attention from the defendants and to put the mob on trial. Barnes told the court that last July the citizenry had been shocked and appalled at Henry Pratt's death, but that their outrage had given rise to an illegal, immoral, and misdirected mob which, to satisfy its thirst for vengeance, had lynched the wrong man. Bill Berry had been murdered by the mob, and the defendants stood before the court now, not because of any wrong doing on their part, but as a result of the Tazewell mob's unquenchable thirst for vengeance.

"Finding they had murdered the wrong man," Barnes told the jury, "the mob set upon the younger brother and were thirsting for his blood to satisfy their vengeance."

In conclusion, Barnes warned the jurors not to be misled by, "specious representations unsupported by facts made by the State's Attorneys brought here to condemn these men."

Barnes looked over the jury and returned to his seat. The jury had heard the final words on behalf of the defendants.

Upon completion of final arguments, Judge Hodges consulted with counsel in his chambers.

He emerged from this meeting and announced that by agreement of parties, it had been decided that the jury would receive no final instructions from the court.

Judge Hodges then proceeded to advise the jury as to the proper form the final verdict should take. The jury would return a verdict of guilty or not guilty for each of the defendants, and for those found guilty, recommend a sentence.

Sometime between 2:30 and 3:00 p.m., the case was placed in the jury's hands, and these twelve men were led from the courtroom to the room in which the fate of the six defendants would finally be decided.

Throughout the day, the courtroom and galleries had been filled with anxious spectators. With the town's population temporarily swelled as it was with parties of dozens of other legal cases waiting to be heard, criminal case #51 had a large audience and had attracted considerable attention. After all, a murder trial was a rare and exciting event - the best show in town.

Although the Morgan county citizenry displayed much interest in the case, there was little or no sympathy for the defendants, possibly a result of pressure from Tazewell county citizens present in Jacksonville for the trial.

The Jacksonville Daly Journal wrote:

> During the trial a strong outside pressure was
> brought to bear against the prisoners by citizens
> of Pekin in attendance, and the public sentiment
> in this city was also decidedly against them, the
> impression having been received that they were
> a gang of desperadoes dangerous to society.

Approximately six months earlier, Jacksonville had been the scene of another murder trial. That case had attracted much attention also. Whether by mannerisms, actions, or handsome appearance, the defendant in that case had infatuated the female population of Jacksonville to such an extent that public opinion, at least among the fairer sex, was almost universally in favor of the accused.

At trial's end, ladies in the galleries had wept, and others had presented the defendant with bouquets. The female population of Jacksonville had become so enthralled with the handsome defendant that they had made it seem almost an insult to have tried him.

This had not been the case in the Berry trial, and one Jacksonville reporter noted the contrast:

> During the whole of to-day the court room and
> galleries were filled with spectators, anxious to
> learn the fate of those six unhappy men. But,
> different from the last murder trial in our city,
> there were no ladies present. These unfortunates
> received no bouquets; there were no fair cheeks
> in the galleries drenched with tears at their unhappy
> condition; they received no gentle caresses and soft
> looks from the fair hands and tender eyes, as did
> as vile a criminal in our city last spring. What
> produced the change we do not know.

A Springfield reporter viewing the scene was more philosophical:

> As the jury retired the crowd remained in breathless anxiety for the verdict that should forever seal the fate of these six unfortunate creatures, or else pronounce them not guilty, and give them their liberty. As we looked at the prisoners, whose lives and honor were hanging as it were by a single thread, we could but wonder at the combination of circumstances and causes, and the criminal depravity of man, that could lead him on, step by step, to such an impending doom as now hung over these men.

What had brought the Berry gang to this end? Was it some strange, combination of circumstances and causes, or was it to be explained simply as criminal depravity? It is doubtful that many spectators that day were as philosophical as the reporter from Springfield, but they were certainly every bit as curious and eager to witness the final verdict.

A large crowd of spectators milled about in the courtroom and courthouse grounds well into the evening. Undoubtedly, many had left the grounds long enough to grab a bite to eat or down a quick drink or two, however, activity around the courthouse continued throughout the night.

Around 7:30 p.m., the reporter from the Illinois State Register telegraphed his home office that a verdict had not yet been reached.

At midnight, the reporter for the Jacksonville Weekly Sentinal reported the same, as the vigil continued through the night.

The crowd was not at a loss for things to talk about. Two and one half days of testimony and arguments had been heard. There were various witness accounts to be discussed and a multitude of opinions to be expressed. There were probably discussions and arguments as well over how the defendants really would react when the sentence was handed down, mainly because of Ike's statement to the reporters that he would "die game" if he received the death penalty. All of this served to spice and flavor the show.

Where the attorneys went to wait the verdict is unknown, and one can only guess at what they might have discussed.

The prisoners, of course, had been returned to their cells in the Morgan County jail where, as the minutes and hours slowly passed, each must have considered and reconsidered the weight of evidence against him as he pondered his fate.

Each prisoner reviewed the evidence against him as well as the arguments made on his behalf.

All of them optimistically clung to hopes of acquittal, except perhaps one - Ike Berry. He knew that the case against him was overwhelming. As the other defendants longed for acquittal, Ike Berry's wishes were more modest. He hoped simply that his life would be spared.

* * *

Throughout the night, the jury deliberated. These twelve men discussed, argued, and debated the relative worth of the testimony they had heard, as well as their respective opinions of what the evidence had actually shown. Perhaps there was debate on the sentences as well.

Hour after hour passed, yet, there was no agreement, no verdict. The jury's difficulty in reaching a verdict must have been a source of optimism for the defense and a cause of concern for the prosecution. Obviously certain members of the jury had not been totally convinced by the State's case. The defense knew the longer the jury remained divided, the better the chance for an acquittal or a hung jury. There was still hope.

But in actuality, there was very little disagreement among the jurors. Early in the deliberations, the jury had agreed as to the guilt or innocence of the various defendants. It had taken little time for them to agree that all of the defendants, except Simeon Berry, bore some responsibility for Henry Pratt's death. As far as Emanuel Berry, Matthew McFarland, Cornelius Daly, and Robert Britton were concerned, there had been quick agreement on their sentences. However, Ike Berry's sentence had presented a problem.

After nearly eighteen hours of debate, ten jurors favored the death penalty for Ike Berry while two jurors stubbornly held out for a lesser sentence. Finally, with the first rays of sunlight creeping into the small stuffy room, after more than eighteen hours of fruitless deliberation, and perhaps with fear of the prospect of a hung jury and therefore a new trial, the ten jurors gave way to the two holdouts.

It was a powerful victory for Isaac Berry, for it was agreed that he would not be put to death, but would be sentenced to life imprisonment. This seemed to be a fair compromise. The jury would not bear responsibility for the taking of a human life, yet the murderer would be removed from society and the time and expense of a new trial would be avoided.

At nine o'clock, on Sunday morning, November 28, the bailiff was informed that a verdict had been reached.

*   *   *

As the news spread, a "concourse of people" began to gather at the courthouse.

By ten o'clock, attorneys, prisoners, and spectators had all been reassembled and court reconvened to hear the verdict.

One Jacksonville reporter noted that Ike Berry "showed considerable nervousness" upon being led into the courthouse.

A single sheet of paper was handed to Judge Hodges by a bailiff. He read the verdict silently to himself and finally aloud for all in the courtroom to hear.

As the verdict was read, two of the Berry brothers, Ike and Sim, expressed relief, if not delight. The other defendants "were apparently indifferent and received their doom carelessly."

Isaac Berry had been found guilty of murder and his sentence set at life imprisonment.

It was noted in one Jacksonville paper that the nervousness Ike had displayed as he entered the courtroom quickly dissipated as the sentence was read.

Robert Britton was found guilty of murder, and his sentence set at 25 years in the penitentiary.

The verdicts for Emanuel Berry, Matthew McFarland, and Cornelius Daly were identical and somewhat shorter than Ike's and Briton's. Each was found guilty of murder and each sentence was set at 15 years in prison.

The jury, apparently obedient to C.A. Roberts advice and recommendation, found Simeon Berry not guilty.

As the shackles were removed, Simeon found himself a free man for the first time in nearly four months.

After the verdict was read, William H. Barnes rose to make yet another motion on behalf of the defendants. Barnes asked the court to grant a new trial, presumably on the grounds that new evidence had become available.

Perhaps because it was Sunday morning and it had been a long weekend for everyone, Judge Hodges agreed to hear the motion for a new trial, but at a later date. He deferred final sentencing until the conclusion of that hearing.

According to law, the sentence handed down by the jury was only their recommendations, and the judge had final say as to the sentence imposed upon a defendant. Court was adjourned.

The courthouse had bristled with activity. Spectators clamored to get outside and spread the news.

The jury had made its departure as the attorneys gathered their books and notes and spoke among themselves.

The Morgan County Sheriff's deputies moved forward to return the prisoners to the jail, while Sheriff Sierso approached Simeon Berry.

Simeon was the only defendant the jury had set free, however, that freedom would not last long. It seemed that back in September, Cassius G. Whitney had foreseen the possibility that one or more of the defendants might be acquitted on the murder charge. He had, as a safeguard against allowing any of these murderers to go free, secured indictments for "assault with intent to kill" against all six of the accused. The indictments, handed down at the same time as the murder warrants, had never been served but had remained safely tucked away in case they were needed.

Whitney now decided that they were needed. The sheriff, having confronted Simeon, informed him that he was under arrest for this lesser offense. His reaction to the arrest was one of disbelief. He was quickly shackled again and led from the courtroom with the other prisoners.

One Jacksonville reporter gave his opinion of the situation as he wrote:

> The shackles were not off his hands but a few
> minutes before they were put on again and he
> remanded to jail. Sheriff Pratt and his friends
> are evidently disposed to pursue these men to the
> bitter end.

The trial seemingly ended as it had begun, with hundreds of curious spectators wondering what fate would befall those six shackled "desperadoes." Nothing had been irrevocably decided.

29

The ultimate fate of the "Berry gang" remained uncertain until 9:00 am on December 14, 1869, when Judge Hodges finally heard the defense motion for a new trial.

To present the defense argument, W.H. Barnes had prevailed upon his law partner, G.H. Lacey.

The court listened as Lacey delivered his "carefully prepared, well written" motion.

Lacey argued that a new trial was in order for three reasons. First, new evidence was available to the defense. They could produce testimony from Simeon Berry and a man named Lane that would shed new light on the case and provide proof of innocence for most, if not all of the defendants.

Secondly, Lacey contended that Henry Pratt's death was not murder, but was "justifiable homicide." Lacey called the court's attention to trial testimony concerning the poor lighting conditions, the distances involved, the fact that the posse had never identified themselves, and that the posse had fired several rounds at Ike Berry as he attempted to flee and avoid a confrontation with his unknown assailants. Perhaps testimony from newly discovered witnesses could give insight into the defendants' state of mind just prior to the shooting and show that none of the defendants intended to harm anyone.

Thirdly, Lacey argued that the form of the verdict was not consistent. The jury had found five defendants "guilty in manner and form as charged in the indictment, but did not affix the same penalty to each." Such inconsistency, Lacey claimed, was contrary to law. If all the defendants were guilty of wrong doing in the death of Henry Pratt, then their sentences should be identical.

For two hours Lacey "argued the case as thoroughly and carefully as it is possible for such a case to be argued." He then relinquished the floor to William Barnes.

Barnes spoke briefly and raised no new points or issues.

By the time William Brown, prosecuting attorney for Morgan County who was chosen to file a reply to the defense's motion for a new trial, rose to reply, the matter had already been decided.

Brown, as one newspaper reported, " did not have much to say, and in fact, it was not necessary."

In his brief address, Brown reminded Judge Hodges of those facts of which he was already aware. Simeon Berry was not a new witness, but had been available to testify for the defense all along. If Simeon Berry had anything of worth to say to the court, why hadn't he spoken in his own behalf earlier? Now that he was no longer in jeopardy, why should Simeon Berry be given the opportunity to tell lies or half-truths on behalf of his friends and brothers when he would not speak for himself?

As for Mr. Lane, he also had been available for the defense if they had desired to use him as a witness. Brown informed the court that this same Mr. Lane had been jailed after refusing to answer potentially incriminating questions against the Berrys at the coroner's inquest into Henry Pratt's death. How reliable would Lane's testimony be anyway?

The "justifiable homicide" issue had been addressed at length during the trial. A duly sworn jury had considered and unanimously rejected it. Why should a new jury be subjected to this ordeal?

As for the lack of consistency in sentencing, Brown pointed out the fact that the statutes allow for a wide range of possible sentences. It was not at all inconsistent, and certainly not illegal for the jury to assign different penalties for the different defendants. After all, the charge might have been the same, but each individual's responsibility for the crime varied. All pertinent testimony had been heard, all relevant issues had been considered, and a just and lawful verdict and sentence had been returned. The issue had been resolved and there was no point in reopening it.

Brown's rebuttal, delivered apparently in a calm matter-of-fact style consumed less then twenty minutes.

The arguments had been presented, and it was now up to Judge Hodges to decide. The Judge announced simply that, "the jury had passed upon the facts and law in the case" and that he could not see any good reason for interfering with their verdict. The verdict would stand. The motion for a new trial was denied.

With the motion denied, the court's attention turned to sentencing, at which time each defendant was given an opportunity to address the court and offer "reasons why sentence should not be passed upon them on the verdict of the jury heretofore rendered against them."

The courtroom listened as the defendants' voices were heard for the first and only time in the trial.

Isaac Berry rose to speak first. Ike told the court that "justice had not been done" and declared that he had always been "a hard working honest man." He denied ever being engaged in horse thievery and stated that he could provide proof. He insisted that he was not guilty of murder, and ended his plea with a request for a new trial so that he could prove his "character."

Apparently, Judge Hodges was not impressed, for he sentenced Isaac Berry to "confinement in the penitentiary for and during the full end and term of his natural life...twenty-four hours of each year [to] be in solitary confinement, and the balance at hard labor."

After Ike took his seat, Robert Britton was called to address the court.

Britton rose, smiled, and informed the court that he had nothing to say.

Judge Hodges promptly announced the sentence: "confinement in the penitentiary for twenty five years, twenty-four hours of each year to be in solitary confinement and the balance in hard labor."

Robert Britton resumed his seat.

Emanuel Berry then rose and in mumbled tone, parroted his older brother in saying that justice had not been done. He then awkwardly informed the court that he had nothing further to say and returned to his seat to hear his sentence.

Judge Hodges announced sentence of "confinement in the penitentiary for fifteen years, twenty-four hours of each year to be in solitary confinement." Presumably, the remainder of the sentence was to be served at hard labor.

Matthew McFarland was called next and he announced that he had nothing to say.

Sentence was then passed. He received a fifteen year sentence, identical to that received by Emanuel Berry.

Cornelius Daly, the last of the new convicts to be heard, had watched as each of his four co-defendants either fumbled his way through a clumsy address, or had nothing at all to say in his own behalf. Each lame address had failed to impress the court, and each defendant had received the exact sentence recommended by the jury. Perhaps he had seen the "handwriting on the wall" and realized what his fate would be unless he was able to speak more convincingly of his innocence.

In either case, Cornelius Daly's remarks to the court were more forceful and aggressive than were those of the other defendants. His speech was lengthy, for this enraged and panic-stricken defendant had much to say.

Immediately upon being informed that it was his turn to speak, Daly "at once rose to his feet and said as much as possible for him to say in twenty minutes time."

Daly's statements to the court resembled more a frenzied condemnation than a logical, reasonable address, but he maintained his innocence throughout.

Daly told the court that he "is an honest man" and like Ike Berry, offered to provide proof. He told the court the other defendants were complete strangers to him until two days before Pratt's death. How could he be considered to have born any animosity toward Pratt, to be a member of the "gang," or to have claimed such strong allegiance to a group of people he had known for so short of time?

After launching a lengthy tirade "against most every person and especially his attorneys, Bassett and Rodecker," Daly appealed for a new trial on grounds that "he had plenty of evidence to prove his innocence but that it was not introduced because his lawyers told him it was not necessary."

Cornelius Daly's address was as impassioned as it was lengthy. In his twenty minute speech he had covered as much as could reasonably be covered.

Judge Hodges remained unconvinced and immediately issued the sentence: fifteen years in the penitentiary with twenty-four hours of each year to be served in solitary confinement and the rest at hard labor.

Following Judge Hodges decree, the courtroom again bristled with activity as the court prepared to direct its attention to other matters.

Spectators to the Berry trial made their way to the exit as a new group of parties to a new set of cases made their way into the room.

Sheriff's deputies prepared the prisoners for return to their jail cells as Attorney Barnes vowed to file a brief with the Illinois Supreme Court in hopes of securing a new trial for his clients. The business of the court in regards to case # 51 had ended. The trial had finally come to an end, and the prisoners were returned to their cells.

The courtroom emptied, and one reporter watching the scene remarked that "they will all be in the penitentiary before tomorrow noon."

30

The long wait was finally over. The trial had resulted in a favorable conclusion for the people of Tazewell County-GUILTY! GUILTY! The cry could probably have been heard for blocks around as the jury gave its verdict.

Justice had finally been achieved. Though it would be a while before anyone could be sure it was working, the wait would be worth it. The people had suffered too much, and a guilty verdict was exactly what they had needed. If the bureaucrats did not use their political power or money to influence someone to turn the gang loose, or at least pardon them, then the people would have gained a milestone.

For the time being however, jubilation abounded as everyone celebrated the victory. There was excitement among the lawmen as well, for they had spent months on this case and it was finally over. One of their own had been avenged. Perhaps the sentence was not what they had hoped for, but at least the guilty would be locked away for years to come. The only thing left was to watch as they were carted off to prison later in the day.

It would be a few hours before the outlaws could be transported to the state prison, so heavy guard would have to continue throughout the remainder of the night or until the prisoners were safely in Joliet.

Sheriff Pratt and Marshal Stone were making plans for their trip. The plans would have to be carefully laid out as there was now great danger from both sides. Heavy guard would be required, for the lawmen knew there were two factors to be concerned with. One was that the Berry gang's family and gang members, what few were left, might try to snatch the men from custody.

There was John Orrel, who alone had to be considered a great concern. Most lawmen were well aware of the escapes he had personally made in recent months, and knew he was a member of the Berry gang. The lawmen were also well aware of rumors about Orrel's attempt to save William Berry, even in the face of hundreds of armed men. Even going so far as to disguise himself in woman's clothing. He could very well be planning an escape for the gang. From all the talk about Orrel, it could be assumed there was a lot of respect for the man's ability and fortitude.

Finally, there was Josiah Combs and old man Lane, two mean old birds who were quite capable of organizing another band of outlaws, just to attack the guards.

Much scrutiny had been given all new arrivals in Jacksonville over the last few days as the lawmen had to wait for sentencing. Each person was carefully observed until the lawmen were sure that person was not a gang member.

The second factor was the people themselves. Decent, law-abiding citizens, who just might decide to repeat the Pekin incident. Caution was truly the order of the day.

At 9:00 P.M., on the 14th day of December, under the cover of darkness, Jacksonville City Police, Morgan County Sheriff's deputies, Tazewell County Sheriff Edward Pratt, and Pekin City Marshal A.U. Stone all heavily armed, cautiously moved the five outlaws from the county jail to the waiting train. It would transport the lot of them far to the north - to Joliet.

Tensely watching everyone and everything that moved, they eased along the streets toward the rail station. The heavily armed lawmen managed to secure their prisoners safely in the railcar that would be home for both outlaws and lawmen alike for the next few hours.

While the lawmen were settling in, the shout of the conductor and the sharp hiss of the steam being released from the iron boiler could be heard. The locomotive belched heavy black smoke and lunged forward jarring all its passengers in its effort to get under way.

The train rolled slowly out of the small central Illinois city, and in one of the cars, several wiry lawmen sat nervously waiting for the train to gain speed so that they might relax their rigid guard somewhat during the long trip. Never before had these men been in a situation where they were so concerned with the security of their prisoners, or, for that matter, their own safety. All they could do now was hope the train reached its travel speed before any of the Berry gang members could sneak aboard and attempt to gain the freedom of the Berry gang members being held in the railcar.

As the train slowly gained speed, the tension ebbed away and the lawmen began to settle in for the long uncomfortable trip.

There had to be many of the same thoughts rushing through the minds of the prisoners. They felt the tension easing as the train gained speed. They knew they would be safe from a mob climbing aboard to lynch them. At that point, they had to be concerned about a mob hiding in the next car, waiting for the train to get far enough from town that shots or screams for help would not be heard.

They might still have remembered the newspaper reports just the past June, about the mob of vigilantes near Indianapolis, Indiana, who had lynched several members of a gang who had robbed a bank in the area. Several local papers had carried that story in June.

That gang no doubt envisioned the same happening to them, not once but twice. Once in Pekin, when the mob had laid siege to the jail, and again as the train slowly edged along the tracks. Yes, worry had to be a great weight on their minds.

For that matter, they also had to worry about the lawmen stopping the train in some desolate area and handing out their own justice. The mere fact that Sheriff Pratt and Marshal Stone were aboard was enough to cause great concern among the outlaws. These two men had reason to do it, and both were certainly capable of it. Every time the two men moved, the outlaws watched with great apprehension. That was something the outlaws would have to contend with until they had been safely locked away behind the iron bars of prison.

That was another worry of the outlaws - what it would be like in prison. None of them had spent more than a few days behind bars and that was only in local jails, where violence was rare. Now they faced the great lockup, where the most dangerous of men had been confined for years.

Only last July, there had been a big write up in the Lincoln Herald about all the violence, and how prisoner discipline was non-existent. There were twelve hundred prisoners in the penitentiary, with only half of them doing any work. The rest were idle, therefore having plenty of time to cause problems. This would be something new to the men, something they had never encountered. They had undoubtedly heard all the tales of torture by the guards as well as the tales of savagery among the inmates, and perhaps there was even fear among the men. Thoughts of escaping had to be prevalent in their minds.

With so much to worry about, outlaws and lawmen alike, there had to be such a silence in the car that the slightest noise would have caused every head to turn almost as one.

Mile after mile sped by beneath the great steel wheels of the train as it raced toward Joliet. The minutes turned into hours, and as the hours wore on, the first gray light of dawn began streaking across the December sky. The rolling hills, almost without notice, changed to the wide-open prairies Illinois was famous for.

On this 15th day of December, it was very chilly, even inside the rail car, for there was no heat. Heat was a commodity reserved for the coldest weather. Fires had to be built in small stoves aboard the passenger cars, and the stoves had to be watched at all times to insure they did not tip over with the swaying of the train.

Cold or not, the train continued its rush through the country side, and it was not long before it was slowing for the city of Joliet. It soon came to a stop, with its stack blowing black smoke thick enough to cut with a knife.

When the smoke finally cleared, there stood the gray stone walls of the prison. No doubt a sense of dread swept over the outlaws as they prepared for their first introduction to life behind those great walls.

The prisoners were offloaded and escorted quickly through the giant gate and into the waiting arms of the warden. The trip was over and it had been an uneventful one, much to the joy of the lawmen, and perhaps the outlaws as well.

The prisoners were safely behind the tall gray walls of the "Joliet Hotel." The same "Joliet Hotel" where William Berry had been delivered by Sheriff Pratt on January 1st, 1868, just seventeen days short of a year before. This time however, there were no executive pardons waiting at the gate for the Berrys. This time they were to stay - this time justice was working.

31

During the next few months, life in and around Pekin slowly got back to normal. That is, if you could call it normal. The people involved in the lynching had been publicly told they had done the right thing, and that they should not be held accountable for the deeds they committed on the night of July 31st, 1869. They were told by the brass, bold vocal inspiration from the Reverend Steele as he preached the funeral of Henry Pratt:

> There lies the conservator of your laws, The protector of your property, shot down like a dog...
>
> How is the majesty of justice of the law vindicated?
>
> The only remedy I know of is in your hands.

In addition, there were the printed words of encouragement and support from the newspapers. As The Jacksonville Daly Journal wrote on August 10,1869,:

> as much as we abhor lynch law, we cannot blame
> them; their lives and property needs must be
> rendered secure in some manner; they had no
> other recourse. We are surprised that similar
> tragedies are not of constant occurrence.
> Murderers and villains are everyday turned
> out upon society by the blundering law. The
> greater the criminal, the more certain he is to
> go free.

Gathering more support from a local exchange group, speaking on lynch law and the causes that lead to its execution, the paper quoted the exchange as saying:

> They happen because the administration of the
> criminal law has become so loose that it only
> acts to prevent the punishment of crime. And it
> is reasonable to suppose that lynch law will prevail
> more and more, until the criminal law is made to
> punish criminals.

The paper continued on by placing the blame upon the laws of the state by likening them to a machine:

> Like a grand and complicated machine which
> will not work, it answers the purpose of show,
> and often amounts to little more.

Another newspaper urged for "leniency for those involved in the lynching."

And finally the Lincoln Herald picked up the story and wrote:

> We are opposed to mob violence, but if there
> ever was a case that demanded anything of the
> kind, it seems to me that this is one. We apprehend
> that but few horses will be stolen in the
> neighborhood of Pekin very soon.

After hearing the preacher, reading the newspapers and receiving the support of other local citizens, the people placed the blame for the terrible incident on the outlaws and put it behind them. They settled back into the quiet routine of farm country living.

However, there were some individual families who would never be able to return to a normal life. These families had been too deeply hurt by the incident to be normal.

The family of Henry Pratt would never get back to normal, for Henry was no longer with them, murdered by scoundrels who would later profess their innocence.

George Hinman, who had received the terrible wounds in the shoulder and head, would never be the same. He would carry the scars for life - not only scars from the bullets, but the mental scars as well - scars caused by the scenes at the site of the ambush, as well as those caused by the horrible siege upon the jail.

There was also the family of Felix Knott, the unfortunate young man who, unable to cope with the scenes at the lynching, had turned his own gun upon himself and ended the mental suffering which so effected him at the time. The former city clerk of Pekin must have had some horrible thoughts racing through his head at the time. Perhaps he was indeed the "unknown person" who had fired the shots into William Berry that night. That might explain why he could not face life afterwards. Whatever the reason, his family would never be the same.

A little further south, in the town where all the misery really began, there were many families that were destined to suffer greatly over the next few years - families like the Berrys' wives and children.

Bill Berry's family especially would suffer. There were Nancy and the two children, left with the farm to manage alone without husband or father.

They were, however, much better off than was the wife of Isaac Berry, who had nothing to help her support the three children they had. Although Ike claimed to be a farmer, he owned nothing at the time of his arrest.

Emanuel's wife and his three children would suffer as well, for he had never amounted to much and had no money or property. Their lives would not be normal for years to come, if ever.

There was Melissa, the young wife of Matthew McFarland, and her four children, as well as Cornelius Daly's wife and two children, whose lives were greatly effected by what had recently transpired.

These were the people who had depended upon their men for their very livelihood. Starvation was certainly something not to be ruled out. It was winter and with no man around to provide for them in this harsh land, death from starvation could have easily come to pass. It would not have taken long for this to be determined, as it was late December and already the cold winds chilled one to the bone.

There had never been any animosity toward the gang's wives or children by the people of the county, and many would no doubt try to help as much as they could. Even this might not be enough, for it was hard enough to care for one family during these times.

The people knew it was not the family's fault that their men were in prison. The men had brought it on upon themselves because of their laziness and their fondness for wine, women, and song. They might suffer in prison, however, their families would suffer far more. The state would feed and house the prisoners, but the families would have to fend for themselves - or take the alternate course and go plead their case to the county authorities to be declared a pauper and placed in the COUNTY POOR HOUSE, the most dreaded place located between Pekin and Tremont. This was the last place a person would allow themselves to be placed if they had any other recourse.

Public opinion was that if one could not make a living for one's self or their family, one had an obligation to go to the poor house rather than have someone else provide for them.

However, it was not yet time to give up, for there was still the chance that they could win a new trial and be set free, or maybe someone would intervene on their behalf and get the men pardoned as in the past.

But as time wore on, winter turned to summer, then back to winter and summer again. It became evident to the families that there would be no new trial, even though attorney Alfred Rodecker had tried desperately to gain one through letters to the courts.

* * *

Two full years passed and the families were becoming desperate, especially Melissa McFarland, who was trying to get her husband a pardon from the Governor. She began by writing to the chaplain of the state prison in Joliet, who Mathew had become acquainted with. Perhaps it was all a scheme on the part of Mathew to get out of prison, but Melissa was very serious about the matter as her family's survival depended upon

her husband making a living for them. A letter to the Reverend
A.T. Briscoe from Melissa McFarland, written on March 6th,
1872, read as follows:

> Dear Sir;
> From the kind words and encouragement I got
> in a letter I received from you some months ago.
> I infer that you feel deeply for the suffering
> Humanity and that you are interested in the well
> being of my husband. I therefore take the liberty
> to forward to you the accompanying petition
> which I have finished circulating in our old
> neighborhood. I obtained the certification of
> Judge Turner, who was at the time of my
> husband's trial, judge of the judicial circuit from
> which a change of venue had taken it to
> Jacksonville, Ills, as to the standing of the
> petitions. I could have got a great many to have
> signed it in the other parts of the county, but my
> object was to get such as was of good character
> & those who were personally acquainted with
> my husband. Now I wish you would forward the
> petition to the governor. I trouble you with it
> because I am advised To send it direct by mail
> would probably not command the attention that
> it would if presented or sent by a person of
> influence.
> For any trouble you may go to for us, I
> commend you to Him who has the very hairs of
> your head numbered!
>
> Yours truly,
> Melissa McFarland
> Wife of Mathew McFarland

It was very apparent that the reverend had compassion for the suffering, for he would be instrumental in writing and presenting many letters on behalf of the Berry gang for years to come.

Reverend A.T. Briscoe was chaplain at the state prison at Joliet, Illinois, where they were incarcerated. Over the years he would write many letters to people in high places to gain a pardon for the men.

On June 7th, 1872, yet another tragic incident suddenly and quite unexpectedly occurred. Word was received from prison that Emanuel Berry had just died. There were many questions on the minds of family members, concerning the cause of his death, due to the harsh and violent lifestyle in prison, but the official cause of death, according to prison records, was that Emanuel Berry had contracted a dreaded disease known as Cerebral Meningitis. Because so little was know about the disease at that time, he succumbed to it. Emanuel "Man" Berry had now paid in full his debt to society.

This would be a terrible grief upon the already suffering family, not for just a few years, but forever, for even though he had not amounted to much as a breadwinner, he was still their husband and father.

His death was yet another directly linked to the incident of July 30th, 1869, when the gang had decided to "stand their ground" against the law. That brought the score to four dead and four wounded. What would the final tally be?

As a result, the families of the convicts pushed harder for the pardons. With all the violence in the prisons, who would die next?

The Reverend A.T. Briscoe began writing with a letter to Judge Thomas on June 9th, 1874, in which he wrote:

Judge Thomas

Dear Sir,
The wife of Mathew McFarland has delivered a
petition to me, asking the pardon of her husband
signed by quite a number of citizens of Tazewell
County- with a certificate attached from Chas
Turner (Judge) certifying as to the characters of
The signers of the petition. Should I not forward
the papers to you, and have you look into and
after them and then have you to use your
influence in obtaining McFarland's pardon. I
shall be pleased to add a certificate as to his
moral character -I believe him to be a soundly
converted man and it well be perfectly safe for
him to have his liberty-again. His wife is a
poor, feeble, impoverished woman and if there
ever was a case- as I understand the destitute
condition of the family that mercy should be
extended, this is one. Please reply as soon as
possible- This petition may be all sufficient. Do
what you can for him.

I am most respectfully
A.T. Briscoe
Chaplain.

Reverend A.T. Briscoe wrote to Judge Thomas on June
15, 1874, apparently in reply to a letter from Judge Thomas
himself. In this letter he answered:

Judge Thomas

Dear Sir:
Your letter of the 12th Inst [sic] and I take

pleasure in forwarding the petition. I can but repeat to you that I verily believe that Mathew McFarland is a safe cause - man to have his liberty. I have known him closely and intimately 4 years. He joined our praying band here May 29th 1870. Since which time I have never seen or known anything to cause me to doubt his sincerity as a Christian I believe in his case he is a soul saved consequently a man made. He has already paid dear enough for keeping a rum-hole for I do not believe he had anything to do with the case of murder - Those that had declared his innocence - Oh! Sir. I do feel that innocent wife and those children have been deprived of the care of a husband and a father - If need be I feel it safe for me to go his security for any reasonable amount to have him released. If he was a real willful murderer I could not feel so.

I am with much respect-"
A.T. Briscoe
Chaplain

A letter writing campaign must have started, for several letters dated within days of each other were mailed to Judges, the Chaplain, and the Governor.

On August 10th, 1874, another letter was sent by Melissa McFarland. This time it was sent to The Honorable William Thomas. The letter was much more pitiful, for her husband had now been in the prison for four and a half years. It read as such:

The Hon. William Thomas

Dear Sir;
My husband, Mathew McFarland, who is an
inmate Of the State Prison at Joilet, frequently
mentions you in his letters to me, as one who
had manifested an interest in his unfortunate
condition and who recommended that a petition
should be gotten up in his behalf which petition
sent to the Chaplain who sent it to you. We
hoping that you would present it to Governor.
Now Dear Sir, for the love of God, if you can do
anything for us, do it. I do not believe that my
husband was ever guilty of a crime of any
magnitude certainly not of murder. For five
years, I've struggled in deep poverty with four
little children, youngest 5 years the oldest 10, to
keep out of the poor house and have succeeded
so far, through we have suffered from hungar
and cold at times greatly. You may think why
don't you go to the poor house. I do not know
why. I have a perfect horror of it. I have
earnestly prayed for grace to submit to it,
because some have said it was my duty to go
there. Yet it seems to me that I had rather die.
Now sir in view of my shattered health the
approaching winter and the difficulty of getting
work. I feel almost in dispair and outside of
God, my hope is alone in you, and should you
restore me my husband while I have breath I will
pray for you.

Melissa McFarland

In this letter to Judge William Thomas she had explained
life without her husband and what was usually expected of poor

people who could not support themselves - going to the Poor House.

Another short letter from the Chaplain to Judge Thomas written on September 29, 1874, indicates that the Chaplain decided to carry the matter of Mathew McFarland right to the top man himself, Governor John L. Beveridge, in the State Capitol building in Springfield. In his letter he wrote:

Judge - Thomas

Dear Sir
Passing through Springfield last week I called
on the Governor, and we had some conversation
about Mathew McFarland. He spoke favorable
with regard to his case. For his wife and
children's sake - I believe he is a safe man to
have his liberty again - I would urge his case. I
believe him to be a soundly converted man, and
that he will here after lead a quite and honest
life. I do hope he may be pardoned. I am sure
you will have no regrets in aiding him in His
misfortune. Will you as soon as possible present
his case to the Governor."

Most Respectfully.
A.T. Briscoe

As one can see by the contents of the letters, only a most cold-hearted man could have ignored these pleas. Apparently Governor Beveridge was not cold hearted.

On November 25, 1874, having served only four years, eleven months, and ten days of the fifteen-year sentence he received, Mathew McFarland was pardoned. That was a great victory for his wife Melissa, who had struggled all those years to gain his release. He was home at last, a converted man.

It appears someone must have taken notice of McFarland's release, for not too many months later other members would be released.

The next to be released was none other than the man known at first only as "Frank"- Robert Britton. He was pardoned by Governor John L. Beveridge on April 22, 1875.

Just two days later, on April 24th, perhaps processing time for the paper work, Cornelius Daly was also pardoned.

Robert Britton and Cornelius Daly would disappear into oblivion as far as can be determined.

Efforts were in the works to try and get a pardon for Isaac Berry by Attorney Alfred Rodecker, who had been one of the defense attorneys at his trial. He prepared a petition, and with it, a thirty-three page letter to the Governor, detailing the whole case from beginning to end. This letter was written on June 5, 1875, however it bore no fruit and Rodecker would write many more letters in Ike's behalf over the years to come.

While everything seemed to be going well for most of the pardoned outlaws, things were not well for Mathew McFarland. The "soundly converted man" as the Reverend Briscoe had written, was in trouble again. He had been arrested and brought before the courts, this time for a seemingly petty offense that may very well have lead to his demise.

On August 20, 1875, nine months after his pardon from prison, charges were filed against Mathew McFarland for the theft of a buggy wheel from W.W. Smith.

McFarland and his accomplice in the matter, Erwin Stockton, were "examined" before a jury in the presence of J.E. Senat, Justice of the Peace, and after examination of witnesses, they were required to post bond. Both men were released after posting $100.00 personal recognizance bond.

Apparently Mathew McFarland never showed up for the court, as nothing was ever filed after that date.

According to information available, he decided to flee the state after the charges were filed for fear of going back to prison. It was rumored around the county that he went "out west and was shot and killed." The validity of this cannot be substantiated.

A sudden interest in the pardon of Isaac Berry took hold, and several letters and petitions began to circulate for his release. However, it was not to be for some time to come.

Petitions were sent to the Governor by Simeon Berry, as they had been for years. Most were like the one he sent in November of 1882. He first filed a public notice in the Pekin Weekly Times, on the 9th, 16th, and 23rd, of November, which read:

> Notice
> To Whom It May Concern You are hereby
> notified that I shall present a petition for the
> pardon of Isaac Berry, who is now confined in
> the State penitentiary for murder, to the Hon.
> Shelby M. Cullon, on the 30th day of November,
> 1882 at 2:00 O'clock P.M. of when and where
> you can appear and resist such application if you
> see fit.
> Simeon Berry

True to his word, Simeon submitted the petition to Governor Cullon in Springfield. The petition is something of a historical marker in itself. The petition said that Isaac was now in the State Penitentiary at Chester Illinois and was about 40 years old. It repeated most of the evidence given at the trial, however at one point the petition read:

after supper, Isaac Berry, R. Britton,
Mathew McFarland and Emanuel
Berry & Simeon Berry were on the
streets of The Village of Circleville talking
together and Isaac Berry & Britton
were mad at W. Shaw for giving false
information and I. Berry said he would whip
Shaw on sight. After talking among the crowd
then Present they agreed to go up & see the
Berry boys mother who lived up the road
about 1 & 1/2 miles. They walked along quitely
not expecting to have trouble with anyone. I.
Berry & Britton were ahead about 100
yards, Isaac Berry had a shotgun and
Britton had a revolver. The other boys were
unarmed. They all walked in this, a respective
position until they passed the house of S.
Renner, Esq. At which place, persons ran
out in the road and said hold on. Simeon
Berry, Emanuel Berry, and Mathew
McFarland stopped and halted.

The petition went on, but here it showed, for the first
time, and in the words of none other than Simeon Berry himself,
that he was in fact with the group when the shooting occurred.
It was quite possible that the witnesses had mistaken Simeon
Berry for Cornelius Daly, for the petition went on to say:

Petitioners avers that the defendants were
convicted more from prejudice than from any
evidence showing guilt of murder. In fact, the
jury convicted Elias Daly who was not
within one-half mile of the place where it
occurred, but was at the very time in bed, W.

Berry's house and knew nothing about it at
the time.

The statements in the petition by Simeon Berry indicate
that possibly an innocent man had been convicted, and that a
guilty one had been acquitted. However, this discovery, so long
after the incident, did not seem to matter, for there was no
action taken in the petition.

Isaac Berry sent out letters, most of which were written
by other people, for he was not one to ably express himself in
writing. This was evident in the letter he wrote to Mr. Benjamin
S. Prettyman, an attorney at law, in Pekin, on Christmas Day,
December 25, 1885, it read as follows, exactly as he wrote it:

December 25, 1885

"Mr. Prety I rite to you in regard to my Case
nowen that you now all a bout it. I have a
hundred dollars in money in the office if you will
git me out I will turn it over to you I dont think
it Would be much trouble to git me out as I have
ben in prison So long Let me hear from you
soon.

I B

Isaac, by this time, had been transferred from Joliet to the
Southern Illinois Penitentiary. From this prison he was able to
enlist the aid of one G.R. Sims, who wrote a letter to Attorney
Prettyman. The letter was written on the letterhead paper of the
Mitchell Pressed Brick Works, located in Menard, Illinois, of
which Mr. Sims was owner.

293

This letter was a reminder to Prettyman that Isaac had promised him a hundred dollars to "git" him out. It was type-written, dated January 28, 1886, and read as follows:

> B. S. Prettyman, Esq.
> Pekin, Ill.
>
> Dear Sir -
> Sometime ago Isaac Berry, a life prisoner in the
> Chester Penitentiary, wrote you a letter
> proposing to give you one hundred dollars to get
> him pardoned. This letter you did not reply to.
> Berry has this amount of money to his credit in
> the wardens office, and but a very little more.
> He will sign an order for same payable on this
> condition, and there will be no doubt of your
> getting it should you be successful.
> At present, Gov. Oglesby is almost ready to
> pardon him, and would if he was convinced that
> Berry had a home to go to and would not re-visit
> his old home in Illinois. He has a married
> daughter doing well at Rising City, Neb.to which
> home he is affectionately invited to come, and
> where he has resolved to go direct. If this fact is
> properly explained to the Governor, and also his
> attention called to the fact that no life prisoner
> has ever served 17 years in this state and Berry
> will have done it next December it does look like
> this case may not be hard to consummate.
> The writer has no interest..save that of pity.. in
> Berry's case, and writes this letter thinking you
> may have overlooked the one Berry wrote.
> Should you reply address your letter to him.

very respectfully,
G.R. Sims

At the bottom of the letter was a hand written note:

His daughters address is
Mrs. Rachel McLeese
Rising City, Butler Co. Neb.

In another of Isaac's letters to the Governor, he invited the governor to come to the prison and see his "farm" on the hillside, where he took care of animals, including bees. He tried to impress the reader that he had a strong respect for living things.

In yet another letter, he describes the prison as "hell."

The prison chaplain wrote another letter to the Governor, in which he urged the quick release of Berry as his "mental state is deteriorating" and he feared he would go insane if he was not released quickly.

On Christmas Day, December 25, 1886, Isaac berry himself writes another letter to then Governor Oglesby. It appeared he must have gotten lonesome on Christmas, for he wrote letters on that day, such as this one:

December 25 1886

"Dear Sir after lingeren hear Since 1869 I
thought I would rite to you and see if you would
ant do some thing for me as my record is good
hear it appears that all the people where i am
sent from Wants me out I hope you will consider
these few lines closely do some thing for me as I
have a Daughter i Braska that needs my help ile
close a hopen to hear from you Soon

Isaac Berry,

Finally, after a petition had reached the desk of the Governor with the names of W. A. Tinney and W.F. Copes, the constable involved in the original shoot out, appearing on it, Governor Oglesby signed a pardon for Berry. He signed it on June 8, 1887.

Isaac Berry was released from prison on June 15, 1887, having served the longest prison term of any inmate in the Illinois prison system at that time. Isaac Berry must have kept his word to go directly to this daughter's for he was not heard of again.

As for brother Simeon Berry, the last of the clan, he lived in Peoria until his death several years after the turn of the century.

Tazewell County Sheriff Edward Pratt lost his bid for Sheriff in 1870, either by vote or by choice, but was elected Sheriff again in 1872. He married in 1874 and served several terms as Sheriff. He lived in Tremont after retiring, and died in 1909.

Pekin City Marshal A.U. Stone quit law enforcement soon after the trail, but took up the badge again the next year. He died quietly at his home in 1876 at the age of 59.

William Berry, who had met his death at the hands of the angry mob on August 1, 1869, had not died an innocent man, as so many have proclaimed over the years. Evidence in the case had proven beyond a doubt that he was just as guilty of killing Deputy Pratt as he would have been if he had pulled the trigger on the fatal shot himself. He had encouraged the men to resist. He had given them guns to use and allowed them to practice shooting at his home. Bill Berry had prepared his men to kill the lawmen he knew would be coming for them.

Had Bill not been lynched, the chances are good that both he and Isaac would have been sentenced to hang. His violent death no doubt played a mayor role in the jury's decision to spare Isaac's life.

William "Bill" Berry's body was finally laid to rest in the Woodrow Cemetery, located within sight of his home. As far as is known, there has never been a marker on his grave. Perhaps not marking the grave was just another way for the people of Tazewell County to try to forget the terrible tragedy lingering in their past.

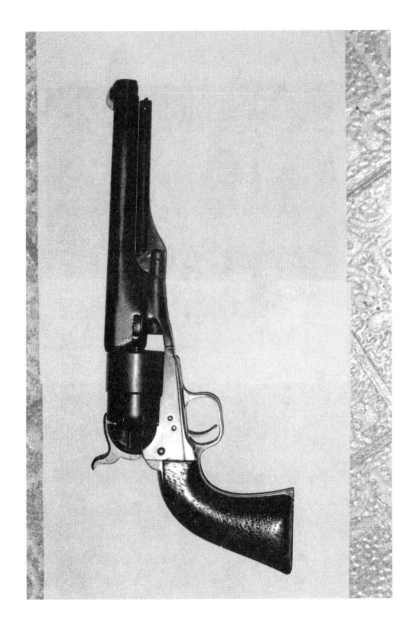

Colt Army .44 caliber revolver, model 1860, owned by WILLIAM "BILL" BERRY when he was lynched -1869. May have been used in the ambush and murder of Deputy Henry Pratt.

WILLIAM FLETCHER COPES, Constable of Circleville, Illinois
emptied his revolver at Isaac Berry during shootout.
Photograph circa unknown, courtesy of Gene Abbott and family.

B

GEORGE WASHINGTON PEPPER, severely wounded with a
knife by Bill Berry in a fight in a saloon in Delavan Illinois on
September 1, 1868, died of his injuries on September 3, 1868.
He is buried in Weyrich Cemetery near Circleville, Illinois.
Photograph circa 1868, courtesy of Mrs. Henry(Margaret) Boorse.

McFarland's Saloon, owned by Matthew McFarland and Bill
Berry, located on East Street in Circleville, Illinois. It was here the
final plans were laid out to ambush the lawmen. Photograph circa
1939, courtesy of Bill Furrow.

Andrew Ditmon's Grocery and Tobacco store located on East Street in Circleville, Illinois, across the road from McFarland's Saloon. William Shaw ran into this store with Ike Berry and Robert Britton chasing him. Photograph circa 1939. Courtesy of Bill Furrow.

Grave marker of Pekin City Marshal Alfred U. Stone, located in Lakeside Cemetery, Pekin, Illinois. He was the only man the Berry boys were afraid of. He led the posse that captured most of the gang. He single-handedly broke up the lynch mob.

F

Grave marker of Henry Pratt, located in Mount Hope Cemetery, Tremont, Illinois. Henry fought in some of the worst battles of the Civil War, only to fall victim to buckshot at the hands of a horse thief named Isaac "Ike" Berry.

Grave marker of Edward Pratt, located in Mount Hope Cemetery, Tremont, Illinois. Sheriff Pratt did what he could to protect his prisoners from the lynch mob, even though they had just killed his brother.

Grave marker of Rachel Berry, located in Woodrow Cemetery,
Circleville, Illinois. She was William "Bill" Berry's mother.
According to cemetery records, the space beside her marker
(arrow) is the gravesite of William Berry. As far as anyone knows,
there has never been a marker on it.

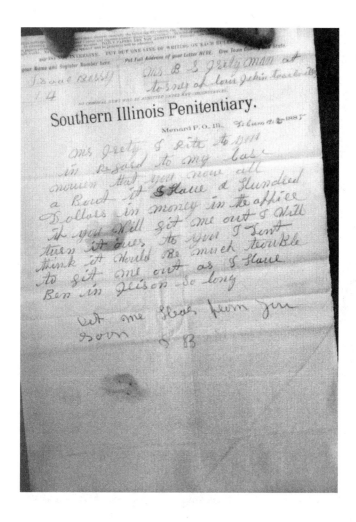

Photograph of letter written on Christmas Day in 1885 by Isaac Berry while still in prison at Chester, Illinois. Isaac, killer of Deputy Sheriff Henry Pratt, spent more than 18 years in prison, serving most of it at Joliet and the rest at Chester. It was the longest anyone had ever spent in an Illinois prison.

Grave marker of George Washington Pepper, located in the
Weyrich Cemetery just west of Circleville. Mortally wounded in a
saloon fight by Bill Berry on September 1, 1868, Pepper died on
September 3, 1868.

K

Grave marker of Andrew Ditmon, located in Woodrow Cemetery just north of Circleville. It was Ditmon's store that Shaw ran to when the Berrys were after him. He was a witness at the trial.

BIBLIOGRAPHY

Peoria Daily National Democrat, 09-03-1868
Peoria Daily National Democrat, 09-04-1868
Peoria Daily National Democrat, 09-05-1868
Peoria Daily National Democrat, 08-01-1869
Peoria Daily National Democrat, 08-02-1869
Peoria Daily National Democrat, 08-05-1869
Peoria Daily National Democrat, 08-12-1869
Peoria Daily National Democrat, 09-15-1869
Peoria Daily National Democrat, 11-28-1869
Peoria Daily Transcript, 07-25-1868
Peoria Daily Transcript, 07-27-1868
Peoria Daily Transcript, 07-30-1868
Peoria Daily Transcript, 08-01-1868
Peoria Daily Transcript, 08-31-1868
Peoria Daily Transcript, 12-21-1868
Peoria Daily Transcript, 08-02-1869
Peoria Daily Transcript, 08-03-1869
Peoria Daily Transcript, 08-04-1869
Peoria Daily Transcript, 08-06-1869
Peoria Daily Transcript, 08-25-1869
Peoria Daily Transcript, 09-16-1869
Peoria Weekly Transcript, 08-05-1869
Peoria Weekly Transcript, 12-16-1869
Pekin Weekly Times, 11-09-1882
Pekin Weekly Times, 11-16-1882
Pekin Weekly Times, 11-23-1882
Jacksonville Weekly Sentinel, 08-13-1869
Jacksonville Weekly Sentinel, 08-27-1869
Jacksonville Weekly Sentinel, 09-24-1869
Jacksonville Weekly Sentinel, 11-26-1869
Jacksonville Weekly Sentinel, 12-03-1869
Jacksonville Daily Journal, 08-04-1869
Jacksonville Daily journal, 08-10-1869
Jacksonville Daily journal, 08-26-1869

Jacksonville Daily journal, 09-18-1869
Jacksonville Daily journal, 11-17-1869
Jacksonville Daily journal, 11-20-1869
Jacksonville Daily journal, 11-23-1869
Jacksonville Daily journal, 11-25-1869
Jacksonville Daily journal, 11-26-1869
Jacksonville Daily journal, 11-27-1869
Jacksonville Daily journal, 11-29-1869
Illinois State Register, 11-26-1869
Illinois State Register, 11-27-1869
Illinois State Register, 11-29-1869
Illinois State Register, 11-30-1869
Tazewell County Republican, 05-14-1869
Tazewell County Republican, 08-20-1869
Tazewell Register, 02-10-1861
Tazewell Register, 05-13-1862
Chapman's History Of Tazewell County, Illinois - 1879
Grant's "Annual Report" of Pekin Police Dept. 1941,
History of Pekin, C.L. Dancey, 1949
Allensworth's History of Tazewell County, Illinois, 1905
Biographical Publishing Co, Chicago, IL, "Portrait and
Biographical Record of Tazewell and Mason Counties,
Illinois 1894
Susquentenial History of Pekin, Chic Renner, 1974
Morgan County Court Case #1138, "Isaac Berry, et al--Murder"
Tazewell County Genealogical Society
Tazewell County Historical Society
Tazewell County Court Records, "Isaac Berry, et al Murder "
Tazewell County Court records, "John Berry - False Arrest"
Tazewell County Court Records, "John Berry - Assault w/Intent
To commit bodily injury"
Tazewell County Court Records, "John Berry - Burglary"
Tazewell County Court records, "John Berry, Jane Berry,
James Dugan, A.W. Brainard - Debt
Tazewell County Court Records, "Mathew McFarland - Theft"
Tazewell County Court Records, "Wm. Shaw - Larceny"

Tazewell County Court Records, "Andrew Ditmon & William Gibbons - Tippling House-Sunday"

Tazewell County Court Records, "John Brownlee - Tippling House/Sunday

Tazewell County Court records, "John & Terry Berry - Toppling House/Sunday

Tazewell County Court Records, "Matthew McFarland et al - Riot"

Tazewell County Court Records, "John Berry - Assault w/intent to inflict bodily injury"

Tazewell County Court Records, "Josiah Combs - Harboring a Common Thief"

Tazewell County Court records, "John Orrel and Henry Orrel - Larceny"

Tazewell County Court records, "John Orrel and Henry Orrel - Larceny"

Tazewell County Court Records, "John Orrel and Harry O'Conner - Larceny"

Tazewell County Court records, "William Berry - Manslaughter - (Pepper)

Tazewell County Court Records, "Docket Book # 7:
    People Vs Wm. Percell - Assault
    People vs James Dugan - False Imprisonment
    People vs John Berry - False Imprisonment
    William B. Parker vs James Dugan - Trespass
    William B. Parker vs James Dugan - Trespass
Tazewell County Court Records, 'Docket Book # 8:
    W.D. Maus vs Thomas Eades - Assumpsit
    Josiah Sawyer vs Thomas Eades - Assumpsit
    R.S.Updike vs Thomas Eades - Assumpsit
    C.B. Cummings vs M.F. Jackson & J.C. Summers - Assumpsit
    Nathan Casswell vs William Berry - Attachment -Trespass
    W.D. Maus vs John & Rebecca Shay - Foreclosure
    Thomas C. Reeves vs Benjamin Priddy - Assumpsit
    Alexander Wynd vs Thomas Eades - Relief

People vs William Taylor Shay - Larceny
People vs Emanuel Berry - Adultery
People vs Isaiah Shay - Counterfeit Money
Nathan Casswell vs William Berry - Attachment - Trespass
R.S Updike vs Matthew McFarland & John A Boyle - Assumpsit
Aaron Shay vs Matthew McFarland - Appeal
Thomas Larrimore vs William Berry & John McBride - Assumpsit
Harriet Mckean vs William Berry - Assumpsit
Peoria, Illinois Library
Pekin, Illinois Library
Delavan, Illinois Library
Tremont, Illinois Library
Morton, Illinois Library
Illinois State Library
Peoria Historical Society
Bradley University Library
Jacksonville, Illinois Library
Washington, Illinois Library
Eureka, Illinois Library
Lincoln, Illinois Library
Bath, Illinois Library
Bloomington, Illinois Library
Illinois State Archives, Cornelius Daly-Executive Clemency File - Bill of Exceptions
Illinois State Archives, William Berry - Executive Clemency File
    Tazewell County Court Transcript
    Petitions for Pardon (6)
    Charles Turner, Letter to Governor R. Oglesby - 12-29-1868
    W. Sellers, Letter to Governor R. Oglesby - 12-29-1868
    C.G. Whitney, Letter to Governor R. Oglesby - 12-29-1868
Illinois State Archives, Isaac Berry Executive Clemency File
    Petition for Pardon - 1875
    Petition for Pardon - 1882
    Petition for Pardon - 1887

Isaac Berry, Letter to B.S. Prettyman, 12-25-1885
Isaac Berry, Letter to Governor Oglesby - 12-25-1886
G.R. Sims, Letter to B.S Prettyman, 01-28-1886
Illinois State Archives, Matthew McFarland, Executive Clemency File
    A.F. Briscoe, Letter to Judge Wm. Thomas, 06-09-1874
    A.F. Briscoe, Letter to Judge Wm. Thomas, 06-15-1874
    A.F. Briscoe, Letter to Judge Wm. Thomas, 09-29-74
    Melissa McFarland, Letter to Judge Wm Thomas, 08-10-1874
Illinois State Archives, Warden's Prisoner Record Book, Joliet State Penitentiary - 1868 - 1880s
Tazewell County Recorder of Deeds;
    File # 58-414
    # 58-441
Rebecca (Counts) Massey, Letter to Mrs. Henry A. Boorse, 11-30-1935 - Relatives of George W. Pepper.
Mrs. Henry A. Boorse, Letter from Rebecca Massey - Personal photographs of George Washington Pepper
Pekin City Directory - 1869-70 (Sellers)
Pekin City Directory - 1861
William "Bill Furrow" - Personal Photographs & Records
Gene Abbott and his sister, Virginia - Photographs of William Fletcher Copes.
Mrs. Marie Pemberton - Personal Family Records
Mildred Fornoff - Personal records - Abstract deed of Circleville.
The Delavan Times Newspaper